Quotes From Clients

John Bartrom, Owner of Jericho Home Improvements

"I FIRED ONE of the biggest ad agencies in Kansas City and hired Rich Harshaw because he understands contractors. It has been a great partnership and one of the major keys of our success."

"We knew how to spend money on advertising before we met Rich. What we didn't know how to do was communicate our unique advantages with power, precision, and passion in our ads. Our Revenue Per Lead (RPL) has almost doubled since we started working with Rich—when people call us now, they already know they want to use Jericho."

"Rich and his team have engineered and orchestrated our entire marketing program. They wrote and built our identity-based website; they handle our SEO, PPC, and online advertising; they handle all of our media buying and write and produce all of the radio and TV ads. They handle our print advertising and helped us increase our trade show results. Their expertise and professionalism are second to none. The results have been nothing short of spectacular."

Leland Smith, Owner of Service Champions Heating & Air Conditioning

"SINCE RICH HARSHAW started handling our advertising, we've actually had to shut it down many times because we couldn't handle all the calls. We've broken monthly sales records several times, including $5.1MM last July."

"Before we hired Rich, our advertising messages lacked focus and power. Now we have a brand that is instantly recognizable; people know that we have the 'World's Friendliest Technicians", and they go out of their way to choose us instead of our competitors. We never did any of that before; we owe it all to Rich Harshaw."

"I just hope this book doesn't do so well that Rich gets too busy to work with us. I've already invited him to our celebration when we hit $100MM, which should be in about three years."

Mark Aitken, Former Owner of Horizon Services (sold company in 2017)

"I HEARD THAT Rich was the best in the business, so I flew him in to put on a weeklong seminar for me and my staff so I could see and decide for myself. I could tell right away that he held a missing ingredient in our planned growth—he knew how to take all the great things that we already do and say them in a way that makes people really believe it. He makes people want to call and buy from us. For the first time I felt like our advertising captured and communicated who we really were."

"Rich bought all of our TV and radio advertising and wrote all the ads we ran for a six year period of time… from the time we were doing about $40MM in sales until we passed $150MM in sales and sold the company. Without a doubt, he was a major factor in our success."

"I paid Rich Harshaw over $1 million to make my company a household name using radio & TV advertising. The results speak for themselves."

Brian Elias, Former Owner of Hansons (sold company in 2017)

"THIS BOOK DETAILS the exact formula I used to grow Hansons to $80MM before I sold the company. Rich Harshaw is a contractor marketing genius."

"Rich Harshaw isn't a 'get one idea from his book' kind of guy. He's more like a 'listen to everything that comes out of his mouth and take detailed notes or you'll be sorry' kind of guy."

"I've paid Rich over $15,000 for one day of his time to get his input on various aspects of our marketing. And that was after paying him six figures to help us integrate our identity into our website and our advertising. When I have questions about marketing, he's my go-to guy."

UNLOCKING UNLIMITED LEAD FLOW

A Blueprint For Remodeling
& Home Services Contractors
To Make The Jump To $10MM+

RICH HARSHAW

ACKNOWLEDGEMENTS

IN ADDITION TO the four company owners mentioned in the Introduction, I'd also like to extend a formal "thank you!" to the small army of people who have helped turn this book into a reality.

Bryan Bauman – All of your aspirations to be my personal Porter Rockwell have been achieved, and then some. Your loyalty is rare. Your diligence is exceptional. Your friendship is treasured. Special thanks for running my company for the last several years, and for your valuable input into writing this book. You are more than a colleague and a friend, you are a brother.

Tim Musch – When you cold-called me and asked me to do a webinar for MarketSharp in 2005, I had no idea that it would lead to more than a decade of seminars, webinars, and this book. Not to mention I made a good friend along the way. Thank you!

The Staff of Think Rich, LLC – Thank you to everyone who has worked for my company in the last decade-plus, especially: Don Byrom, the master of design; Katie Colihan, guru of customer support and getting things done; Dave Moffitt, copywriter extraordinaire; Leslie Gerbrandt, wizard of special projects; and Elizabeth Hulett, accounting genius. Special thanks to Nick Nordstrom, copywriting Phenom, for channeling your inner Rich Harshaw to edit this book.

Clients – Thank you to the hundreds of clients, past and present, who have trusted us to help you generate leads and grow your businesses. We consider it an honor to serve you.

Family – Finally, thank you to my wonderful wife Tonia, and my six delightful kids: Sam, Kelsie, Ben, Jonah, Grace, and Luke. You are the reason I do what I do. Thanks also to my parents, Curtis & Janice Harshaw, who continue to put up with me for some reason.

CONTENTS

Introduction

AS OF THE date of this writing, I've been a professional marketing consultant for 25 years. During that time I've helped thousands of companies—mostly small ones—in every imaginable industry to increase lead flow and sales by writing better ads, creating more effective websites, negotiating more efficient media schedules, and so on.

In 2005, thanks to a foot in the door from then-stranger, now-friend Tim Musch of MarketSharp, I became heavily involved in the remodeling industry. I found myself consulting with owners of small companies who were stuck in the sub-$5MM range, and who struggled to find enough leads to make the jump to higher sales and profits.

Then the recession hit in 2008, and I witnessed a lot of these companies—even many of the larger ones—start to teeter and fall. The 1st and 3rd largest Four Seasons Sunroom dealers were both my clients at the time, and I watched in helpless shock as both of them shriveled up and went out of business. They weren't the only ones. The next few years were hard on the industry.

In 2011, something happened that changed everything for me: **Mark Aitken**, owner of Horizon Services, hired me to help his (*not* struggling) company make the jump from $44MM to $100MM. I had never met anyone so obsessed with and committed to doing *everything* right. And I had never met anyone so confident that he would reach his goals—and quickly, too. I discovered that it was entirely possible to build a recession-proof company that could grow exponentially and withstand any challenge.

I subsequently ended up working with the owners of several other companies who were cut from the same cloth. Their personalities were different, but they all shared a single-minded focus on excellence. These inspiring leaders were **Brian Elias** of Hanson's, **John Bartrom** of Jericho Home Improvements, and **Leland Smith** of Service Champions Heating and Air Conditioning.

They taught me, first and foremost, that success in the remodeling and home services industry starts with what I now call "The $10MM Mindset", which is covered in detail in Section 1 of this book. Without that mindset, nothing else matters and there is no chance of making it to the next level. Owners who don't have it are doomed to mediocrity and are subject to the ebbs and flows of external factors such as seasonality, weather, and the economy.

But what I really learned from these four intrepid leaders was how to unlock unlimited lead flow. All four already provided outstanding service which gave them great reputations in their communities. They already charged premium prices which gave them the financial resources to implement across-the-board best practices. And most significantly, they were all eager (yes, eager!) to spend huge amounts of money on marketing and advertising to consistently stoke their growth engines.

This book is not theory. It's not hype. It's not wishful thinking. It's a blueprint for remodeling and home services companies to unlock their own unlimited lead flow and make the jump to $10MM.

Are you ready to make the jump?

SECTION 1
The $10MM Mindset

CHAPTER 1
Why A $10MM Company?

JOHN WAS RUNNING late for our meeting.

I had flown in the night before in preparation for that days' discussion about his remodeling company's TV and radio advertising for the upcoming year. After a restful night's sleep at a nearby hotel, I arrived at his office a few minutes before our 9:00 am start time. I let myself into his conference room, got my materials ready, and waited.

After a few minutes, I glanced at the clock on the wall—9:00 am sharp.

No John.

9:05. 9:10. 9:15. Still no sign.

Finally, at 9:17, John rushed into the conference room wearing blue jeans and a polo shirt. He apologized for being late, and explained that he had stopped by the vet's office that morning on the way to the office.

"The vet?" I asked. "What's up?"

It seems that his dog—apparently a really big dog—had swallowed a bee two days before… and when stung, had gone into anaphylactic shock.

John had rushed the dog to the emergency vet, where multiple procedures and surgeries were administered in an effort to save the dog's life. The dog survived the attack—barely—and was now in recovery after having been transferred to a second facility.

The cost to save the dog? About 15 grand.

Later that day, John and I talked about writing some radio spots to highlight the "Go Orphan" project his company supported in Haiti. Every year, John's company donates hundreds of thousands of dollars to their cause, including money for full-time caregivers called "mamas" who watch over and teach Haitian orphans. There is one mama for every 10 orphans, and that year, they were sponsoring 39 mamas. They donated enough money for enough mamas to take care of 390 children for an entire year.

Later that day, John whizzed me to the airport in his fresh-off-the-lot Maserati a little earlier than we had planned. He said he wanted to hit the gym before heading home to spend time with his kids.

Let's start this book with a simple question: Why would you want to own a $10MM (or more) remodeling or home services company in the first place?

To a lot of contractors, $10MM sounds like a pipe dream. Doesn't running a company that big bring lots of extra stress and headaches? Wouldn't it be better to just stay small and more manageable?

Think of it this way: you're going to work 40, 50, 60 hours a week no matter what your sales are.

Why not makes as much money as possible during those hours?

The truth is, the difference between owning a $3MM remodeling or home services company and a $10MM one is **night vs. day.**

But to enjoy the spoils (read: healthy profits) of a $10MM company, you have to build you company the RIGHT WAY—the way I'm going to show you in this book.

If you build up to $10MM *the right way*, your whole world changes:

- You can afford to make everything in your company <u>GREAT</u>, and do *everything* right; you never have to cut corners on *anything*.

- You can treat your employees better than anyone else. You can pay them so much that they'll never want to leave because it would require them taking a sizeable pay cut. They'll work hard because they'll want to stay.

- You can also give them Fortune 500-level benefits: company cars, paid vacation, full health insurance, matching 401(k) plans, and trips. Stuff almost none of your competitors offer.

- If you mess up or make a customer mad for some reason, *you just pay to have it fixed.* You don't have to risk your reputation by getting in "pissing matches" with angry customers. You just smile, fix the problem, and move on.

- You can afford to use the best materials, and you can hire all the best people. That means you can offer (and actually service) warranties like nobody else.

- You can afford to hire specialists, consultants, and experts to solve any problems you (inevitably) encounter.

- You can build a company with a loyal customer base and have huge brand equity in the marketplace. You can legitimately sell your company because those assets are **tangible and valuable**. The cold hard fact is it's almost impossible to sell a $2MM remodeling company to anyone but an uncle with a drinking problem.

- Your referrals will shoot through the roof.

- On a personal level, you'll be rich.

- And the profits on a $10MM company? $1MM, bare minimum. Usually closer to $2MM. Per year. *Net* profits.

Now let's get really personal:

- If YOUR dog swallows a bee and almost dies due to anaphylactic shock, you can easily afford the $15,000 vet bill to save his life.

- You can build your dream house in whatever neighborhood you want and drive whatever cars you want. Like John, who drove me to the airport in his new Maserati.

- You can sit in box seats or front-row seats for any sporting events you want, including the World Series. $8,000 per ticket is affordable when you make $1.6MM a year in personal, take-home income.

- You can go to Maui twice in less than three months; once with your sales staff who qualified for the incentive trip you offered and paid for, and once with your entire family for 10 days because… well, Maui.

- If your parents are elderly and need special care, you can be the sibling who everyone counts on to "just take care of it," whether that means medicines, in-home care, nursing facilities, or anything else. A few of my clients take great pride in being able to perform this duty.

- You can contribute as much money as you want to whatever causes you want. All of my clients with over $10MM in sales are generous philanthropists. Yes, philanthropists.

Like I said, it's a whole new world.

I'm going to show you how to achieve it.

That's what this book is all about.

CHAPTER 2
Stuck

'VE BEEN WORKING with remodeling and home services companies for over 20 years now—and exclusively since 2005. For the most part, they are owned and operated by hardworking, honest people who have dedicated their working lives to their businesses.

But the majority of them have been small businesses—ranging from under $1MM to maybe $4MM or $5MM. I worked with one company for a while that got up to $8MM before their lack of systems and financial controls killed the company.

Then, in early 2011, I was hired to work for a big HVAC company that was doing $44MM in sales.

I quickly found out that the company wasn't just bigger—they were bigger for a reason. Their mindset was completely different. They weren't satisfied growing to $44MM and staying there. They wanted to get bigger… and bigger… and bigger… and bigger.

And they had both the money and the cajones to pull it off.

This HVAC company paid me $40,000 to put on a four-day seminar for the owner, his three-person marketing staff, and a few of his friends who owned non-competing businesses.

Satisfied that I knew what I was talking about, they then agreed to a $15,000 a month consulting contract to help them get to the next level. That was more money than their other three marketing staffers were making combined.

They hired me because they felt like they had hit a marketing brick wall. They were spending millions of dollars on traditional advertising—with the majority of their budget going into direct mail and newspaper ads.

But you can only put so many ads in the paper, and you can only mail to the homes in the zip codes you service so many times. So the logical next step, they thought, would be to have me write better ads.

The idea was simple: If they were spending $1MM in the newspaper and $2MM on direct mail, they figured my improved ads and mailers would pull 5%... 10%... maybe even 20% more leads. Then that $180,000 a year they were paying me would be chump change.

Those first six months, I wrote tons of new ads for them. It was great stuff, and sure enough, leads went up, and everyone was happy.

Then we sat down in November to work on the budget for the next year.

As I looked over their financials, I was baffled. The conversation went something like this:

Me: Why are you only spending $56,000 on radio?

Client: We can't track how many leads come from TV or radio, so we gave up on it. We're on one station now as a favor to our service manager's sister.

Me: Would you consider spending more?

Client: We hate things that can't be measured. We know exactly how many leads we get from every single newspaper ad. We know exactly how many calls we get from direct mail. We like that.

Me: But you want to get to $100MM, right?

Client: Yes.

Me: Ok. What about this Pay-Per-Click budget? Why is it only $20,000 a month?

Client: Because that's how much we allocated for PPC.

Me: That seems awfully low for a company your size. Do you have to limit the spend to certain times of day? Or to certain days of the week?

Client: No, we just run it until it runs out.

Me: When does it usually run out?

Client: (checking reports) It looks around the 10th or 15th of the month, depending on the weather.

Me: (speechless)

Remember, this was a big company run by smart people. They were aggressive and passionate.

But this was the first time they had ever grown a company to $44MM—they were in uncharted territory. They didn't know what came next. Just 15 years earlier, they were two guys with a truck, some old tools, and a telephone. They had built their mini empire completely from the ground up, but knowing how to run TV, radio, and internet campaigns isn't something you "just figure out."

They needed help, so they reached out to an expert. Because of the success of their company, they could afford the best (i.e., me).

Fast-forward seven years: They reached over $150MM in sales and sold the company to a private equity firm for about seven times earnings, which hovered around 20%. Do the math.

You probably have a smaller company, but you're smart and capable, too. I'm guessing you'd like to grow your business, but probably aren't sure how to get over the next hump.

I'm here to be your marketing expert. I know how to get you where you want to go.

- Maybe you've been stalled out in the $2MM to $5MM range for several years now.

- Maybe your sales are higher than that, like the client in the example—but you're still stuck at a certain sales and profit level.

- Or maybe you're still a "little guy" doing under $2MM… but want to do more. *Much* more.

The reason companies stall is always the same: **they don't have a reliable way to generate enough leads to sustain more sales.**

They can barely make the phone ring enough to support $3MM in sales. Reaching $10MM? It seems like a pipedream.

That's when they stall out. They just stay in a narrow range that only moves up or down due to external factors like the economy or the weather.

This book is for owners who want to find new ways to GROW. To grow fast…and to grow with predictable control.

Here's what the typical sales growth of remodeling and service companies looks like:

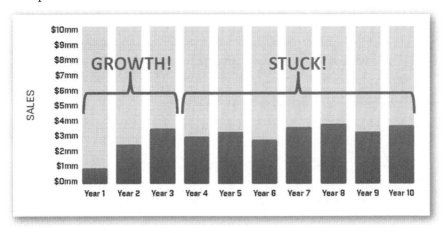

To get to the next level, you have to know how to *keep your leads pipeline full at all times.* You've got to find a way to unlock unlimited lead flow. And for most companies, that means jumping off a cliff into terra incognita.

Many try TV and fail. They try radio and fail. They try online marketing and can't get enough leads.

And so they settle into their comfortable pattern of never really growing. They're stuck.

Most Companies Are One- (Or Two-) Trick Ponies

Those comfortable, stuck patterns usually involve having success with one (or maybe two) marketing tactics. It could be direct mail… or home shows… or telemarketing… or newspaper.

I don't mean that they don't TRY other things. And I don't mean that they don't have some success with multiple things.

What I mean is their <u>bread and butter</u> is usually just one or two things.

That's dangerous in two ways:

First, what if that one thing quits working for some reason? The home improvement industry is littered with guys who crashed when the telemarketing rules changed. And other guys who flamed out when newspaper quit working. Or who are struggling to hold onto the glory days of canvassing.

And second, it's dangerous because it's usually stagnating. You do your "thing" as much as you can do it—but that "thing" can't generate $10MM worth of business. It maxes out at $2MM. Or $4MM. Or whatever.

It's not scalable.

It all comes down to unlocking a predictable, reliable, cost-effective—and scalable—flow of leads. To get to $10MM, you're going to have to have more than one or two reliable lead generators.

I will cover most of the usual ways of doing marketing that most companies are using in the last section of this book. But I'm only going to cover them briefly and only to give you some ideas and suggestions for how to maximize your return on them. I'll cover things like direct mail, canvassing, social media, referrals, home shows, and referrals.

But those are NOT the things are going unlock unlimited lead flow.

What is going to make the difference will be covered in the first five sections of this book—your mindset, your identity, your website, online lead generation, and radio/TV.

For most companies, those will be your $10MM pillars that will give you virtually unlimited leads.

When we introduced our methods to the HVAC client in the example, here's what happened:

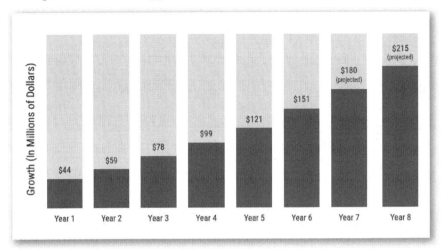

How did they grow so fast? They did lots of things right. Lots of things. You don't grow from $44MM to over $150MM by being stupid and messing stuff up.

But look what we ended up spending in a couple of key categories:

Year	Marketing Budget	TV/Radio	PPC
Year 1	$4.5MM	$56,000	$189,000
Year 2	$6MM	$1.00MM	$1.4MM
Year 3	$8MM	$3.00MM	$1.7MM
Year 4	$10MM	$4.4MM	$2.2MM
Year 5	$12MM	$5.2MM	$2.6MM
Year 6	$15MM	$6.1MM	$3.2MM

Since about 2010, I have specialized in working with larger companies to help them really dial in their marketing. I've personally handled millions upon millions of dollars of marketing budgets on behalf of these clients.

This book is going to show you how to do what they do.

I've worked with a $70MM window, siding, and roofing company.

I've worked with a $41MM HVAC company (not the same one from the example).

I've worked with a $12MM (and insanely profitable) kitchen and bathroom remodeling company.

I've worked with one of the most well-known and highly respected replacement window companies in the world—a name you know for sure—that does hundreds of millions in annual sales.

Just to name a few.

But in that same time, I've also continued to work with hundreds of smaller contractors. The little guys.

The stuck guys.

And I've found that if a little guy who is stuck can *shift his mindset*, he can become a big guy.

I've also found that the marketing formula is always the same. But you have to be willing to do things differently if you want to make the jump from little guy to big guy.

With this book, you will learn how to make that jump by unlocking unlimited lead flow.

CHAPTER 3

The 4-Step Formula To Get To $10MM

RECENTLY, I TOOK my wife to lunch at Panera Bread. I ordered half a sandwich and a bowl of soup; she got a salad and a Diet Coke. The total bill: $24.95. For two people.

As we sat down to eat, I couldn't shake the thought that I had just paid over twelve bucks per person. For lunch.

I'm not cheap, but still. $9.49 for a salad? $5.29 for a bowl of chicken noodle soup?

Wendy's was only 100 yards away—we could have been in and out for around $10 total.

Oh, well. Happy wife, happy life, right?

Later that evening, while half-watching TV while reading something on my phone, my wife suddenly and enthusiastically shouted, *"Hey, I LOVE that salad! This is the commercial that made me want to go to Panera and get one!"*

I looked up, and sure enough, there was the $9.49 Strawberry And Poppyseed salad my wife had from Panera sitting on my TV, tempting women (and a few men) all over the Dallas-Fort Worth area to buy one.

And found in that stupid little story is nearly everything you need to know to grow to $10MM. Or $20MM.Or $70MM. You name it.

Here is the 4-Step Formula:

1. **Sell awesome stuff that people genuinely love.**

2. **Charge high prices.**

3. **Master the internet.**

4. **Use radio & TV advertising.**

In that order.

Okay, there wasn't any internet in that Panera example. Relax—we'll get to that in a minute.

One of my clients started his kitchen and bath remodeling company in Kansas City in 2008—right as the recession was just getting started.

Despite that, in just four short years they had topped $10MM in sales (Year 1 - $1.5MM; Year 2 - $3.5MM; Year 3 - $6.8MM; Year 4 - $10.1MM). Now they hover in the $12MM range while increasing their profitability every year.

They are the clear #1 kitchen and bathroom remodeler in KC—the next closest competitor only does something like $2MM.

Here is their 4-Step Formula for success:

1. **Sell awesome stuff that people genuinely love.**

2. **Charge high prices.**

3. **Master the internet.**

4. **Use radio &TV advertising.**

In that order.

I won't go into detail about everything they do to build AWESOME kitchens and bathrooms that people genuinely love. That could be an entire book. And I'll touch on it in a future chapter.

But I will tell you this: They have **raised their prices by 15% an astounding FIVE times** since starting the company.

That means a bathroom that used to be $10,000 now sells for about double that—$20,000.

Which is basically like charging $9.49 for a salad. Or $5.29 for a bowl of soup.

I'll also tell you that they poured **all of their profits** for the first few years of the business into radio and TV advertising. **All of it.**

They were spending $1MM a year on advertising long before they were doing $10MM in sales.

That's HOW they got to that level.

And now the owner drives a Maserati and shrugs his shoulders when writing a check for $15,000 to save his dog that swallowed a bee.

The formula for making the jump to $10MM is simple—but like anything else in life, there are details you need to know.

They're ALL in this book. I'll walk you through everything you need to know to break out of your current comfort zone and double, triple, quadruple your sales.

It's not pie-in-the-sky BS. It's what companies hire me to do. This company hired me because they wanted to grow—in sales AND profitability.

I'll give you a few ideas about how to create an awesome company and how to raise your prices… but honestly, that's something you're going to have to bring to the table.

The majority of this book is going to focus on the marketing part of the equation. How to master the internet. How to master radio and TV advertising. Then, at the end of the book, I will briefly cover some additional marketing topics like direct mail, home shows, canvassing, and more.

At the end of the day it comes down to this: The companies that will break through and make the jump are the ones who can figure out how to create a predictable, reliable, cost-effective—and scalable—flow of leads.

Unlimited lead flow.

CHAPTER 4
Is $10MM In Sales Even Realistic?

BEFORE WE GO any further, I need to address some important questions I get from contractors who are excited about the idea of growing to $10MM in sales, but have concerns:

- "Why would I <u>want</u> to grow my business to $10MM? I make plenty of money now."

- "I've been in business for 22 years and I'm only at $3MM—sounds like you're selling magic beans."

- "Nobody in this market does $10MM—I don't think it's even possible."

I already answered the reason WHY you would want to grow to $10MM in the first chapter. The short recap is: You can afford to do everything right in your business, and you have enough money to buy pretty much whatever you want.

If you're not motivated by that, call Tony Robbins. I can't help you.

If you don't <u>want</u> to run a $10MM company, that's up to you. Nobody's putting a gun to your head, forcing you to do so.

As for the **"Is it possible?"** question, it depends:

If you're running a roofing company in Coffeyville, KS (shout out to my parent's hometown, population 10,295), you probably can't do $10MM. There's probably not $10MM total in the entire town including all the change in their collective couch cushions.

But if you run a remodeling company in any city of any size at all, it's not only possible—it's practically inevitable if just follow the 4-Step Formula I gave you in Chapter 3:

1. **Sell awesome stuff that people genuinely love.**

2. **Charge high prices.**

3. **Master the internet.**

4. **Use radio &TV advertising.**

Think about it for a minute. How much business is there, IN TOTAL, in the city where you sell stuff?

If there are <u>two</u> companies doing $3MM, <u>five</u> companies doing $2MM each, and <u>100</u> smaller companies doing $15MM in combined sales, that's $31MM.

You only need to capture a third of that.

Yes, if you take a full third of the sales in your market, other companies are going to suffer and go out of business.

But what do you care?

You're already better than them, right? Good grief, if you don't think so, why are you even reading this?

You already genuinely offer the best value in the marketplace (*not* price—<u>VALUE</u>), right?

Then it's not a sack of magic beans. It's just math.

The goods and services are already being sold by somebody. Why not just sell most of it yourself?

To make this happen, you're going to have to come to grips with words like dominate, monopolize, and market leader.

Earlier I told you about a company I helped take from $44MM in sales to over $150MM in six years.

Some of that growth came from spreading into new markets.

But most of it came from OWNING and DOMINATING the markets they were already in.

They have <u>over</u> 20% market share in four of the counties they service, including an astounding 37% market share in the county they've been in the longest.

You can make a veritable fortune with 37% of the market.

And because they follow the 4-StepFormula (great products, high prices, master the internet, TV advertising), they are the most expensive company in the area—by a long shot.

Don't tell them it's magic beans. It's calculated. It's systematic. It's expected.

THAT'S THE FIRE SWAMP! WE'LL NEVER SURVIVE

NONSENSE! YOU'RE ONLY SAYING THAT BECAUSE NO ONE EVER HAS

Do yourself a favor. **Don't let anyone else define you.** You can do whatever you want. And if that includes growing your remodeling or home services company to $10MM in sales, then go for it.

Is it possible? Yes.

Is it easy? Well, actually, yes.

As long as you have a great company and charge high prices—those are the hard parts—and you're willing to follow the marketing programs outlined in this book, it's easy.

But honestly, most companies I see in this industry settle for less and end up getting stuck. Here's the model that most companies are using without really knowing it:

1. **Sell pretty good stuff that keeps most of your customers happy.**
2. **Charge middle-of-the-road prices or slightly higher.**
3. **Generate a few leads from the internet.**
4. **Stick to one or two "bread and butter" lead generators; ignore radio & TV since they don't work.**

That is the wrong formula for getting to $10MM and living the lifestyle you really want. That is the formula for making a living and doing okay. That's the formula for "$2.7MM in sales after 33 years."

Unlocking unlimited lead flow and making the jump to $10MM starts with the right mindset, and that starts with the expectations you place on yourself.

CHAPTER 5

Demanding Excellence Is The First Grand Key

To BUILD A great company that's worthy of $10MM in sales, here's an attitude you have to adopt: ZERO TOLERANCE for anything but excellence.

You must demand excellence and peak performance as cornerstones of your company culture. You must have zero tolerance for anything less.

Here's an example:

One of my big clients in the HVAC industry was dealing with a rash of rear-end collisions in his service fleet. As a result, he had video cameras installed on the dashboard of each vehicle that would continuously record both forward and backward. In the event of a collision, the cameras would detect the impact, and save the recordings so they could see what was happening during the crash.

Even with the cameras installed, there were still 12 collisions in three months. The videos revealed that it was the technician's fault nearly 100% of the time. They just weren't paying attention while driving.

So he made the following announcement at the next technician meeting:

"If you're in a rear-end accident, here's what you do: Get your personal belongings out of the truck, lock the keys in the cab, and go the F&!# home. You're fired!"

That's what you call zero tolerance.

Rear-end collisions stopped immediately.

Translation: If I can't trust you to pay attention when driving (and your own safety is at stake), how can I trust you to pay attention when repairing/replacing a customer's air conditioner?

The owner of the company told me that story the first time I visited his office. While I was there, he gave me a tour of the facilities.

As we walked down a set of back stairs, he stopped when he noticed a dime-sized spot on the carpet. He looked at his assistant and demanded, "What happened here?"

Zero tolerance.

Then we went into his warehouse. It was immaculate—and HUGE. It looked like a Home Depot, but much, much cleaner and brighter. Then he spotted a 15-inch scuff mark on the floor. He looked at the warehouse manager and asked how it had gotten there (the pallet jack), why it hadn't been cleaned up yet (it just happened less than five minutes ago), and why it hadn't been cleaned off as soon as it happened (no comment).

Zero tolerance.

A few minutes later, as we walked down a long hallway, he somehow spotted a company truck outside—that was 50 yards away through a glass door—that had some paperwork laying on the dashboard. That was a big no-no. You can't have ANYTHING on the dashboard. Somebody ran off to find the culprit so it could be removed.

Zero tolerance.

You might think everyone would hate working for a "zero tolerance" boss like this.

Actually, quite the opposite.

The people who hate this kind of scrutiny either never make it through the hiring process, or they wash out within weeks of starting.

And everyone else—the ones who conform to the culture of excellence—absolutely love working there. They are part of the fastest growing company in the industry. They make more money and have better benefits than their peers. (And way cleaner trucks!).

I've personally worked with this company for many years now and never had a problem with the owner at all. He's demanding. He's intense. He's a taskmaster. And as long as I continue to deliver great results, on time, he'll keep treating me well and paying me good money to do it.

Here's the reality when it comes to creating an exceptional company that's worthy of doing $10MM or more in sales: Most of what needs to change is between your ears.

It's a mindset. It's a mentality.

There's also the small issue of marketing—unlocking unlimited leads. We'll cover a lot of that, too. In detail.

But for now, do a self-introspection: are you a "zero tolerance" kind of guy (or gal)?

If not... this book and mentality probably isn't a good fit. How could you improve in this area?

Are you willing to learn and grow?

A couple years ago I got a call from a former client—the owner of a $65MM exterior remodeling company.

Something was a "little off" in his sales presentation. He wasn't sure exactly what it was, so he wanted me to take a look at it.

A few days later, he flew to my home office in Texas with his top two executives. He paid me $15,500 to let them give me their sales presentation, so I could provide suggestions on how to make it better.

Over the course of six hours, I identified two or three dozen (mostly) teeny-tiny adjustments that I felt, collectively, would move the needle.

After the meeting, I typed up the notes and created a 17-page document that gave an analysis of all 48 pages of their iPad pitch book, and where the changes needed to occur... as well as specific things the reps should say as they talked through any particular slide.

All in a day's work.

What impressed me most about this was the owner's willingness to open up and ADMIT he didn't know everything.

The guy was doing $65MM a year and he made his VP of Sales sit there and listen to ME for six hours.

In other words, he's open to suggestions. He values an outside opinion. He wants to double- and triple-check his own thoughts—and the thoughts of his staff.

This is a characteristic I see far LESS OFTEN in far smaller companies. The guys who are "stuck" are a lot more likely to be "know-it-alls." They are more likely to be cynical toward the ideas and concepts in this book. They tell me they've "tried that stuff and it didn't work." It's hard for them to accept that maybe they were doing it wrong.

Do you demand the best? Do you put systems and checklists in place to make sure that excellence happens all the time and in all areas of your company? Are you open to input?

Again, the point of this book is not to give you a step-by-step of how to do this. It's a marketing book. But you have to find a way to deliver the best products and services for top dollar if you're going to have a chance.

CHAPTER 6

Becoming Irreplaceable—The Ignition Code

H ERE'S THE REAL reason you want to offer the best products and services in the entire industry.

Confidence.

I'm talking *"Arthur Fonzarelli, Tom Brady, Greg House, and Jack Reacher all wrapped into one"* kind of confidence.

If you don't know who those people are, look them up. You'll get the point quickly.

There's an old movie called *The Transporter* starring Jason Statham that offers a great metaphor.

The opening credits of the movie shows the lead character driving a black, late-model 7-series BMW through the streets of an unnamed French town on a summer morning. He's dressed in a black suit; he wears black gloves and dark sunglasses. He looks very official.

The camera focuses in on a huge clock on top of a building; then, just as the clock moves into the 10 o'clock position, the camera pans down to show the car stopping in a circle drive in front of the building. An alarm sounds and four masked men come running out of the building carrying what appear to be sacks of cash.

It's a bank robbery, and we are figuring out that the lead character, "The Transporter," is apparently the getaway driver.

But instead of speeding away the moment the four money-bag-toting bandits get in the car—the ringleader in the front passenger seat, and the other three in the back—the driver just sits there. Doing nothing. While the armed guards pour out of the building and surround the vehicle with guns drawn.

Here is the dialogue that ensues:

Ringleader: Move it! Let's go! Move, move! In the car! Let's go. Let's go!

The Transporter: There's four of you.

Ringleader: You can count. I'm impressed. Now drive.

The Transporter: (calm, facing forward) Rule one—never change the deal. The deal was transportation... for three men with a combined weight of 254 kilos.

Ringleader: Yeah? (pointing gun to The Transporter's head) Well, this is a new deal.

The Transporter: (expressionless, staring straight ahead) An extra 80 kilos means we'll not make your destination on the gas I have allotted.

Ringleader: (getting agitated) So we'll stop and get more gas!

The Transporter: Every stop we make exposes us. Every exposure increases the risk of getting caught. An extra 80 kilos means the Koni shock absorbers I installed for this job will not give us the ability to outmaneuver any police that might be chasing us. Which means if there is a chase, we lose our advantage, which also increases the possibility of getting caught. I don't want to get caught (turns head to look straight into the gun barrel). You don't want to get caught.

Ringleader: (extremely agitated) Just drive the car, man or you're gonna catch a bullet through the brains!

The Transporter: (facing forward again, expressionless) And who's going to drive?

Henchman From Back Seat: Shoot this (expletive)! I'll drive.

The Transporter: (glancing to a keypad on the center console) Not without the ignition code you won't (turning again to face the gun barrel). Three men. 254 kilos. That was the deal.

Ringleader: Argh! (turns and shoots henchman in the back seat; others throw his body out of the car)

Ringleader: Three men, 254 kilos.

The Transporter: Seatbelts.

One of the most ridiculous and insane car chases then ensues. The Transporter outmaneuvers dozens of cops while driving the wrong way through town, evading pedestrians on sidewalks, triggering hidden obstacles that pop out of the street, backing off a bridge onto a random car transport truck, and barely speeding in front of a train without getting hit. Among other things. All while keeping perfectly calm, cool, and collected.

In other words, The Transporter wasn't just talking the talk. He could walk the walk. Or drive the drive, so to speak. He was that good.

(If you would like to watch this clip, you can find it at UnlimitedLeadFlow.com/book. Bookmark that page because I've put tons of extra resources, videos, case studies, and examples on there that will enhance your understanding of the concepts in this book).

The most critical line from above—and the one relevant to our discussion about making the jump to $10MM—is when The Transporter calmly stares down the barrel of the gun and asks "**And who's going to drive?**"

This is David Lee Roth-in-1984-level confidence.

It's a belief that you are so good at what you do—so far superior to any other choice the homeowner could possibly make—that you're willing to ask for an extremely high price while looking them calmly in the eye without blinking.

The key—in case I haven't been perfectly clear—is to actually BE THAT GOOD.

You can't fake being height-of-his-powers David Lee Roth. Or Tom Brady. Or Magic Johnson. Or Usain Bolt.

You have to actually be that good.

More specifically, this good:

In other words: The "best of the best" succeed because they have the ignition code.

Do you?

CHAPTER 7
Proof That Your Customers WANT To Pay More

B UT WHAT IF nobody is willing to pay for that ignition code?
I get this objection all the time, and it's nonsense.
I know it's hard for you to believe that people WANT to pay more money than you're charging right now.

I mean, you already struggle to get your salespeople to sell at your current prices.

But the fact is that people are paying exorbitant amounts of money for all kinds of luxury items in every category you can imagine. This phenomenon has been going on for about three decades now.

I'm not even talking about super rich people who can afford whatever they want.

I'm talking about regular people who live in nice, normal houses in nice, normal neighborhoods that make nice, normal incomes.

Ever hear of Callaway Golf? Or Victoria's Secret? Or The Cheesecake Factory?

These brands have already cashed in on regular people's desires to pay extra for premium products—and they've done it to the tune of BILLIONS of dollars.

It's simple economics:

In the last 40 years, the average middle class family enjoyed a doubling of real per-capita income… while cost of living remained basically flat, in real terms.

Therefore, the amount of money available for "new luxury" has exploded.

That doesn't mean that everybody is now eating caviar at every meal and driving Bentley's to drop off their kids at soccer practice.

It means that people have the money to pamper themselves with luxuries on certain purchases *that are important to them.*

Take Victoria's Secret. They took ladies underwear from a utility item women bought off the rack at Montgomery Wards to something extraordinary that women really wanted. The average price of a Victoria's Secret bra is TRIPLE to QUADRUPLE what you can pay for a "plain" one at Wal-Mart or Dillard's. But women would rather "treat" themselves.

And it's not just the ladies; there's a reason you dudes buy Big Bertha drivers and Callaway irons. Who cares if it's $3,000 a set—it's worth it!

And guess what?

These same people are DYING to fork over huge sums of cash for the best roof. And the best windows and siding. And the best kitchen and bathroom. And the best air conditioning repair. And not just the best products—the best service, too.

Look, not everyone eats at The Cheesecake Factory. I get it.

And not everyone is going to pay you $1,200 for a window when Window World is advertising them for $189.

But believe me: There are more than enough people who will. Enough to get you to $10MM in sales and enjoy all the benefits we talked about in Chapter 1.

There are plenty of people who want the ASSURANCE that you will do it PERFECT (and that you'll bend over backward to make it right if you do mess up) instead of paying some dude from Craigslist to do it… who might also murder their children.

All of this has been documented in an excellent book called *Trading Up: Why Consumers Want New Luxury Goods—And How Companies Create Them.*

The book is now more than 10 years old—but don't worry, it's not outdated. Not even a little.

To spare you from having to buy and read an entire book, I found a clip on YouTube of the author giving a speech in 2006—again, a bit dated, but the point is still as valid today as ever.

Just go to YouTube and type "Michael Silverstein: The American Consumer." Then click the video and start watching at the 1:15 mark. There's also a link to the video at UnlimitedLeadFlow.com/book.

To get to $10MM in sales, your company is going to have to become part of the new luxury.

Sure, you can just sell more of the low-margin, copycat windows and reach that figure. Or try to land remodeling jobs by being "price competitive." Or advertise a $5,995 complete AC system.

But you won't have the margins to sustain a great company and put a million dollars a year in your personal coffers.

The first step is to build a great company and create that "ignition code" advantage.

Then—and only then—you will need to raise your prices to reflect your newfound swagger.

Keep this in mind: Only 1% of contractors ever make it to $10MM. If you're already at $2MM or $3MM, you just might have the right stuff to get there.

CHAPTER 8

Why You're Chicken To Raise Your Prices (And How To Do It Anyway)

Raising your prices is the easiest and most crucial factor in building your remodeling or home services company to $10MM. It's also the scariest part. Ignition code be damned.

If you think your prices are already high, you'll still probably need to raise them *again*.

At a minimum, you need to shoot for a 2.5-to-1 ratio of price to cost… 3- or 3.5-to-1 would be even better.

In other words, if the hard costs (materials, labor) are $5,000, you should be selling it for $12,500 to $17,500. And trust me—that extra $5,000 in the spread (between $12,500 and $17,500, per job) could buy you a TON of TV advertising that would allow you to destroy your competitors.

I fully realize that most of your other competitors are selling that "same job" for $5,000 to $10,000.

I put "same job" in quotation marks because we both know that most of those jokers are only putting $3,500 of cost into it. They shortcut everything, from material quality, to quality control, to installer ability, to (lack of) warranty. They couldn't care less.

And they're probably only marking the job up by double, if that. They're selling $3,500 job cost for $5,000 to $7,500. As long as they can afford to take their wife and kids to Applebee's on Friday night, they're good.

Even your higher quality competitors who DO spend $5,000 on the cost only have the stones to charge double, or maybe a little more—$10,000 to $12,000.

Question: Are any of them doing $10MM in sales?

No. No, they are not.

Never forget my simple 4-Step Formula to get to $10MM:

1. **Sell awesome stuff that people genuinely love.**

2. **Charge high prices.**

3. **Master the internet.**

4. **Use radio &TV advertising.**

You have to have the ignition code—that's Step 1.

Because I promise you this*: If you're not a high-price, high-quality provider in the market, you'll never get to $10MM.*

You won't even have a chance.

I'll give you the benefit of the doubt: I'll assume that you offer exceptional quality and service to your customers. And if you don't now, you're at least committed to doing so in the near future.

After all, Step 1 is to "Sell awesome stuff that people genuinely love".

But even if you do, chances are high that you're not selling at the coveted 3.5-to-1 ratio. Here's why:

Your salespeople are <u>scared to death</u> that they will lose the sale! They're CHICKEN!

They have that terrified look in their eyes. They already struggle to close at the prices you already have that they already *think* are too high. They are SURE that if you make them ask for even MORE money, the customers won't just say NO... they'll actually laugh in their faces! Or get mad. Or kick them out of the house!

Meanwhile, Disney World charges $325 for a four-day pass, even though I can buy a full one-year pass Six Flags (good at 13 different parks) for about $80.

Do you think the lady at the ticket counter at Disney World gets all nervous, starts sweating and stammering, and apologizes when asking for $325 per person for a four-day pass?

Are you kidding me?

Talk about an ignition code.

That's because Disney World is committed to selling awesome stuff that people genuinely love and have massive brand authority thanks to decades of... wait for it... being on radio and TV.

I'll convince you to get on radio and TV later on in another section of this book. It's non-negotiable if you want to join the $10MM club. I will also give you some pointers on providing a Disney-like experience.

Right now, I'm giving you the 30,000-foot view on how to raise your prices. That consists of the following:

1. Be better than everyone else. It's not that hard. The majority of your competitors suck. I mean that, and you know it's true. Ignition code.

2. Clearly articulate how you're different and why you're better in all of your marketing. This is harder, but I can help you do it. It's the essence of Section 3 – "Identity." We'll get there soon enough.

3. Master the internet and spend a butt-ton of money on radio and TV to get people to believe you're not only better, but that they'd be a complete fool to choose anyone BUT you. You will learn how to do that in this book, too.

4. **FIRE EVERY SALESPERSON WHO IS AFRAID TO ASK FOR THE SALE AT YOUR NEW, HIGHER PRICES.**

That's right, FIRE THEM.

In my experience, you cannot remediate cowards. There's a good chance you'll have to fire your sales manager, too.

I know you like some of these people; you've become friends with them.

But I promise you they are in the way of your success. Not all of them. But a lot of them are. Somebody's got to be the adult in the room. And that person is you. Make the hard decisions.

You might have to handle some of the sales calls yourself for a while. Hopefully <u>YOU</u> believe in your pricing (and your awesome products and service).

You might have to take two steps back to move 10 steps forward.

You might have to gut your entire sales team if you really want to get to $10MM. They don't just hand out $10MM in sales to anybody.

Don't worry. Selling for ultra-high prices is not hard when you have the right product and you do the marketing the right way.

Marketing brings the right people to you. Then just type in the ignition code.

CHAPTER 9
Financing: Your Secret Weapon To Higher Prices

$8,214.70.

M Y WIFE COULDN'T think of a good way to deliver the shockingly bad news: She'd just gotten the quote from the dentist. To fix all the things wrong with my family's teeth was going to cost about the same as a pretty good used car for a teenager.

Eight-thousand two-hundred and fourteen dollars!

And seventy cents!

After switching to an insurance plan that our previous dentist didn't accept, it took nearly two years to finally get around to finding a new one. Sure, you're supposed to go to the dentist every six months. But what's the worst thing that could happen after two years? A few cavities?

Well, when you have six kids, the answer is *a lot more than a few cavities*. I was informed that two of my teenagers needed their wisdom teeth out. Another one had a gap in her front teeth that needed be closed. An assortment of fillings, root canals, and extractions were needed. And, the dentist warned, I really needed to get my old 1970s-era silver fillings replaced before they cracked and fell out of my face.

Because, you know, you wouldn't want your fillings falling out of your face.

My immediate instinct was to prioritize: Which kids had the worst problems that needed to be fixed the most urgently?

Then my wife handed me a brochure from the dentist stating that they offered multiple financing plans, including—among others—12 months, no interest if paid in full.

I pulled out my iPhone and did the math: $684.56 a month. A pretty nice car payment—but all things considered, doable within my budget. To be sure I wouldn't hit the dreaded "interest kicks in" part of the plan, I rounded the payment up to $750 a month for 11 months and told her to "GET ALL THE WORK DONE."

Here's what you need to know about my financial situation: I'm no Bill Gates, but I live in a nice home in a nice part of town. I drive reasonably nice cars, and I take vacations with my family. In other words—**if you have a great company that sells for high prices, I look an awful lot like YOUR TYPICAL CUSTOMER.**

And your customers, like me, are going to spend a heck of a lot more money with you when you offer them financing.

Why a discussion on financing right here in the front of the book?

Simple: If you're selling at super high prices (like I have basically commanded you to do), you're going to need all the tools for selling you can get.

And trust me—nothing moves the needle quite like offering financing.

But the truth is, almost ALL contractors use financing the WRONG way. Yes, that means you. You're almost certainly doing it WRONG.

Don't worry, though. I'm about to fix that.

As we shift the discussion to financing of home improvement projects, let me dispel a couple of myths right up front. Please keep an open mind, because there's a good chance you believe one or both of them:

Myth #1:"My Customers Don't Want/Need Financing."

Fact: Either they're lying, or you're making bad assumptions based on faulty logic. Nobody—and I mean nobody—wants to take $8,000 to $40,000 out of their savings to buy new windows (or kitchen, basement, siding, HVAC system, or whatever). Nobody. Just because they CAN afford it doesn't mean they WANT to.

And just because they don't ASK for financing doesn't mean they won't be THRILLED when you offer it. According to industry statistics, 38% of homeowners said they would not have made their purchase without financing, and 42% chose a contractor primarily because of promotional financing offers.

Myth #2:"Financing costs too much, so it should only be used as a last-ditch option."

Fact: Financing doesn't cost you money... it <u>makes</u> you money. Check out these mind-blowing stats I collected from a major home improvement financing company:

- **$5,519** – Average sale with "no interest if paid in full in 12 months" offer

- **$6,804** – Average sale with "no interest if paid in up to 36 months" offer

- **$7,466** – Average sale with longer term, low APR finance offer

Stats are unavailable on what the average sale is when no financing is offered at all. But let's use our noggins and common sense and assume it's lower. For sake of argument, let's conservatively guesstimate $4,500. That's about a 67% increase in average ticket (with long-term, low APR) over no financing. Assuming the cost of financing to you is about 5.5% to 6% (about $450 on a $7,500 sale), can you afford NOT to offer financing?

Don't Use Financing As A Last-Ditch Option. Make It Front And Center.

But just offering financing isn't enough. ***Commit*** to financing. Instead of using it a last-ditch effort to salvage a deal that's slipping away, <u>*start with this discussion*</u>:

> *"Mr. and Mrs. Prospect, we offer several financing options to make this project affordable. How much money do you feel would fit comfortably into your monthly budget to make this project happen?"*

When you <u>lead</u> with financing, you immediately feel the homeowner's tension melt away. Instead of sticker shocking your customer at the end of the presentation with a price tag of $12,500 for new windows (and trust me, they were expecting a MUCH lower number when you walked into their house), you simply work the terms of the financing to fit their pre-agreed-upon monthly payment.

One-call closes go up. Overall closing ratios go up. Average sale prices go up. And best of all, profit margins go up. ***YOU MAKE MORE MONEY… with the exact same prospects you already have!***

When I discovered the sales-propelling power of financing, I instantly started encouraging my client to PRO-ACTIVELY offer it.

Here's an example. A good-size closet organization company told me their average sale was about $2,800. They signed on with our preferred finance partner and reported that their FIRST attempt to use it resulted in a $7,700 sale. That's nearly THREE TIMES their average. According to the client, their customer said, "Well, since the payment is so low, let's go ahead and do all three closets right now instead of one."

But that's just the tip of the iceberg.

I work with an HVAC company in California that's already doing north of $40MM in sales. Their top sales guy has perfected the art of offering financing THE RIGHT WAY. He brings it up at the beginning of the meeting. He makes it the first and second option. He only talks in terms of monthly payments. He reluctantly accepts cash only in cases where the customer insists.

And his average sale is $24,000.

The rest of the sales staff? With one notable exception, they hover around $13,000 per sale.

When I found this out, I immediately put together a full-blown training course outlining *Mr. $24,000*'s methods for the rest of the sales team to follow. We created scripts and forcedthe salespeople to memorize and use them. Success followed shortly thereafter.

(Note: Don't assume that just because somebody in the company is doing it right that everybody else is going to automatically catch on. They might. But they might not. Institute training to make sure).

Offer financing. Offer it early in the presentation. Talk about it in the middle of the presentation. Give them monthly payment options at end of the presentation.

Want to hit $10MM? Don't neglect financing. It's an important weapon.

Conversion rates will go up. Average tickets will spike. And you'll be well on your way to breaking the eight-figure barrier.

CHAPTER 10

You Have To Budget For And Buy Your Leads

J UST ONE MORE thing in the "$10MM Mindset" section before we get to the marketing part.

You MUST have the mindset that you're going to <u>spend money</u> to buy leads.

I learned this the hard way many years ago. I was working with an $8MM home improvement company that had about a $100,000 a month marketing budget. My job was to work with the owner to allocate the money and make many of the various media buys.

After a couple of months, the owner got me on a call and was steaming mad—he was reviewing his numbers and saw that his leads and sales were down. The reason was simple: I hadn't spent all his budget. The money I thought I was "saving" him in advertising was actually COSTING him big time. He not-so-patiently explained to me that he has to BUY EVERY SINGLE LEAD HE GETS.

Lesson learned.

What about you? Do you *look forward* to spending money on advertising and marketing, so that you can buy the leads you need to grow your business? Naturally, you want to spend your money smart and get as big of a return as possible. That's a big part of this book.

But don't forget—to get to $10MM, spending money is NOT optional. It has to be done. End of story.

With that in mind, here's the big question: How much should you spend on marketing, as a percentage of sales?

Ten years ago, the most common answer I'd hear from remodelers was 10%. In other words, if a company was selling $100,000 a month, they'd shoot for a $10,000 monthly marketing budget. A $4MM company would budget $400,000 for marketing and advertising.

The truth is that 10% is the bare minimum you should be budgeting. Large companies can get away with 10%, but here's a hard truth: If you want to get to $10MM, you're going to have to plow some of your profits (read: take-home money) back into marketing for a few years until you get there.

If you're doing $2MM or $4MM, you might need to spend 12%, 15%... even 18%. You won't take home as much money right away, but long term you're going to be killing it. That's part of the mindset.

But whenever this question of <u>budget as a percentage of sales</u> comes up, there are always a handful of companies that shudder at the notion of even 10%; for this select group, even 5% seems like way too much. They give me answers like 2% or 3%... and seem outraged at the thought of spending a penny more.

And whenever I hear those lowball answers, I automatically know that these are companies that get the majority of their business from a combination of **repeat and referral business**. Always. Without fail. Usually, when pressed, these companies will proudly declare that 60%... 70%... 80% or more of their business comes from these two lead sources.

And unbeknownst to them, this equation—3% marketing budget, 75% of business from "repeat and referral"—is killing their chance to grow their business.

Wait... what?

Aren't repeat and referral leads the holy grail of remodeling lead sources? Wouldn't all remodeling companies KILL for a profit machine that continuously churns new business out of old business? Wouldn't it be great to free yourself from the shackles of the lead generation treadmill?

Actually, no. The problem in a nutshell: Companies that rely so heavily on repeat and referral business lack the ability to significantly grow their business.

Here's why:

They Don't Understand Their Real Numbers: If a company's doing $2MM in sales, and $1.5MM comes from repeat and referral... and they spend 3% on marketing, that's actually the equivalent of spending 10% to 12% on marketing. Why? Because that 3% ($60,000) is being spent to generate the $500,000 in sales that are NOT coming from repeat and referral. And in my experience, these kinds of companies usually have ONE major thing they're "good" at—usually home shows. Which leads to the next problem...

Their Mindset Prevents Growth: These companies inevitably assign the 3% marketing budget against ALL sales, which causes them to draw a false (and deadly) conclusion: "Any marketing activity we engage in should have a comparable 3% lead cost or we will refuse to participate." This is a death-spiral mindset that at best will prevent growth...and at worst cost you the business you already have (see weathering downturns, below).

Not Scalable: This means a business that can, by definition, only grow very slowly. You can only generate so many referrals and repeat purchases. If you want to grow from $2MM to $3MM, you can't magically generate an extra million dollars in sales from referrals. Realize if you're getting the lion's share of your business from repeat and referral, that means you're already really good at it... and you aren't going to find a lot of table scraps on the floor. If you want to grow, you're going to have to conquer the internet AND advertise—and advertising of any kind is going to cost you a heck of a lot more than 3%.

Can't Weather Downturns: But you are comfortable with your $2MM company, you say...and you're not really interested in adding another million dollars in sales. Fair enough. But what happens if you experience a dip in repeat and referral business for some reason? You'd be surprised at how many of these companies end up talking to me for this very reason. Then when I bring up alternate lead generation activities that cost as much as 20% to 30% to START (i.e., before they optimize and settle back into the 10% to 15% range), they freak out. Rough waters ahead.

Prices Not High Enough: Here we go again. I've also found that high-percentage of "repeat and referral" companies frequently have low prices, relative to their competitors. This is often a major reason why they have so many people coming back in the first place. That's not a bad thing, in and of itself. But if your prices are low because you don't have to spend the same money on advertising that your competitors do, then you're going to be in bad shape if and when you're forced to jump into the lead generation pool later. You simply will not be able to afford it. Meanwhile, your higher-priced and lead-generation-savvy competitors are going to eat your lunch.

So, what's the takeaway? What is the actionable next step?

First of all, if you fall into the category of companies that are fortunate enough (yes, fortunate!) to generate a ton of business from repeat and referral, check your pricing. This is a serious issue. I'd immediately raise your prices by at least 10%, with a goal of ultimately raising prices by 25% to 50%. You don't want to raise prices so quickly that your salespeople freak out and die on the spot… and you don't want to alienate the customers who are coming back and sending their friends. But if you have quality products, treat your customers right, and stand behind your work, you will be able to raise your prices WITH NO PROBLEM.

Next, you'll need to absolutely MASTER internet lead generation and selling. It's not optional, and it's what a huge part of this book is all about.

Once you've spent all the money you possibly can on internet lead generation, the next step is to start with a FARMING marketing activity with 10% to 20% of your marketing budget. By FARMING, I mean advertising activities that are designed to generate a few leads now, and **lots of leads in the future.**

Later on in this book I will talk you into radio and TV. Don't worry, I'll give you all the details, overcome all your fears, and get you into the right mindset to actually make the jump to $10MM or more in sales.

Finally, keep an open mind. Just because you've always been able to get away with a 3% or 7% marketing budget, realize that getting to the next level is going to cost more.

But oh, the rewards.

SECTION 2

Identity – The Case For Doing Business With Your Company, And The Foundation For All Your Marketing

CHAPTER 11
Standing Out From The Crowd

'D NEVER BEEN less impressed with a restaurant in my entire life. If you could even call it a restaurant.

Several years ago, an employee and I had just flown cross country for a seminar in San Francisco—something like a four-hour flight. After the usual luggage shuffle, taxi cab ride (this was before Uber!), and hotel check-in, I was exhausted. All I wanted to do was get a good meal and catch some shut eye.

Upon checking in, the lobby clerk informed us that the hotel restaurant was closed, but we could still order room service if we wanted. Maybe it's just me, but I can never seem to rid my room of the smell of Buffalo wings and burgers after ordering room service. So we asked about nearby dining options.

The clerk told us there was a Mexican restaurant within walking distance less than a quarter mile away.

Perfect.

The clerk said to go out the side door, walk toward the soccer complex, and up the little street to the right. That's where we'd find the restaurant.

We did exactly that…except there was no restaurant.

All that was there was a combination soccer complex and golf driving range. No restaurant in sight.

We walked to back to the hotel and kindly informed the hotel clerk that his directions didn't lead us to food. The clerk then clarified that the restaurant was INSIDE the combo sports facility.

Now, if we were to play a word-association game, how long do you think it would take you to pair the terms "restaurant" and "combo sports complex"?

Exactly.

But, hey—we were starved and desperately low on options. We walked back up the little street to the right, went INSIDE the soccer facility, past the golf clubs, and found what can best be described as a crusty indoor taco stand.

There was no sign, inside or out—no wonder we missed it the first time. A guy behind the counter wearing a nametag identifying him as "José" made eye contact with me a split-second before I could dial 1-800-DOMINOES on my cell phone.

Thoughts of food poisoning-induced projectile vomiting on unsuspecting seminar attendees swept through my mind as I smiled and politely told Jose that "I guess I'll try the chicken fajitas."

Jose was ecstatic. I think we might have been the only customers that week. As we sat down and rationed our sodas (NO FREE REFILLS!), we discussed what kind of bad karma might result from simply running out of the place. We had already paid, so they couldn't call the cops on us. But ultimately, the thought of potentially crushing Jose's spirit was enough to resign us to whatever fate awaited.

Then Jose brought our food to us. I looked down at the plate and didn't know what to think. I was simultaneously dazzled and puzzled. Amazed and confused. Delighted and bewildered.

Jose, it turns out, was an Artist. With a capital "A."

I wasn't looking at a pile of tortillas, shredded cheese, and chicken. I was staring at what could be best described as an angel that had escaped from some kind of heavenly wedding ceremony, crashed into a wall, and wound up on my dinner plate. It was far too nice looking to consider actually, you know, *eating* it.

Naturally, I became fast buddies with José. I wanted to know all about this (what I dubbed) "Wicked Angel Fajita" he had served me.

He explained that it was just a little something he liked to do to make his job a bit more interesting. He liked seeing people's faces when they were expecting chicken and he instead served them an edible doily. He said he'd been doing it for years and he was pretty well known for it.

I did manage to get proof of the second coming of Michelangelo on my crummy pre-iPhone-era camera phone, which you can see above (Sorry for the UFO-sighting-quality photo. I swear it was really cool).

This got me thinking: when was the last time you were so blown away by something you bought that you had to immediately take a picture and text it to your spouse? When was the last time you experienced service that was so unbelievable you had no option but to brag it up to your friends? When was the last time you experienced something so flipping COOL that you were compelled to post it to Facebook or Tweet it out to the world?

Yeah, same here. Pretty much never.

Here's the good news: Achieving "Wow," as innovation guru Tom Peters would say, is actually pretty easy to do… and generally doesn't cost all that much. In the spirit of José the Fajita Artist, and in following with the first step our 4-Step Formula to get your business to $10MM (sell awesome stuff that people genuinely love), I'd like to introduce you to the concept of IDENTITY.

Definition of Identity:

Words, phrases, and images… articulated with power, precision, and passion… that instantly and definitively communicate who you are, how you're different and better, and what customers can expect when doing business with you.

Sounds easy, simple, and intuitive, right?

Not really.

There's a 50% chance that you HAVE an identity… but only a 1% chance that you're actually communicating it in a way that customers and prospects can understand.

In other words, you're almost surely using PLATITUDES in your marketing instead of IDENTIY.

What's the difference?

Let's find out.

CHAPTER 12
Platitudes Are Murdering Your Marketing

S PEAKING OF FOOD...

In case you weren't aware, Papa John's Pizza has better ingredients, and therefore better pizza.

And I'm sure the first time you ever saw or heard that slogan, you immediately wised up to all that crummy pizza you had been buying from the likes of Pizza Hut, Dominoes, or the local pizza joint and switched to Papa John's.

After all, if Papa John's *says* their pizza is better, it <u>must</u> be true. Right?

In the late 1990s, Pizza Hut certainly didn't think so. At the time, their virtual monopoly in the pizza world had been decaying for several years, and they decided to fight back the American way—by suing their rivals. In the crosshairs was (relative) upstart Papa John's and their misleading, blatantly FALSE slogan, "Better Ingredients. Better Pizza."

Much of the case revolved around the difference in the way the two chains prepared their sauces. A scientist was brought in as an expert witness by Pizza Hut to testify that both sauces, in fact, tasted identical.

It was proven that neither product was actually fresh—they both sat around for weeks before being deployed onto a pizza. After weeks of trial and millions of dollars in legal fees, the judge ordered an injunction against Papa John's entire "Better Ingredients. Better Pizza." campaign.

Papa John's immediately appealed on the grounds that the judge had simply gotten the law wrong.

They argued that "truth in advertising" laws hinged on a definition of "puffery" and "puffing." According to these laws, they were free to PUFF all they wanted… which is the act of making statements so vague, ridiculous, outrageous, or opinionated that they could not possibly be taken seriously by customers.

Otherwise, BMW would have to empirically prove that their automobile was indeed THE ultimate driving machine. American Airlines would have to prove that they indeed understand why each and every one of their customers flies. State Farm would have to demonstrate that they are, in fact, there for you "like a good neighbor."

Or, in other words, nobody believes platitudes anyway, so go ahead and use them all you want.

The appeals court agreed, and green-lighted Papa John's to puff away. And with that, it became legally official: Platitudes are disregarded by the buying public as throwaway statements that mean nothing, prove nada, and influence nobody.

You can use them in your advertising all you want, without recourse.

Which is why you probably have tons of them in (gulp) YOUR marketing.

When you say "high quality" or "best service" or "best installers/technicians" in your marketing, those things may have a deep, rich meaning to you. Your life's work has probably gone into delivering the highest quality or the best service or in training your technicians to be the absolute best.

But to the listening public, they're just empty phrases—*they're platitudes.*

Would you ever expect a company to advertise anything OTHER than they have the best workmanship or best service or whatever? Of course not!

But you know what? If you look at 95% of marketing and advertising—including, probably, your own—you'll see it's absolutely LOADED DOWN with platitudes.

By definition, **platitudes are words and phrase that are drearily commonplace and predictable.** They lack the power to evoke interest because they are so flagrantly overused. Yet companies state them as if they were original and significant.

You can find platitudes EVERYWHERE. On mailers.On TV commercials.During radio ads.Plastered all over company websites.

To successfully implement the 4-Step Formula to get to $10MM, you must ELIMINATE platitudes from your marketing without remorse.

Charlie Brown's Mom

Do you remember watching those Peanuts cartoon specials on TV back in the '70s that featured Charlie Brown and Snoopy? Remember what would happen in those cartoons whenever one of the kids would talk to an adult?

Whenever the adults would speak, you wouldn't actually hear the words they were saying; instead, all you would hear was "*Waaawawaaaawawaaaaawaaaa!*" That's exactly what it sounds like you're saying when you have platitudes in your marketing.

Is this making sense to you? Is it evident that platitudes might be a problem for you now, and a tremendous competitive advantage if you could figure out how to fix it? You've got to find ways to communicate your TRUE IDENTITY with power, precision, and passion.

We'll get to HOW to do it in just a minute...

CHAPTER 13
The Curse Of Knowledge

B UT FIRST: WHY are these platitudes still so common? I mean, given that they don't work in marketing. Why is nearly every contractor website, mailer, and home show booth still crammed full of them?

In seminars with contractors, I answer this question by playing a fun little game called **"tappers and listeners"** that I discovered in a book called "Made To Stick" by Dan and Chip Heath.

It's simple: I tap a song on a table with my knuckles (I'm the tapper) and the seminar audience tries to guess what song it is (they're the listeners).

The only clues I give them is that the song will be traditional. Something that everybody knows, like "Happy Birthday" or "Take Me Out To The Ball Game." No modern pop music or rock or country or anything that would require knowledge of a certain genre.

As I tap, I ask them to raise their hand if they know the song... but NOT to shout it out (so as to ruin the game for everyone else).

And I always get a room full of blank stares.

Out of 100 people in a room, anywhere from zero to five will THINK they know it, and half of them will be wrong.

I tap the song again. Same song. No variance. I assure them that they've all heard the song hundreds of times.

Taps.

Blank stares.

Then I reveal the title: "The Star-Spangled Banner".

You know… our National Anthem, which has been played and sung—and in some cases butchered—at every major sporting event for the last 50 years.

Then I tap it again, for a third time.

I see eyes light up. Smiles appear on faces. Heads nod in recognition. Once they know what song the taps are supposed to be, everybody gets it.

Here's the point: When you're the tapper—like I was—it's impossible to NOT hear the tune in your head as you tap it out. Not only do you hear the tune, but you hear it in full stereo surround sound—with the orchestra.

As a listener, on the other hand, you only hear a monotone set of like-sounding taps. You're only being given a small fraction of the information needed to decipher the song—the basic melody.

But look at what you're NOT getting—no individual notes, no words, no rhythm. Just taps.

This illustrates a problem known as the "Curse of Knowledge."

When you know something, it's nearly impossible for you to imagine what it's like NOT to know it.

The result, as marketers, is we tend to impose our level of understanding on other people. We write the words High Quality or Best Service on an ad and we hear them in our heads with the full orchestra in surround sound. The words have deep, rich meaning to us.

Meanwhile, the ad reader only hears a few seemingly discombobulated taps.

Hold that thought on The Curse of Knowledge. Now I need to introduce you to another concept, then I'll tie it all together.

CHAPTER 14
Confirmation Bias: Finding And Pointing At The Showerhead

MANY YEARS AGO, when my children were all still very young, my wife and I decided to put our sanity to the test by embarking on (what turned out to be) a 4,975-mile cross-country trip in a silver Chevrolet 15-passenger van.

After two relatively uneventful days of driving, we were descending out of the mountains into the little community of Ogden, Utah and started looking for a hotel. This was before mobile devices allowed you to check and book hotels on the fly, so we had to actually stop in and check availability.

And as fate would have it, the first place we found was a Holiday Inn Express. It met our basic requirements—relatively new, free breakfast, and a swimming pool.

As we checked in, I couldn't help but notice a sign on the counter showing that Holiday Inn Express was the home of the "Stay Smart" showerhead by Kohler.

The sign showed a picture of a giant showerhead that appeared to be bigger, badder, and bolder than any regular showerhead could ever hope to be. I didn't pay that much attention—just another sign on another counter—no big deal.

When we got to our rooms, the kids immediately started jumping between the beds, turning on the TV, and generally wreaking havoc like kids do when they're releasing 11 hours of pent-up energy.

Next to the TV on the dresser I spotted another sign showing the picture of the hulking showerhead and inviting me, at my earliest convenience, to check out the "Stay Smart Bathroom," featuring the "Stay Smart" showerhead by Kohler.

"Okay," I thought. *"I'll bite."*

As I walked into the bathroom and flipped on the light, I was met by another sign—the third one now—on the counter informing me that the Stay Smart Bathroom had more pleasant surprises. This included a bowed-out shower curtain rod, plush, oversized towels, designer toiletries (i.e., fancy soaps, shampoos, and lotions). And of course, the centerpiece of the entire bathroom, the Stay Smart showerhead by Kohler.

I turned toward the shower area to at last behold this marvelous Stay Smart showerhead in all its glory and splendor.

But the curtain was closed.

As I whipped it open, I could hear angels sing and bright lights coming from the heavens as I witnessed the supernal beauty of... the Stay Smart showerhead by Kohler. Want to know how I knew it was the Stay Smart Showerhead by Kohler?

They put a sign on it—just to erase any doubt.

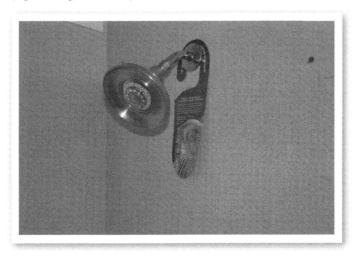

This is the actual picture of the actual Stay Smart Showerhead in my room in Ogden, Utah. As you can see on the lower left-hand part of the sign, the showerhead provides three luxurious-sounding settings: "Invigorating," "Revitalizing," and "Rejuvenating."

I locked the door, stripped, and turned on the water. I considered my options. Was I in the mood to be invigorated or revitalized? Or was I up for some rejuvenation? After mulling over my choices, I set the showerhead to "Rejuvenating."

I'm not going to lie: That was one delightful shower.

That is, until my wife started banging on the door, telling me that the kids were starving and destroying the room… and to get my butt out of there and do something with them! I ensconced myself in the luxury of an oversized, 100% cotton towel, got dressed, and took the kids to Pizza Hut. (Take that, Papa John's!).

So… what's the bright idea here? And how does this all relate to YOUR marketing?

The hotel's marketing campaign worked on a principle called "confirmation bias," which means that **people tend to seek out and believe evidence that supports their existing beliefs, and they tend to ignore or minimize evidence that goes against their existing beliefs.**

Confirmation bias is what causes a naive mother to believe her beloved teenage son when he claims that the marijuana found under his mattress "must have been a friend of a friend of a friend's that he barely even knows and who he'll never invite over to the house again."

Yeah… right.

It's what makes people who hate Donald Trump love his tax plan when they're told that it is Bernie Sander's tax plan.

That's confirmation bias.

Here's what's interesting: in business, you can set your prospects' beliefs <u>for</u> them, and then supply them with the evidence to support those beliefs.

That's exactly what the Holiday Inn Express was doing in this story. They tell you their showerhead is the greatest thing since sliced bread.

They have a sign in the lobby telling you how great it is. Then again in the bedroom. Then again in the bathroom. Then again hanging from the showerhead itself.

By the time you actually get in shower, you not only <u>notice</u> the showerhead (when under normal conditions, it would go completely and utterly unnoticed), you also interpret the evidence (large size, luxurious-sounding settings, high water pressure) as proof that that it actually IS the greatest showerhead ever. Or at least a darn good one.

You NOTICE it and you LIKE it.

This is what you should do with YOUR business: **Point to your showerhead.**

Yeah, I know you don't have a showerhead in your business (unless you're a bathroom remodeler, lol).

But you probably have *something* that's at least semi-awesome. Or, hopefully, something that's REALLY awesome.

As you'll remember, Step 1 of our 4-Step Formula was selling awesome stuff that people genuinely love.

But don't assume because you're selling something awesomethat people are going to automatically notice it, appreciate it, and like it.

Chances are, they won't.

That's where marketing comes in.

You have to figure out what your "showerhead" is and point at it like crazy.

If you do this, then customers and prospects will begin to believe that it *really* is great, and find evidence to support that it's everything you've made it out to be.

This is the birth of an IDENTITY.

To make this work, though, it's a pre-requisite that whatever you're pointing at HAS to be impressive.

What if you hopped in the Holiday Inn Express shower—after all the hype on the signs—only to find a dinky, calcium-encrusted showerhead with no water pressure?

Not only would you notice it, but you'd hate Holiday Inn Express for lying to you.

Let me give you an example to help you understand.

One of my clients, a kitchen and bathroom remodeler, only hires master craftsmen to work for them.

The problem is that "master craftsmen" is a platitude. It sounds good enough, but nobody really knows what that means or if it's any better or different than what any of their competitors do.

The "Charlie Brown's Mom" way to advertise would be to simply use the platitude. Tell people online, in print, and on the airwaves that "We only hire master craftsmen."

But we have to explain to the jury what that means so we can get past the platitude and communicate with power, precision, and passion. Here's what the radio script says:

Do you know what a 'master craftsman' is? If you're about to remodel your kitchen or bathroom, you should. A master craftsman is somebody with at least 10 years of experience… and who has completed at least FIVE HUNDRED projects. He understands every aspect of the job, and maintains a quality score of 99%. At (Company Name), we ONLY hire master craftsmen. In fact, we have over 50 of them on our staff. They are absolute _experts_ on kitchens and bathrooms—not just "jack of all trade" carpenters. That means the same person will be working on your kitchen or bathroom from start to finish—to make sure that EVERYTHING is done exactly right, with precision, down to the last detail. Master craftsmen at (Company Name). They're a lot harder to find… and they cost more to employ. But just wait until you see the final result.

BOOM! There's a showerhead—master craftsmen.

And guess what? We can do the same thing for other points of differentiation, too. I'll talk more about that in the upcoming chapters. Visit UnlimitedLeadFlow.com/book to see and hear more TV and radio ads for this and other campaigns.

Now it's time to tie all these concepts together and create an IDENTITY.

CHAPTER 15
Your Identity

BEFORE WE TACKLE the concept of identity, let's first review what we've covered leading up to it:

- Standing out from the crowd is imperative. Just like the wicked angel fajita.

- Platitudes won't cut it. But practically everyone's using them anyway. Charlie Brown's mom.

- The curse of knowledge. It's hard to know what it's like to not know what you know.

- Confirmation bias. Find the showerhead (fajita, whatever) and point at it.

Which brings us to identity. By way of review from Chapter 11:

Definition Of Identity: Words, phrases, and images… articulated with power, precision, and passion… that instantly and definitively communicate who you are, how you're different and better, and what customers can expect when doing business with you.

Let's break that down and make sure it's sinking in…

- **Words, phrases, and images:** A lot of the heavy lifting is going to be done with words, particularly headlines. But images can play an important role in conveying your identity, too.

- **Articulated with power, precision, and passion:** Look at most marketing writing; it's stale and full of platitudes. We have to find colorful words that express deep meaning—with specificity—and let your passion shine through.

- **Instantly and definitively communicate:** We want the reader/listener to recognize what you're trying to say in a split second... without question or ambiguity.

- **Who you are, how you're different and better:** What exactly are the benefits of doing business with you instead of any other choice or choosing not to buy anything at all?

- **What customers can expect when doing business with you:** What will the experience be like? What can they expect? How will it be different?

Let's jump straight in with an example that will make this all crystal clear.

Here's a screen shot of a website from a company called Upscale Remodeling. Let's see if we can detect an identity:

Let's go through this using the criteria I listed above.

- **Words, phrases and images:** The images here look cookie-cutter; they don't show anything particularly interesting, and certainly not stunning. It's very amateurish. The headlines are uninspiring and boring.

- **Articulated with power, precision, and passion:** Instead of passion, we find platitudes. "You can be sure it's done right!" and "Oldest, full-service remodeling companies!" Yawn. Boring. There is absolutely no power here whatsoever.

- **Instantly and definitively communicate:** In a split second, my best guess is that this is another remodeling company of no particular distinction.

- **Who you are, how you're different and better:** They only give me platitudes that are not believable; I have not been promised any particular benefit other than the typical clichés every other remodeler talks about.

- **What customers can expect when doing business with you:** Remodeling will be done—but how and to what extent it will be different is impossible to tell.

When developing an identity, I always consult with the owner of the company to dig down deep and find out what makes the company really tick. What do they do that's different? What are they passionate about—and how do they show it?

In talking with this company's owner, Steve, I found a person deeply committed to remodeling… and especially to extraordinary quality standards.

He's been in the industry literally since he was nine years old, when he would follow his dad around to jobsites to listen and learn. Steve is a guy who puts systems in place to make sure that everything gets done right. He is a person committed to giving the customer a predictable, no-stress, no-surprises experience.

Based on this, here's what we came up with for a website homepage:

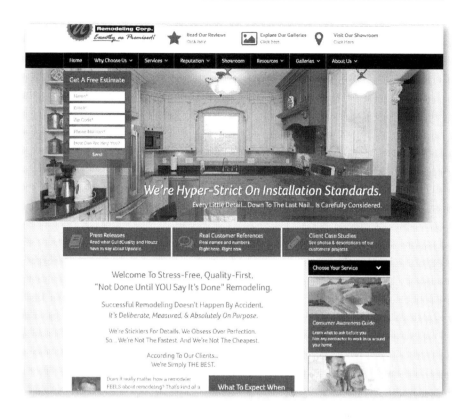

Important note: the top photo is what we call a "slider," meaning that it shows on the screen for a few seconds, then changes to a different photo with a different headline. This is an important tool in communicating identity. Let me show you the other sliders:

We Focus On Every Single Detail Of Every Single Job.
That's How We Guarantee 100% Satisfaction—Start To Finish, No Exceptions.

Everything You Need In Our 3,600 Square Foot Showroom.
Don't Run All Over Town—Just Stop In Our Showroom & Explore The Possibilities.

Our Warranties Have Backbone & Teeth—Not Loopholes.
When We Say It's Covered, You Can Take It To The Bank.

What are you learning, as a visitor on this site, as you watch these sliders scroll by on the screen?

Well, for starters:

- You get a visual representation of the kind and quality of work they do—kitchens, bathrooms, living rooms.

- They are extremely detail oriented, down to the last nail.

- They are fanatical about communication. There will be no surprises.

- Everything is covered by robust warranties.

- They have a showroom that will keep you from running all over town.

So now review the definition of identity... how are we doing? I'll wait, review it.

- **Words, phrases and images:** CHECK

- **Articulated with power, precision, and passion:** CHECK

- **Instantly and definitively communicate:** CHECK

- **Who you are, how you're different and better:** CHECK

- **What customers can expect when doing business with you:** CHECK

Verdict: We're doing GREAT.

Now let's look at the main headlines—the ones <u>under</u> the sliders.

Welcome to Stress-Free, Quality First, "Not Done Until YOU Say It's Done" Remodeling.

(Can you feel the passion and the commitment?)

Successful Remodeling Doesn't Happen By Accident. It's Deliberate, Measured& Absolutely On Purpose.

(Power, precision, and passion to spare!)

We're Sticklers For Details. We Obsess Over Perfection So... We're Not The Fastest. And We're Not The Cheapest.

(Any idea what you might expect if you do business with them?!?)

According To Our Clients...
We're Simply The Best.

(You might be thinking this is a platitude—and it would be if it were the only claim we made. But after the bold, powerful, passionate statements above, it actually becomes a **summarizing CAPPER!**)

Some people look at this example and instead of learning from it, they try to tear it apart.

They say, "I don't like the way the site looks." Or "I would never use those words to describe my business." Or "There are too many words there!"

First of all, realize that an identity is like a fingerprint. Every company's identity will be different because every company is different. Your company's identity should be based on who YOU are, what YOU do, and how YOU'RE different. There's no such thing as a "one size fits all" identity.

Next, websites can be made to LOOK in any of thousands of different ways! Honestly, this website is one of our oldest ones right now (as I write this); we actually have built many, many websites that I feel look better than this one. But this one looks good—**and it works!** We recommend updating the look and feel of your site every two to four years, even if the content doesn't change... just to keep up with the latest looks that customers expect. Don't get <u>too</u> caught up on the look.

As for the wording... we have to use words to communicate our meaning. Yes, pictures have their place, and they are important. But the tool we have to really communicate with power, precision, and passion is WORDS! They allow us to paint detailed, personalized pictures on the mental canvas of the reader. We'll talk more about this later.

To explorethe identity in this website in more detail—and to see more identity case studies—go to UnlimitedLeadFlow.com/book.

Once you have a powerful identity, you can use it in EVERY aspect of your marketing. It becomes the HUB of everything you do. Need a TV or radio ad? Pull it from your identity! Need a mailer? Or a home show booth? If you have a good identity, you can create those very quickly.

To wrap up: Everything depends on your identity. Let's now work through creating one for YOU.

Right here.

Right now.

CHAPTER 16

Creating An Identity, Step One – "What Makes Your Company Tick?"

THERE ARE THREE steps to creating a powerful identity, and we're going to go over them in each of the next three chapters. They are:

1. What makes your company tick?

2. Build a case.

3. Communicate with power, precision, and passion.

As we go through these sections, I'll give you some examples that will help make the concept of identity come together for you.

Let's start with—what else? —Step One, "What Makes Your Company Tick?"

It's a deceivingly simple question. As you will see in a minute, you're going to have to dig a little bit below the surface to get the answers you'll need to create a powerful identity. But you won't really need your shovels until Steps Two and Three.

With Step One in mind, consider these questions to get started…

- **What do you already do that customers like?** There is a reason your customers like you—what is it? Write down anything that comes to mind. Don't worry about writing down platitudes right now—we'll fix those later. This is your STARTING point!

o   Do you treat people better?

o   Do you not require money up front?

o   Do you refuse to play sales games?

o   Do you have a higher level of workmanship?

o   Are you a stickler for details?

o   Are your warranties better/longer than others?

o   Are you more convenient?

o   Do you communicate better than most companies?

o   Do you use higher quality materials?

o   Do you get the job done faster?

o   Do you have better payment terms?

o   Do you use (or not use) subcontractors?

o   Something else?

Write down whatever you can think of, then go back and put them in order from most important to least important.

Here are some more questions that might yield the same (or similar) answers. Sometimes asking questions from a different angle spurs different thoughts…

•   **What do you take particular pride in?**

•   Are there details that you handle (or pay attention to) better/more than anyone else?

•   What do you deserve to win an award for (even if such an award does not actually exist)?

•   If you could teach a class to other companies (not geographically competitive), what topic do you have the expertise to teach them?

•   **What makes you better and different than most of your competitors?**

- If you asked your customers the number-one reason they chose youBEFORE the job started, what would it be?
- If you asked your customers the number-one reason they chose you AFTER the job was completed, what would it be?
- What are the main points of differentiation you talk about in your sales presentation?
- **What are you really, really good at?**
- What have you spent years/decades perfecting?
- What have other companies unsuccessfully tried to copy or steal from you?
- **What do you want written on your tombstone?** (I'm not trying to kill you off! But a tombstone is a place where you have very little space to say something very profound—think about it).
- **What are you absolutely unwilling to fudge on?**

Ask yourself these questions, and then ask your employees. Ask your sales manager and your controller. Ask your general manager. Ask your salespeople. Ask the receptionist. You can even ask your vendors.

Once you have a list of answers—just jot down *anything* that comes to mind—go back and prioritize them.

You should have at least five items on your list, and maybe as many as 20 or 25. Make sure to write them all down!

Once you have your list, you'll be ready to build a case, which is Part Two of creating an identity. But before we go there, let's crack open a couple of case studies.

Case Study #1 – Video Game Manufacturer

You might think it's weird to give an example outside of your industry. But in my experience, it's often easier to see and understand the *principles* when you're looking at something you're not so close to. (Don't worry, I'll also give you a contractor example in a minute).

Heads up: I'm going to give you these case studies in pieces, as we go through each of the three steps. I'll start them right now, and then show you how PartsTwoandThree of creating an identity apply to these cases as we get to those chapters. In other words, <u>pay close attention</u>!

The year was 1997. I was less than three years into my career as a marketing guru, and still eight years away from specializing in contractor marketing.

Actually, guru status was the farthest thing from my mind. My main objective was to extend my winning streak with this client, Dynamo, Ltd.

The company manufactured coin-operated amusements… stuff like pool tables, air hockey machines, foosball tables, and so forth.

Earlier in the year, I had hit a home run for them with a product called "Top Brass Pool." I created an effective advertising campaign that convinced owners of bards, bowling alleys, restaurants, and even gentlemen's clubs that they could make more money from their pool tables by upgrading their green-felt and wood-colored pool table (50 cents per play) to a fancier blue felt and black laminate ($1.00 per play).

When truckload-sized orders started pouring in, my client was thrilled. They had been literally on the brink of bankruptcyseven months earlier (when they first hired me). Now they were flush with cash—but also overflowing with great expectations.

They tasked me with helping them sell more video game cabinets. Think of a Pac-Man or Frogger or Donkey Kong machine—essentially a wooden box with a computer screen and some joysticks and buttons and some electronic stuff inside. They manufactured these raw "boxes" and sold them to the video game companies who then loaded the software (games) in them and plastered the sides with eye-catching graphics.

As I sat down with them to go through an Identity Consultation, I started with the usual line of questioning: What makes your cabinets better or different? Why would somebody want to buy them instead of the overseas models that cost half the price? What makes your cabinet so darn special?

Immediately they focused in on QUALITY. Nobody—and I mean nobody—I was told, built a higher quality, longer lasting video game cabinet than Dynamo. They seemed incredulous that I would even ask—the answer was obvious, wasn't it? Everybody just KNOWS that

Benz is the best car, right? Same thing with Dynamo cabinets, at least according to the half-dozen executives at the conference table.

I asked *what they meant* by quality. What, specifically, were they proud of? Unwilling to fudge on? What would they win an award for—if such an award existed? And so on, through all the questions I just asked you above.

They got stuck. They couldn't get past the generic (platitude) answer, QUALITY. And that's okay, because we can take platitudes and FIX THEM and make them into a better, more powerful answer in the next chapter, when we talk about "building a case."

Let's put a pin in this for now—we'll circle back around to this case study in each of the next two chapters. But for right now, I want you to see that the "What Makes You Tick?" question yielded the answer of "quality."

Let's now look at an example of a contractor.

Case Study #2: Heating And Air Conditioning Company

This company, Service Champions, came to me a couple of years ago as a referral from my biggest client. They saw the work I was doing—particularly in radio and TV—with that client and wanted to get on the train.

I quickly found out how *different* two companies can be—even though both companies are in the same industry and are far and away the biggest and best companies in their respective markets.

The first company—my biggest client that had referred Service Champions to me—was all about convenience and quality. They guaranteed their appointment times. They came any time, day or night, at no extra charge. They trained their technicians for 150 hours a year… a phenomenal feat.

But when I sat down with my new client, I was blown away at how different—and how AWESOME—*they* were (too).

They invited me to attend their monthly "all company meeting" (literally, every employee attended) so I could see what they were all about. The plan was to then sit down with the owner and marketing team afterward to discuss their identity as we kicked off the relationship.

To say I was blown away by the meeting would be a massive understatement.

Long story short, they barely talked about goals, numbers, and strategic focus like I had expected. Instead, they talked about employees—showed pictures of people's dogs and kids. They told stories about how many people they had done "good deeds" for. They profiled certain employees and talked about their personal lives—hobbies, vacations, passions, music interests, and families.

Web Extra: To read about this meeting, go to UnlimitedLeadFlow. com/book, and find the article titled "The best way to manage your business." You'll be glad you did.

But that meeting was only the appetizer for the identity meeting that followed. When I asked them what made them different and better, their answers inevitably pointed to one thing: their technicians.

Their technicians were nicer, friendlier, cleaner, and kinder. They showed up on time and respected people's property. They did good deeds for their customers. Basically, they had hired and trained a giant troop of Boy Scouts.

What about convenience? What about quality? What about training? What about being on time?

They assured me they did all those things. But they also barely seemed to care about any of it. Their main thing was this army of angels that they were sending out to service their customers' air conditioners.

That was the one thing they would NOT fudge on.

That might seem like an odd thing to put all your chips on—until you understand that their customer base is predominantly older people. People who value the look and appearance and demeanor of the person entering their home.

And so it was. Their identity was to be based on their technicians.

We'll also come back to this case study in the next chapter. I'll show you how to take these raw qualities—superior workmanship for the remodeler, and boy scout-like technicians for the air conditioner company—and turn them into rock-solid identities.

CHAPTER 17
Creating An Identity, Step Two – "Build A Case"

REMEMBER THE OJ Simpson trial? For some of the younger bucks out there, you might have to Google it. The rest of you remember it for sure.

First, OJ hired the best attorneys money could buy.

Those attorneys then sold a jury of 12 people a story that got him off the hook, despite overwhelming evidence that he had murdered his wife and her alleged lover. The trial dragged on for weeks... then months... as the attorneys trotted out piece after piece after piece of evidence to support their case. The entire nation hung on every detail for nine full months until the "not guilty" verdict was rendered.

But think about it: What if OJ's attorneys got up there, and instead of building a meticulous case, just spewed a bunch of platitudes?

"Come on... he couldn't have done that! He's OJ! The Juice! He runs through airports! He's the 2,000-yard Buffalo Bill! He's a movie star! There's no way man! He wasn't even there that night. He was out somewhere else. He just couldn't have done it."

As ridiculous as that sounds, that's about as good of a case as most businesses ever prepare to defend and sell their product. They just offer a non-compelling, surface-level laundry list of platitudes and hope that someone will give them money. As if just being there—just being in business—makes them entitled to our business!

Look at what OJ's attorneys <u>did</u> do: they got all kinds of forensic reports, alibis, expert witnesses... and <u>everything</u> to prove that he couldn't <u>possibly</u> have done it. They defined the important issues and brought in experts to teach the jury what they needed to know about said issues:

- They had a guy who was a **glove expert** who showed how and why the glove found at the crime scene couldn't possibly have been OJ's... it was too small!

- They had **blood splatter experts** who testified that there's no way that that the blood would have splattered the way it did if OJ had done it. They gave the jury a crash course on blood splatter-ology. See, if OJ would have stabbed someone, the blood would have splattered over there, not here.

- They had a **shoe expert** testify that bloody footprints left by OJ's size 12 Bruno Magliboots were not necessarily made while OJ himself was wearing them.

Whoever heard of a glove expert or a blood-splatter expert outside of a court case? Who knows, they probably make good money for their strange but expert knowledge. But hey… after hearing their testimony, the jury felt like they knew enough about gloves and blood splatters, and the relevant issues surrounding it that OJ got off scot-free.

That bell that just went off in your head was your brain connecting the concept of "Point at the Showerhead" (aka confirmation bias) and building a case!

Since the jury (your prospects/customers) **don't know what to look for** when it comes to buying (windows, roofing, HVAC, siding, bathrooms, electrical service, etc.), it's up to you to tell them.

In other words: Educate the jury. Show them evidence. Prove it to them.

So here we go: Think of your business as being on trial. Because it *is* on trial—in the court of consumer opinion.

Your product or service is the defendant.

Your customers are the jury.

You (and your marketing) are the attorney.

And it's a life or death sentence.

It's really that simple. If you can prove your case, you will win. If you can't, you will lose.

To start this process, fill in the blank:

Your company is being put on trial in a court of law, and you have to prove that you _____.

Fill in that blank with *whatever you came up with in Step 1*. For the manufacturer, it would be "build the highest quality cabinets." For the HVAC company, it would be "have the best technicians."

What would it be for *your* company? Well… look at the prioritized list you just created. Start with the first thing.

Now answer these important questions:

- How, specifically, do you do that?

- What, exactly, do you mean by that?

- Compared to what?

- Do you have any examples?

- What evidence can you provide to prove your claim?

- What stories can you tell to back it up?

- Can you provide witnesses?

Remember, OJ's attorneys didn't just say "the glove proves he's innocent." That's about like saying "buy from us because we have high quality."

Nope. Instead, they explained why the glove was important, how sizing of gloves affects fit, and specifically how and why the glove couldn't have been OJ's. They had experts there to educate and testify.

So how does this translate into your marketing? Easy.

The first step is to challenge yourself to hyper-specificity. Get your shovel out and start digging for details.

Exactly how big is the showerhead? How does that compare to normal showerheads? What materials is it made out of, and why are those materials the best? How many settings are there, and what are they? Compared to what? What is the pattern of the holes/nozzles? How much water pressure does it deliver, and how does it achieve it?

I worked with a roofing company that insisted that their identity would be basedon how meticulous they were about quality. Okay, good start! But we need to be more specific. Upon further questioning (pummeling, actually), they said they followed the manufacturer's installation guidelines to the "T."

Imagine a radio ad: "We follow all manufacturing guidelines to the "T."

(Yawn. Zzzzzz.)

This is when I bring out my hammer and start pounding. Or my shovel and start digging. Depending on which analogy you prefer.

Watch the questions I ask, and how they progressively reveal more and more details. The client knew all this information the entire time—they just needed me to beat it out of them. (Curse of knowledge, anyone?)

Me: Give me one good example of "following the guidelines" and why it matters.

Them: We use six nails per shingle—like the manufacturer specifies.

Me: So, how many nails would other companies use?

Them: Only three or four.

Me: So what?

Them: Well, it technically voids the warranty if they use less than six nails.

Me: But does it cause any actual damage? Like, is the roof actually worse when they use three or four nails instead of the specified six?

Them: Absolutely! Cutting back on the nails weakens the entire roof and makes it far more susceptible to wind damage, hail damage, and natural wear and tear.

Me: Okay, but does that affect the lifespan of the roof? By how much?

Them: (Looking at me like I'm an idiot) Of course! Our roofs last the full 30 to 50 years they should, depending on the product and the warranty. When the other guys cut those corners, their roofs might last 20 years, but typically more like five to 10 years. It's a big difference.

Me: So why would they cut that corner? I mean, I know it probably saves them time and money. But like how much?

Them: Ummm... probably on a standard size roof, it might save them something like $12 to $20 on nails, and probably, $100 or so on labor. Maybe more.

Me: The roofing company might save$100 to $150 by cutting that corner, then?

Them: At least.

Me: How would the customer even know if they were being cheated on nails like that?

Them: They would never know. When the roof starts to go bad early, they would never even suspect that it was a nail problem.

Me: Are there other things other contractors might cut corners on, too... that would save them a few bucks here, a few bucks there... that add up to a lot of money on a given roof?

Them: (almost peed themselves as they started listing all the ways roofers cut corners).

Okay, now we are getting somewhere! Look at this radio ad we could then write based on what we just learned:

Hi there, Robert O'Leary here from ABC Home Improvements... and I want you to know that it's the little things that count. Anyone can SAY they treat their customers right, but when it comes to roofing, siding, and windows, it's hard to know for sure if a contractor is treating you right or not. If a contractor uses four nails per shingle when they're supposed to use six, how would you ever know? If a contractor uses a cheap $4 tube of caulk on your new windows instead paying $9 a tube for the good stuff, could you tell by looking? It all comes down to details... and TRUST. At ABC Home Improvements, we only do things one way—the right way. We never cut corners. We never skimp on details. We never do less than the job requires. That's why we offer the best warranties, and have the happiest customers. If you're in need of roofing, siding, or windows, give us a call at (phone number, web address).

BOOM—specificity. Ask the right questions, get the right answers.

The second thing is creating and presenting compelling EVIDENCE to prove your points.

What I'm talking about is stuff like…

- Online reviews
- Real customer references
- Project photos with descriptive captions
- Case studies
- Awards and accolades you've received
- Demonstration videos

I'll cover each of these points in the next section of this book, which talks about the imperative elements of a website. For now, I want to impress upon you one super-important point about evidence: You must assume that the jury (prospects) know absolutely NOTHING about what you are selling.

Just like the OJ jury knew nothing about blood splatter, glove fittings, or bloody footprints.

Web Extra: You can't just SHOW them the evidence—you have to explain it to them. Go to UnlimitedLeadFlow.com/book and read "rifle vs. shotgun" to get additional perspective on this. I tell an interesting story about the time I sat on the jury of an actual murder trial, and the marketing lesson I took away from that experience.

For now, I want to revisit my two case studies, then move on to Step 3 of creating an identity for your company—using power, precision, and passion in your writing.

Case Study #1 Revisited – Video Game Manufacturer

If you recall, when we left off, my client had just incredulously told me that they were the high-quality leader in their industry of manufacturing video game cabinets.

Like in the example I just gave you about the roofer with six nails instead of four, I pressed them for SPECIFICS.

First, they explained that the cabinets were held together by 13 screws per side (26 total), not eight like their competitors. Okay, that's a pretty good start.

Plus, they used a specialized screw-head that a kid couldn't undo with a screwdriver from his dad's toolbox. Apparently, this was a big problem with delinquent kids who loved to destroy stuff for no reason. Also, a good point for our case.

Got it. What else?

Well, they also used "cleat and bracket" construction I was told. That's a woodworking technique that uses a protruding piece of wood on one side to connect to the joining piece of wood for added strength. Kind of like a jigsaw puzzle.

One of their executives was growing tired of the questioning as he whined, "But everybody else also uses cleat and bracket construction. That's just how you build cabinets."

Great. What else?

After about 15 minutes of meandering and unproductive discussion, one of the executives mentioned, almost apologetically, "Well, we use dowel rod construction."

Dowel rod construction? What's that? I mean, I know what a dowel rod is… but what does it mean in video game cabinet construction?

Short answer: They sink a ½" hole into one side of the wood, and another ½" hole into the adjoining piece of wood… then stick a 1" hardwood dowel rod in there, secure it with industrial strength wood glue, and let it dry. This adds a ton of lateral support, and improves the overall structural integrity of the cabinet.

That sounds pretty good. In fact, that sounds really good.

"How many dowel rods do you use," I asked?

Silence.

They looked around the table at each other and shrugged their shoulders. Nobody knew.

I asked them who *would* know, and they said a guy named Dan ran the machine that drilled the holes. They picked up a phone, and two minutes later Dan walked into the meeting.

"I have no idea," said Dan.

"Can you go count?" I asked.

A few minutes later he came back and looked down at a piece of paper where he had taken some notes.

"172," announced Dan.

"172 what?" I asked.

"172 hardwood dowel rods in every cabinet," he replied as he handed me a gherkin-sized dowel rod to emphasize the point.

"Holy crap. How do you even fit 172 of these into a single cabinet?" I wondered aloud. "How many dowel rods do your competitors use in their cabinets?"

(Silence. Head shaking. Awkward pause.)

"They don't use any."

Showerhead located. Commence pointing.

Case Study #2 Revisited: Heating And Air Conditioning Company

Now let's find that showerhead for Service Champions, the heating and air conditioning company. Remember, they're the ones who essentially hired a big bunch of boy scouts to perform service for their clients.

In this case, when I started drilling them for detailed information about HOW their technicians were better and different, it didn't take long to strike oil.

First, before anything else, they won't even consider a candidate who can't pass a drug test and background check. Failure on either one of those fronts is an automatic disqualification.

If a candidate makes it past that hurdle—and you may or may not be shocked how many do not—they interview the candidate. But instead of worrying about their experience and skillset, they are mostly looking for how well the person communicates with the interviewer. They are looking for pleasing personalities, lots of eye contact, and plenty of smiling.

Of course, they don't TELL the candidate that's what they're looking for—but you'd better believe it is. Their philosophy is that it's a lot easier to train naturally friendly people to be technicians than it is to train good technicians to be friendly.

The other thing they're looking for during interviews is appearance. This company has a strict "clean-cut" policy, which means no facial hair, no earrings, no visible tattoos, and conservative hair styles. Uniforms must always be clean and well-kempt, so the clothes that the candidate wears to the interview say a lot about whether or not they will be hired.

If you don't like that… fine! You just can't work for this company. It's a free country.

Are you starting to get an idea of what kind of people they hire? And how they run their company? And what the customer can expect when opening the door to a Service Champions technician?

Finally, if a candidate makes it through all those requirements, they'll hire them on and pay them while they go through training for 12 weeks. If bad qualities manifest during the training period—anger issues, being late, poor communication skills, etc.—then they'll be let go.

Only those who can truly be considered a "Service Champion" are allowed to be seen by customers.

So… what does that look like in an advertisement? You'll find out in the third and final installment of this case study at the end of the next chapter.

CHAPTER 18

Creating An Identity, Step Three –
"Power, Precision, Passion"

L ET'S REVIEW: So far, I've asked you to define your differentiators (case points), to get as specific and detailed as possible, and to gather evidence for each point.

To take the court case analogy a step further, all of that, collectively, could be considered "discovery" and "case preparation."

But at the end of the day, it doesn't matter how solid your case is if you can't present it in a powerful, convincing way.

That's where Step 3 comes into play: **Power, Precision, And Passion!**

The "3 P's" are the presentation of your case. It's like finding an attorney that can skillfully persuade the jury to believe the evidence you're presenting.

But before we delve too deep here, I want to quickly point out to you that these three elements—*power, precision, and passion*—are not the same thing. They are separate and independently important. Yet when used together, they will make your marketing irresistible and compelling.

Let's discuss each of them separately, then together.

The Psychology of POWER

As a general rule, people want to be told what to do. They don't THINK they want to be told what to do. But trust me, they do.

Why? Because in most cases, they have no idea what to do on their own!

People are looking for a lighthouse in the dark. They are looking for an authority. They want to find somebody with a credible opinion, so they don't have to go through the trouble and possible missteps of forming their own.

Think about it. When you walk into a Best Buy, do you want the guy to give you 1,000 technical specifications on every TV in the store? Or do you just want him to tell you which one to buy?

Do not forget this: **People want to be told what to do!**

To give you a fuller, richer idea of what I mean when I say POWER, here are a few synonyms; read this list and let the meaning sink in deep:

Influential	Commanding	Forceful
Aggressive	Intense	Inexorable
Controlling	Compelling	Persuasive
Potent	Strong	Sway

People are drawn to powerful people!

The truth is that when you speak with power, people tend to believe you are powerful. They are attracted to you. They look to you as an expert.

When you speak with power and confidence, your character and competency are not questioned. After all, anyone who speaks with THAT much authority must know what they're talking about, right?

Bottom line: People want a credible authority to tell them what to do.

When you speak with power, you will stand out from the crowd… *because it's such a rare quality.*

The Psychology of PRECISION

I talked at length earlier in the book about platitudes and why they're worthless in marketing.

But why, exactly, are they worthless?

It's because people have a subconscious "platitude filter" built into their brain. We've heard so many platitudes so many times from so many sources that we just expect to be gently "lied" to by everyone. It's in the unwritten social contract.

When you see a commercial for Papa John's Pizza, you don't get all bent out of shape that they say "Better Ingredients, Better Pizza." You *know* it's a platitude. You don't consciously use that word, *platitude*, but you intuitively know it.

By the same token, you don't expect BMW to literally have *THE* Ultimate Driving Machine. Or to literally "Be Lovin'" McDonalds. And you know that Budweiser is not *literally* the King Of Beers.

People know this. They filter the platitudes out, and for the most part, just ignore them.

People also intuitively know that they can LIE using generalities, but have tell the TRUTH when they use specifics. Why? It's too easy to get caught lying when using specifics.

Remember the roofer who uses six nails per shingle? If you tell somebody you're going to use six nails per shingle (precise language), people will then start looking for precisely six nails. They'd kill you for using only five, even if other roofers only used three or four. You're the one setting the standard—you have to live up to it.

If, on the other hand, you say "we follow manufacturer's standards for installation," nobody knows what that means. You could use two nails or 20 and nobody would know if you were actually doing it right or wrong. They wouldn't even know to ask or look.

That's the difference between precision language and vague language.

Here's a list of synonyms for the word PRECISION to help deepen the meaning:

Exactness	Definite	Rigor
Correctness	Sure	Attention
Meticulous	Accurate	Particular
Careful	Perfect	Strict

Another thing to keep in mind is that people tend to "believe what they see, not what they hear." Why do you think politicians rarely put their big promises in writing? When you do put it in "black and white," it becomes a de facto promise.

The Psychology Of PASSION

Bottom line: people tend to believe others who seem to really believe what they are saying. Passion is a master key to persuasion.

> *"What convinces is conviction. Believe in the argument you're advancing. If you don't, you're as good as dead. The other person will sense that something isn't there, and no chain of reasoning, no matter how logical or elegant or brilliant, will win your case for you."*
>
> *(Lyndon B. Johnson)*

Passion is what separates a good attorney from a great one. It's what wins championship trophies and Academy Awards. It's what all exceptional salespeople have in spades.

And it's sorely, obviously, and painfully lacking in just about all marketing communication—especially written marketing.

I've given you lists of synonyms for power and precision—why stop now? Here's the list for PASSION:

Fervor	Affection	Energetic
Enthusiasm	Intense	Emotional
Excited	Zeal	Eager
Conviction	Stirring	Spirit

The idea with passion is simple: to hit an emotional note with the prospect so they start to FEEL the way you FEEL about what you are selling. Ultimately, passion is about word choice, tone of voice, and the feeling communicated in your voice.

Principles of Power, Precision, And Passion

It is not the intention of this book to teach you how to become a master copywriter. So instead of covering this copywriting in tremendous detail, here is a list of guidelines to help you increase the level of power, precision, and passion in your marketing.

Be Specific: As stated previously, specificity is hyper-important; it's the foundational concept for communicating power, precision, and passion.

A remodeler who wanted to emphasize that he's available any time, day or night, to make sure that your job is done right created this banner to display at a home show:

Ruin My
Vacation.

Interrupt
My Dinner.

Wake Me
Up At 2AM.

My Only Concern Is That Your Job Is

100%
PERFECT.

MY CELL NUMBER IS
(971) 285-0770

It's one thing to tell people you have low prices. It's quite another to tell them specifically how and why you achieve those prices:

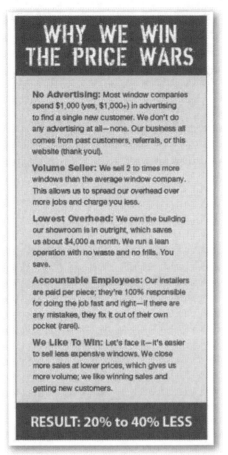

Or how about instead of telling your website visitors that you "believe in doing things the right way" you told them this:

"From age nine, my dad taught me that when it comes to remodeling, only absolute, unqualified perfection will do."

Use Absolutes: I'm talking about words that most **marketers shy away from** because they don't want to paint themselves into a corner. Words like *always, never, exactly, insist, every,* etc.

When you use absolutes, "We do the job right the first time" becomes "We always insist on doing every job exactly right the first time."

"We pay attention to details" becomes "We sweat every single detail on every single project to ensure a 100% perfect job every single time, start to finish… and beyond. NO EXCEPTIONS.

See the boost in power?

Tell The Story: Nothing captures the detail and nuance of how and why you are better than telling stories that illustrate your case points. Obviously, you have to careful and sensitive about WHEN and WHERE to tell stories… but nothing is more powerful.

I'll tell YOU a story to illustrate this point:

One of my clients, Energy Swing Windows, had just been awarded the BBB's coveted "Torch Award" for the second time. As you're probably aware, this is a pretty big deal—they don't just hand out these awards to anyone. So to capitalize on his second award in four years, the owner, Steve, wrote an advertorial (newspaper ad that looks like a news article) talking about his achievement.

The original ad is on the following page:

It's a pretty straightforward discussion of what they won and what their business philosophy is.

Good enough, right?

Wrong.

My blunt response to the ad: "I'm sorry Steve. I'm glad that your company won the BBB Torch Award for the second time. *But I hate to tell you—nobody cares. It's boring.*"

The fatal flaw with the ad is that as an article (remember, it's an advertorial), it doesn't even come close to covering information <u>that anyone gives a proverbial rat's butt about.</u>

To remain relevant, newspapers (and other media outlets), must provide their audience with credible, timely, and interesting content. Advertisers, on the other hand, are frequently more focused on delivering their selling points, which leads to content that's not very engaging.

Long story short: *This ad sounds like it was written by and for employees of Steve's company—not for the readers.*

The above critique isn't just for advertorials, either. It's just as true for a "traditional" ad or website as well.

I challenged Steve to find a way to reposition the Torch Award—instead of telling people <u>THAT</u> he won it, help them understand <u>WHAT THEY DID</u> that allowed them to be eligible for it.

Since the Torch Award is given to businesses that "put ethics at the forefront of business decisions," I asked Steve to <u>give me a concrete example</u> of a time when his company did just that. I challenged him to think of a real-life situation where it would have been easier and cheaper to cut losses and walk away… but where they instead specifically decided to do the go above and beyond the call of duty, ethics-wise.

Immediately he started telling me a story about a time when their supplier messed up a door order TWO times in a row—first by cutting it too short, then by sending in the wrong material (steel instead of fiberglass). The client was upset, but agreed to sign off on the second door as long as Steve gave him a big discount. Instead, Steve ordered and installed the RIGHT door—on the third attempt—then REFUNDED ALL the client's money. Every penny of it. Between the lost labor, the messed-up doors, and the customer refund, they took an $8,200 loss on the project.

The solution to Steve's boring BBB ad? Just tell THAT story!

Local Window Company Loses $8,200 On Botched Project—
Owner Says He'd Do It Again In A Heartbeat

By Nancy Boyer
Energy Swing Staff Writer

The driving philosophy at Energy Swing Windows is to always do the "right thing". And sometimes doing the "right thing" means taking a large financial hit to ensure complete client satisfaction. That was the situation in which Murrysville-based exterior remodeler, Energy Swing Windows, found themselves during a recent fiberglass entry door installation.

Company Orders Beautiful Entry Door For Client, But Encounters Major Issue

The process began as any other at Energy Swing Windows. Chris Saxton, an experienced Client Consultant helped homeowners choose an entry door that was the best fit for them, and hashed out all the finer details, like color, hardware, and glass style. Then an Energy Swing Project Manager took precise measurements of the custom-sized door, before finally placing an order with their door supplier.

Fast forward a few weeks to when Energy Swing receives the door from the supplier and sends a crew of its certified employee installers to the clients' home for installation. The fiberglass door along with two sidelites and decorative glass looks perfect with the exception of one glaring issue—it was cut too short.

New Door, New Problem: Supplier Sends Second Door In Right Size, Wrong Material

Frustrated by the supplier sending the wrong size door, Energy Swing President, Steve Rennekamp, vows to make it right by re-ordering the door and sending his installers back to the home for a second install day. This time, the door is perfectly sized to fit the opening in the house, but Rennekamp's crew finds another huge mistake—what was supposed to be a fiberglass door was, in fact, a nearly identical door made of steel.

Discouraged Homeowners Agree To Keep Steel Door Only If Given A Discount

Energy Swing was prepared to order the door for a third time

but the homeowners were willing to accept the steel version of their door, on the condition that Energy Swing reimburse them a portion of their investment because steel doors are generally less expensive than similar fiberglass doors.

Owner Decides To Give Them All Their Money Back

Embarrassed by the onslaught of errors from his door supplier, Rennekamp did what he claims he would "do again in a heartbeat"—he gave the clients all of their money back for the project. "When you consider all the doors we had to order and all the trips we made, we took an $8,200 loss," said Rennekamp, "but we've built Energy Swing Windows on the principle of providing 100% client satisfaction, and that's what it took this time. It's why we've won two Torch Awards."

Rennekamp was referring to the *Better Business Bureau Torch Award for Marketplace Ethics* that Energy Swing was awarded twice—in 2008 and recently in December 2012.■

Exclusive Offer For Murrysville Star Readers

15% OFF
Energy Swing Windows,
Entry Doors & Patio Doors
– or –
0% Interest
Financing For 60 Months
All Offers Expire April 12

724-387-2991   EnergySwingWindows.com

Have A Strong Opinion: As previously discussed, people are drawn to those with an authoritative opinion. If you don't have one, don't expect to win. If you do have one, make sure you communicate it with power, precision, and passion. Like so:

"**FLAWLESS.**"

My Methodical, "Thoroughly Thorough,"
Borderline-OCD Processes & Procedures
Will Ensure Your Project Is *Flawless*... **EVERY TIME.**

Greg Schantz, Owner

- *"Before I Started This Company In 2001, I Was A CPA for 17 Years. My Personality & My Training Only Allow Me TO Do Things One Way: THE RIGHT WAY."*

- *"I Shut Down The Jobsite In Disgust, Ripped Out The Entire Floor, And Started Over Again From Scratch."*

- *"If You Pay $43,000 For A New Kitchen And Aren't 1,000% Thrilled With The Results... DON'T COME CRYING TO ME. There's A ZERO PERCENT Chance I Did The Job."*

- *"Our Thrilled Customer Rate Is An Even 100% Because I Insist That Every Detail Is 100% Right 100% Of The Time."*

- *"Our Last BBB Complaint Was NEVER."*

Tell It Like It Is; Don't Mince Words: What I'm talking about here is one step up from being authoritative—telling it like it is, in no uncertain terms. It goes without saying that only somebody who is an authority would have the guts to speak so candidly:

- *"I Honestly Couldn't Care Less If You Go With Another Remodeler Who's Cheaper Than Me."*

- *"Why On Earth Would You Pay $1,200 For A $525 Window? You Wouldn't... Unless You Were Duped By A Fast-Talking Salesman."*

If you don't believe me, then explain how Donald Trump became the president of the United States. He spoke up and said things with confidence and power. That's how.

Maybe you hate Donald Trump. Maybe you love him. It doesn't matter here. He just happens to be the most conspicuous example of gaining authority by speaking with power and passion, and not mincing words.

Become A Consumer Advocate: If you really want to be convincing, become a consumer advocate. What I'm talking about, figuratively speaking, is to get up from the opposite side of the "sales table" and walk around to the prospect's side. Let them know you're on their side—trying to help them make the best decision for THEM.

Frequently this means exposing the negative aspects of your industry. You know, the things that you should have fixed way back in Chapter 7, when we talked about creating something that people really want to buy.

Here are few examples to help you understand this concept:

- *"$13,800… For Replacement Windows?!"*

- *"Most Window Companies Send Their Salespeople To Weeklong Sales Bootcamps (You Don't Stand A Chance)."*

- *"How Much Should You Pay For A Good Replacement Window? $199? $1,200? $600?"*

Use Plain English: There is a common misperception that professional writing must be verbose. People think that writing with big words and long-winded sentences will make them appear smart.

A quote from legendary advertising pioneer Rosser Reeves best sums up my position on this:

"Let's say you've got $1,000,000 tied up in your little company and suddenly, for reasons unknown to you, your advertising isn't working and your sales are going down. And everything depends on it. Your future depends on it, your family's future depends on it. I walk into this office and sit down in this chair. Now, what do you want from me? Fine writing? Do you want masterpieces? Do you want glowing things that can be framed by copywriters? Or do you want to see the #!@%$&#@! sales curve stop going down and start moving up?"*

The reality is you don't need to use big words and "glowing things" to sound smart. Here are some ideas for you:

- **Use short sentences:** An average of 17 words is good; 25 is difficult. Don't try to stick two thoughts into one sentence. Use two short ones instead.

- **Use simple language:** Prefer the familiar word to the far-fetched. Prefer the concrete word to the abstract. Prefer the short word to the long word.

- Use **personal references**: examples: names, pronouns, andhuman-interest words. Thebest word you can use is…. **YOU.**

- Use **live words** – *verbs*. Most writing contains nothing more than nouns and adjectives, glued together with the prepositions *is, was, are, and were.*

- Don't try to be **cute**; it won't help your case: *"I'm not saying charming, witty, and warm copy won't sell. I'm just saying that I've seen thousands of charming, witty, and warm campaigns that didn't sell."* (Rosser Reeves again)

- Be **specific and quantify** everything.

- **Long copy vs. short copy**: Say as much as needs to be said, then quit. A good, easy-to-read format will allow you to use more text. Use video or audio to say what might be too burdensome to read.

- Use **emphasis tools** to allow the reader to "hear" your voice tone and inflection while reading… like **Bold**, *italics*, <u>underlined</u>, ALL CAPS, and (parenthesis).

- Use **punctuation** to allow your reader to "hear" your pausing and pacing:

	Between Words	Between Sentences
Normal Pause	White space	Period
Shorter Pause	Hyphen	Semicolon (or colon)
Longer Pause	Dash	Paragraph

Again, this book isn't about copywriting. Take the ideas and guidelines above as just that—ideas and guidelines.

For more detailed instructions on writing in a plain and effective style, I highly recommend a book called "The Plain English Approach To Business Writing" by Edward P. Bailey, Jr.

Let's wrap up this chapter—and this section—by completing our two case studies. Now you're going to see power, precision, and passion in action!

Case Study #1 Conclusion: Video Game Manufacturer

Okay, so let's take a look at how the manufacturing company integrated all that power, precision, and passion into their advertising.

Remember, when we left off in the last chapter, I had just discovered that they had 172 hardwood dowel rods in every cabinet. That, in my opinion, was kind of a big deal.

To prove the client absolutely did NOT think it was a big deal, let's look at the ad they came up with prior to hiring me. This is what they were running in the leading industry magazine, which was distributed to over 5,000 potential customers (original is full color with an orange background):

Remember, this was 1997—we can give them a break on the graphic design. But still, the headline is unforgivable: HS-27 Cabinet.

Did you notice the third bullet point there? "Built with both cleat and dowel construction."

This is why manufacturers shouldn't be allowed to create their own marketing. It's all about the technical specs and details. There's no sizzle. There's no great promise. And there certainly isn't any showerhead being pointed at. Power, precision, and passion are nowhere to be found.

I went back to my office and threw the piece below together. Not to be put into the next edition of the magazine, but to be faxed (hey, it was the '90s!) out to a list of possible customers they kept in-house:

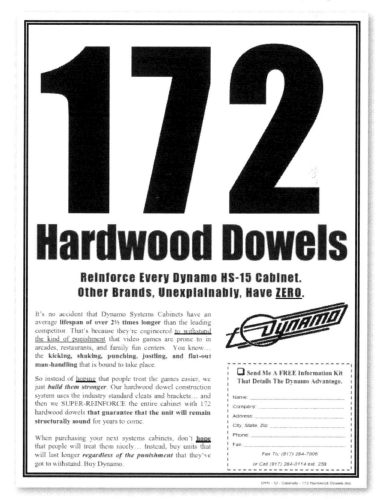

I'll be honest with you. Over 20 years later, I still LOVE this ad. Power out the wazoo. Precision to spare. Passion oozing all over the place.

First, the "172" punches you in the face. What a great way to get the prospect's attention!

Then the subheadline excoriates the competition: "Other Brands, Unexplainably, Have ZERO."

The text then builds a strong case using passionate language designed to convince the reader to believe the claims are true. Remember, your court case is only as good as your attorney's ability to deliver it.

We Had The Biggest, Fattest Guy We Could Find Jump Up And Down On Our HS-27 Control Panel For 12 Minutes...

Just To Make Sure It Could Endure Any Punishment Your Customers Could Dish Out.

Our 272-lb. Punishment Test Failed—So We Re-engineered The Darn Thing.

That's right. The big, fat guy BROKE the control panel clean off after 12 minutes of jumping up and down. Sounds like a story of failure, right? Wrong! That gave us all the information to re-engineer, reinforce, and FIX the problem before it got to one of your arcades.

We Go The Extra Mile To Make Sure That Dynamo Is The Best Stuff On The Market.

Our "fat guy" test is just one of the things we do to make Dynamo products the best on the market. We're not interested in selling to operators who are fly-by-nighters looking for the cheapest stuff available. But the other 99% of you know that quality counts... and makes you far more profitable in the long run.

Buy The Cabinet That Passed The "Fat Guy" Test. Buy Dynamo.

Granted, it took us two tries. But it passed for a whopping 15 minutes before we let the fat guy off. No breakage. That's Dynamo quality. Insist on it.

For A FREE Video Of The Big Fat Guy Test Call (817) 284-0114 ext. 212

DYN - 12g - Cabinets - Biggest Fattest Guy.doc

The results of sending this fax were so immediate and overwhelming, that we created an entire fax campaign. Here are a couple of other sample pieces:

The Biggest Threat To Your Video Cabinets COULD BE An Allen Wrench & Screwdriver That Some 13-Year Old Kid Took From His Dad's Toolbox.

26 Phillips Head Wood Screws Hold Some Brands of Video Cabinets Together.

Scary thought, but it's true: some brands of video game cabinets are extremely vulnerable to vandalism. In fact, brands make vandalism tempting to kids who are normally good—because the screws that hold it together are just sitting there begging to be tampered with. The screw heads are exposed so that any kid with a screwdriver can dismantle it in just a few minutes.

The Good News?
Logic Board Thieves Will Make You Forget About Your Vandalism Problems!

The real problems with some of those other brands really starts when logic board thieves get hold of them. The only thing protecting the logic boards are two allen head screws (easily accessible from outside the cabinet) and

one measly simple slide bolt—which can easily be jimmied open by any novice would-be thief. Simply put, you are asking for trouble with these brands of cabinets.

Want To Break Into A Dynamo Cabinet? Better Bring A Crowbar, A Chainsaw, and A Pick-Axe.

Dynamo cabinets are instantly recognized by thieves as OFF LIMITS. It's just not going to get broken into. And over the course of the cabinet's lifetime that can mean savings of thousands of dollars per cabinet to operators. Put your money where it will stay put: Dynamo.

For A FREE Comparison Checklist
Call (817) 284-0114 ext. 212

DYN - 13d - Cabinets - Biggest Threat Is Allen Wrench.docDYN - 13d - Cabinets - Biggest Threat Is Allen Wrench.doc

This is how you turn a money-losing company into a company with a $7MM profit in just under 10 months. We repeated this process of injecting power, precision, and passion into the marketing for every product line, including pool tables, air hockey, video game cabinets, and foosball. The owner ended up selling the company to Brunswick for $35MM in 2003.

Case Study #2 Conclusion: Heating And Air Conditioning Company

What about the friendly technician HVAC company? What does power, precision, and passion look like when put into their advertising?

Let's take a look. Below are some scripts for a couple radio ads. Keep an eye out for the "3 P's."

(You can listen to these ads—and more—at UnlimitedLeadFlow. com/book).

"One In A Million" (60 Seconds)

You've heard the phrase, "one in a million," right? What about "one in 500?" This is Leland Smith from Service Champions Heating And Air Conditioning, and it takes about five hundred candidates to find just ONE outstanding technician. When hiring, the first thing we do is make sure they're friendly and courteous. If not, it's over right there! Then they have to pass a background check and drug test… which might not sound like a big deal… but only about one out of 10 actually pass both! Next, we test for the right aptitudes, skill sets, and work ethic. If they pass all that, we put them through a rigorous 12-week training course to learn how to do things the Service Champions way, and over half wash out of that! All in all, it takes about 500candidates to find that one OUTSTANDING technician. So when you open your door to a friendly, smiling Service Champions technician, you'll know you're looking at the best of the best of the best. Call Service Champions at 777-7777 in either the 714, 949, or 562 area code… or you can find us online at ServiceChampions.com.

"We Only Hire Friendly People" (60 Seconds)

This is Leland Smith, owner of Service Champions Heating And Air Conditioning, and I want you to know that we have the world's friendliest technicians. And here's how we do it: **We only hire friendly people!** It's the VERY FIRST THING we look for during interviews. If they're not friendly, it's a deal breaker! They think we're checking their experience and technical abilities… but we're really seeing if they smile or not. We're checking to see if they are polite. We want to know if they are approachable, outgoing, responsive, sociable, open, pleasant, and kind. And if they are… and ONLY if they are… then we take a look at their technical abilities. But I'm telling you, if a guy's a jerk. No job. If a guy won't smile. No job. If a guy's not polite. No job. The result is an entire team of over 100 friendly technicians. The world's friendliest technicians. Call us and see for yourself. Right now, you can get a precision tune-up and professional cleaning for just $77. Call Service Champions at 777-7777 in either the 714, 949, or 562 area code… or you can find us online at ServiceChampions.com.

"A Troop of Boy Scouts" (60 Seconds)

I was talking to one of my friends recently who said he had just had Service Champions to his home for a heater tune-up; he was raving about how great the technician was—clean-cut, friendly, and extremely courteous. I explained to him how we only hire techs who are courteous, clean, kind, cheerful, friendly… and who do good deeds for our customers because they WANT to… not because they HAVE to. My friend got an amused look on his face, then started laughing. "Leland," he said, "it sounds like you've hired a troop of boy scouts, not technicians!" I thought about it for a minute, smiled back at him, and said, "Guilty as charged." Don't get me wrong—our technicians are experienced professionals who are extremely good at tuning up, repairing, and replacing heating and cooling systems. But they're also the most clean-cut, friendly, helpful, courteous, kind, and cheerful bunch of young men you'll ever encounter. And yes, they also do good deeds for free, including helping little old ladies across the street! Call Service Champions to schedule a precision tune-up and professional cleaning for just $77… Our number is 777-7777 in the 714, 949, or 562 area code… or find us online at ServiceChampions.com.

And here's what they look like in print (originals are full color with a bright red background; see them and others at UnlimitedLeadFlow. com/book:

Here's an important word for you to latch onto: PRICE CONDITIONING.

Okay, so that's two words.

Remember earlier in this book when I challenged you to raise your prices, and then raise them again? The operative principle was that to have enough budget to do EVERYTHING RIGHT, you were going to have margins that more than just pay your bills.

The biggest concern, of course, when it comes to raising prices, is whether or not you'll actually be able to sell at those higher prices. That's fair if you're only thinking of things the "old way," (i.e., without an identity).

But here's what happens when you integrate your identity and corresponding evidence into your marketing. People not only know you exist—they also understand that HOW and WHY you are head and shoulders above the competition. Your identity allows you to begin to PRICE CONDITION at every step of your marketing program. It's the key to selling at higher prices.

CHAPTER 19
No Identity, No Premium Prices

M OST COMPANIES *SORT of* have an identity. They just don't tell anyone about it until… drum roll please…. THE SALES MEETING!

If YOU are waiting until the sales meeting to begin to talk about how and why you're different and better, you're losing out. Big time.

Not only will you MISS sales opportunities (see my story about Rodney Webb in Chapter 21), you'll also make your salespeople's jobs way harder than necessary.

Think of it this way:

If your prospect knows essentially NOTHING about you until the sales meeting, yoursalesperson has to educate them. They have to get the prospect all the way from point "A" on the selling spectrum (knowing diddly squat about you) to point "Z" (knowing who you are, why you're better, and willing to plunk down the cash even though your prices are higher).

That's why it normally takes two to three HOURS to sell somebody something. It's why you have to spend so much time telling your company story and explaining exactly how the extrusions on your window are different and better. You have to do all this because THEY JUST MET YOU! There's no pre-existing trust. There's no definitive feeling ahead of time that you're the one to buy from.

A strong identity, woven throughout your entire marketing program, allows you to educate your prospects every step of the way. This allows them to understand how and why you do things—and why you're probably more expensive.

In other words, they have already received the arguments in your case. They *already* understand it costs more money to put six nails in a shingle or 172 dowel rods in a cabinet.

But now that you've given them something other than price to consider, guess what? They'll consider more than just the price. Which is when you magically start selling for higher prices. They're not just "okay" with six nails or 172 dowel rods—they *insist* on having it that way (and are willing to pay extra for it).

Some Things Never Change

This reminds me of one of my earliest contractor clients, way back in 1996—a company in Ft. Worth called Lon Smith Roofing. At the time, they were the largest residential-only roofing company in the country—somewhere around $50MM in sales.

That was back before the internet was relevant for marketing, and when the Yellow Pages were still mega-important. And back then, when Yellow Pages were important, it was absolutely critical your Yellow Pages ad was packed with your company's identity.

Of course, most companies' ads were terrible—full of platitudes and generalities and Charlie Brown's mother. In those days, we could ALWAYS get a <u>five to 20 times increase</u> in leads from Yellow Pages just by rewriting their ads using the same principles we've already covered. It was easier than stealing candy from the proverbial baby. I'm not kidding.

The only problem was that Lonnie, the owner, absolutely HATED the Yellow Pages. The roofing section back then was 60 to 70 pages thick (in a book that was so big it came in two 5" thick volumes). But Lonnie never purchased an ad. He only had the free line listing that you got just for existing. We tried to convince him to take out an ad in the next year's book, but he flat refused.

"All we ever get from the Yellow Pages is broke people and tire kickers," Lonnie said. "Everyone calls and just wants to know 'how much will it cost for a new roof?' We can't sell over the phone like that. The calls are worthless. We never convert them, so we stopped running ads years ago."

Huh?

Think about it: How would callers know to ask any question about roofing OTHER than *"how much will it cost?"*

Seriously. How on earth would they know? They've never bought a roof before. They know nothing about what makes a good roof a good roof. Of course they're going to ask about the price—it's the only question they can think of to ask!

I explained it to Lonnie then. And I'm explaining it to you now. It is your job to educate the consumer to know what to look for, what to look out for, what makes you better and different, and what they can expect when doing business with you.

You know… identity!

You cannot expect the jury to walk into the courtroom already knowing how gloves are supposed to fit. Or how blood is supposed to splatter. Or what kind of footprint a Bruno Magliboot makes.

It's YOUR job to explain all that.

When your marketing has an identity with power, precision, and power, your salespeople's job becomes infinitely easier. Instead of taking them "A to Z," they only have to take them from "L, M, N, O, or P" to "Z." In other words, HALF THE WORK HAS ALREADY BEEN DONE.

Identity. There is nothing more important to your marketing success.

And it all starts with your website.

SECTION 3

Your Company Website – The Keystone Of Your Entire Marketing Program

NOW THAT YOU'VE got the $10MM mindset and you've discovered to how create an identity for your company, it's time to actually create marketing that will be seen by your prospects. Before we get too far, let's review our formula so you can see where we are.

The 4-Step Formula to get you company to $10MM:

1. **Sell awesome stuff that people genuinely love.**

2. **Charge high prices.**

3. **Master the internet.**

4. **Use radio & TV advertising.**

First we'll cover creating a website that turns lookers into buyers (chapters 20 to 26), then we'll talk about how to drive traffic to your website (chapters 27 to 32). Let's get started!

CHAPTER 20

"What Happened To All My Leads?"

So far, we've touched on the first two steps in our 4-Step Formula to $10MM. Those involved 1) selling awesome stuff people genuinely love and 2) charging higher prices.

Now we'll focus on Step 3—mastering the internet.

The best place to start is with Kevin Bacon.

A few years ago, I was watching TV with my family when a commercial came on promoting a show starring Kevin Bacon called The Following. I guess it had been a while since I had seen Kevin Bacon because my reflexive comment when I saw him was "Wow! Kevin Bacon looks hammered! How old is that guy now?!" His youthful Footloose days were clearly behind him.

The question had been strictly rhetorical; I could tell just by looking that Bacon, at the time, was probably in his mid-50s. Nevertheless, within a matter of seconds my wife called out, "He's 54."

I'll give you one guess how she knew so quickly how old he was. (And, no, she's not the former president of the Kevin Bacon fan club).

Tick Tock. Tick Tock.

Okay, time's up. If you said, "Googled it on her iPhone," you'd be close. Actually, she asked Siri.

Google is how just about every man, woman, and child today discovers information about nearly anything he or she could ever want to know about. I know this isn't a news flash, but the internet is now literally in the palm of EVERYONE's hand. And from a marketing perspective, that literally (yes, REAL literally, not HYPERBOLE, *literally*) changes everything (yes, *everything*).

I'll prove it to you: Let's go back in time to about 2004 to 2006. Let's say you placed an ad in your local newspaper (or TV or radio or whatever advertising you did then) that would, at that time, reliably generate 10 leads for you.

Given that historic lead costs has been about $250 to $300 each, let's say that it cost you $3,000 to get those 10 leads.

Now here's the important question: If you were to spend that same $3,000 on that same advertisement today, how many leads would you realistically expect to generate?

I've asked this question at scores of seminars all over the country, and the audience generally tells me the answer is now one or two leads. Same money spent, same media as before—now instead of 10 leads, it's just a couple. Many contractors even cynically insist that the answer is ZERO.

So the operative question is *"What happened to all the leads?!"* Surely there are still people buying windows, siding, remodeling, air conditioners, and roofing. So why aren't they responding to your advertising anymore?

Answer: Kevin Bacon!

See, back then, when somebody wanted to look something up online, they would generally have to LOG ON to their DESKTOP computer and DIAL IN on their modem. And even though laptop computers were being widely used by 2005, wireless internet was still a rarity—about only 30% of private homes had it.

Then in 2007, the first true smartphone (the iPhone) was introduced. Right about that time, wireless internet started becoming more commonplace. Apple launched the iPad in 2010, and by 2013, instant-access internet was available on multiple devices. At home, at work, and on the go.

I know—it seems like we've had iPhones and wireless internet forever. But we haven't!

So back then—before the iPhone—when somebody *thought* about replacing their windows (or siding, or remodeling their kitchen) they usually wouldn't take any immediate action. They'd have the thought, consider their options for a moment, then forget about it.

Then, the next day (or week or month) they'd see your ad in the paper and think, "Oh yeah, I need to call about that."

Boom—10 calls.

Here's what happens NOW to the 10 people who USED to see your ad:

- One or two of them still see your ad and call—just like in the good old days.

- Four or five of them already looked it up online when they first had the thought… and contacted SOMEONE ELSE before they ever saw your ad.

- Two or three of them see your ad, remember they are in the market, look you up online, don't like what they see on your website, and decide NOT to call you.

- One of them sees your ad, looks you up online, and calls you.

In case you're not catching on, all of this is just another way to say that you'd better have your internet marketing act together. But for some reason, the majority of remodeling companies and contractors I've seen over the last several years just aren't getting the job done. Overall, it's getting better—but there is still A LOT of room for improvement.

To make matters worse, instead of shoring up their internet marketing, most remodeling company owners keep asking me the same old tired question: *"How can I make my ads generate more leads?"*

Look at the numbers above again—asking me how to write a better ad that generates more leads **isn't even the right question anymore.** The smart companies are asking these questions instead:

1. How can I make my website work better, so it converts more of my web visitors into actual, legitimate leads?

2. How can I get more of the people who are searching online for what I sell to find my website?

The answers to these questions are complex. And it takes time and intelligence to implement effective strategies. I'll cover the answers to both questions in detail in a bit.

But trust me—these are the FIRST AND SECOND questions you'd better be asking yourself now if you want to continue to compete and thrive in your marketplace.

The days of simply "slapping up a website" and calling that "internet marketing" are long over.

CRITICAL POINT: Bad experiences you might have had with internet marketing providers and website builders does NOT diminish the need to find good answers to these questions.

Again, I'll discuss detailed solutions to all of these problems in this book. For now, just realize that when you place an ad and get far fewer leads than you'd like—it's Kevin Bacon's fault.

CHAPTER 21

Falling In Love – The Purpose of Your Website

I N THE OLD days, the most important part of the selling process was the sales meeting itself.

A good salesman could dazzle and amaze the prospect. He could take the prospect from knowing nothing about your company or products to making them fall in love and sign a big, fat check. All in a span of two to three hours.

Those days are basically over.

Yes, you still need good salespeople. But if you don't make people FALL IN LOVE with your company and your products **BEFORE** the sales meeting ever occurs, you'll be missing 50% to 90% of your opportunities.

Getting prospects to fall in love with your company, so they are practically begging for your business BEFORE the sales meeting?

Sound impossible!

Stick with me. It's not only possible—it's imperative that you learn to do so.

In today's "Kevin Bacon is 54" internet-connected world, people don't want to wait until the sales meeting to decide if they want to do business with you. They want to know ahead of time. And the companies that figure out how to facilitate that "falling in love" are the ones who win. Period.

Your Website Is The Key

First of all, realize that just about every single customer you'll ever get is going to visit your website.

That's pretty obvious. But have you ever stopped to ask yourself this question? *WHY are they visiting your website?*

Answer: They hope to find something to validate their decision to consider buying from you. To receive this validation, they need to get as much information as possible about your company—and they want to get it RIGHT NOW (while they are on your site, actively thinking about it).

In other words, they are doing some due diligence. The problem is that most websites are pathetically devoid of any REAL information. Instead, they're filled with platitudes that tell people nothing. As such, the prospect can only HOPE to get a feel for the company based on things like the design quality of the site, any posted job photos, and other surface-level breadcrumbs.

Here's a novel concept: **help prospects do their due diligence!**

Consider that most people…

A) Have NEVER before bought what the type of product you are selling

B) Have ZERO idea how to evaluate a contractor

C) Are skeptical because of the industry's overall poor reputation

D) And can only guess at how much the project will cost

It's no wonder people are starving for information. Yes… STARVING!

Think about it this way: How many pianos have you bought in your life?

I ask this question at seminars. A few people have bought two or three pianos. But 85% have never bought ONE.

Probably including YOU!

Now imagine that your little son or daughter has gotten pretty good playing on that $149 keyboard you bought for Christmas last year. So much so that they're ready to graduate to a "real" piano.

You walk into the piano store. You see pianos of every variety and color. You see pianos for as little as $1,999 and as much as $30,000— and everything in between.

Which piano do you buy?

Or more to the point—do you even know WHAT QUESTIONS to ask the salesman?

Guess what? Now you know what 85% (or more) of <u>your</u> prospects feel like! Remember the "tappers and listeners" game from earlier in this book? Remember the "Curse of knowledge?"

When you know something, it's nearly impossible for you to imagine what it's like NOT to know it.

This is why your website is so crucial to your success. It's your chance to set out a massive "information buffet" the prospect can choose from and feast on.

To stick with the metaphor, your "information buffet" should contain far more choices than any normal person could reasonably consume in one sitting. You want to stock the buffet full enough so they can pick and choose what <u>THEY</u> find to be delicious (helpful, relevant, interesting, thought-provoking). Make sure they walk away stuffed—and satisfied. Don't force them to wait until the sales meeting to get a bite from you. Give it to them right here, right now, on your website.

The rest of this section will talk about what kind of stuff to put on the buffet... and how to present it all in the most attractive way possible.

The 93% Guy

I used to speak at the same events as my favorite sales trainer in the remodeling industry, Rodney Webb. He's a super smart guy with some really awesome sales techniques that I believe in and whole-heartedly endorse.

Rodney claims (and I believe it) that he was so good at selling that he became known as "The 93% Guy." Meaning, he closed 93% of his sales appointments.

One day as we were both waiting back stage for our turn to speak, we got into a friendly little discussion. Or debate. Or whatever. He said something to me like, "I don't like giving all this information away up front, in the marketing, because it 'steals the thunder' of the salesman when he gets into the house."

I responded by asking him a question: "Rodney, you're the 93% guy. That's awesome! But what percent of deals do you close when you don't even get in the home and have a chance to make a sales presentation?"

His response: "Huh? What do you mean?"

Exactly!

You will always close 0% of the deals you don't get a chance to sell to. And I'm telling you here, now, that if your website isn't working like it should, you will MISS 50% to 90% of the opportunities you SHOULD be having.

Stated differently, which would you rather close: 35% of 100 prospects... or 93% of 20 prospects?

It's a no brainer. If your website does its job, you WILL get more sales meetings.

Your website is your first and best opportunity to make prospects **fall in love with your company**.

Your Website Is Like A Shoe Store At The Mall

Imagine you want to buy a new pair of running shoes. You go to the mall, since they have several competing shoe stores—you'll be able to look around and find the right shoe at the best possible price.

When you get to the mall, you naturally first go to the store that's closest to where you came in. Once inside that first store, you see the usual, expected large displays of shoes on a couple of the walls, and various types of athletic apparel in the middle area. You head to the wall of shoes, look for the section you're interested in (running, in this example), then glance around to see if any particular shoe or shoes catch your attention. If so, you pick up the display shoe and check the price. If it's something you like—and the price is right—you ask the worker if you can try on a pair.

What happens next is where things get interesting—and a lot like your contracting or remodeling company.

Even if you find a pair of shoes you like—and you believe the price is fair—chances are extraordinarily high that you'll leave the store, walk down the mall, and look at another store.

But why?

The second store looks very similar to the first. It too has a wall of shoes, a section dedicated to running shoes, and a nearly identical lineup of brands, colors, and styles. All priced within 5% of the first store.

Then you'll leave THAT store to go check out a third. And a fourth, if the mall has that many shoe stores.

Why didn't you just buy from the first store? You didn't leave the first store because you didn't like it. You didn't leave the first store because they had a terrible selection. And you didn't leave the first store because you felt like their prices were too high.

You left the first store because you wanted to make sure you were getting the best shoe for you at the best price available. **You wanted to see what options existed.**

Consequently, you end up buying the shoes from the third store. Or the second. Or maybe you go back to the first.

If you were paying attention, you realized somewhere in the middle of that story that your website is like one of the shoe stores, the mall is like Google, and your prospective customers are the shoe shoppers.

And just like shoe shoppers, your prospective customers browse around from site to site to site… just to see what's available and to see what your competitors' sites look like. Then when they find that your website—pretty as it may be—looks and smells and feels ESSENTIALLY EXACTLY like all the others, the prospect calls whichever one they happened to look at last. Or whichever one <u>happened</u> to seem best.

The problem is you are *not* exactly like your competitors. You're better than them. You do things differently. You work harder, pay more attention to details, have more experience, treat people better, warranty the work longer, and a dozen other things.

You know, your identity!

Your website's job is to convince people beyond any doubt that you are the best choice. It should communicate your advantages in clear, compelling, passionate language. Don't save "the good stuff" for the sales meeting. Put it all out there on your website.

Give people enough information, enough evidence, and enough proof that you're the best choice. Make them unequivocally fall in love with your company before your sales rep ever sets foot in their home.

If you don't consciously plan this out, you'll end up looking exactly like all of your competitors: one of many indistinguishable pretty faces in the crowd. You might get picked—but you might not. It's a crapshoot—and that's assuming prospects even find you in the first place (That's a whole other discussion for later in this book).

If your website doesn't pass the "fall in love" test, then **<u>fire it immediately</u>**. It doesn't matter how new it is, how much money you spent on it, or how much you like the person who created it. Kick it to the curb and start over.

Too much is at stake. Too many qualified visitors will "step into your store," look around, then click to another site and never return. Not because they didn't like what they saw. Not because they liked somebody else better. **But because your site lacked the power, precision, and passion to make them fall in love.**

Here's how to "fire" your lackluster website…

CHAPTER 22
Fire Your Underperforming Website

MAGINE YOU'RE IN the market to hire a new salesperson. After checking around, you luck out and hear about a guy who's been in remodeling sales for 15 years. He recently moved to your city because his wife got a promotion at her job, and he's looking to get back to work. He comes in for an interview and says all the right things. He looks the part. He clearly knows the industry.

You call his former employer and get a good report—this guy knows how to close. You negotiate a modest base salary and generous commission package and he signs on. You put him through your closing methodology training and he quickly absorbs everything.

In other words, everything is perfect.

After a few weeks of training and shadowing your top producer, you hand him 10 leads… and he only comes back with one sale. Your company's historic closing ratio is 32% first-call close, and 40% after reeling in stragglers.

Yikes.

Week two doesn't go much better: 12 issued leads, two sales. He's new, so you cut him some slack.

Week three: 11 issued leads, one sale. You start to panic. You have your sales manager troubleshoot and discover that the guy isn't following your sales protocol at all. He talks too much, doesn't ask enough questions, and gets flustered after practically any objection.

By now you've got six weeks and over $10,000 invested in his hiring, training, leads, and salary. Do you cut him loose? Do you give him more chances? Do you try to build a time machine so you can go back and start over?

The obvious answer is you FIRE HIM, ASAP!

Not only is he underperforming your averages by a huge margin, he's also costing you tons of money in lost revenue. If your average sale is $10,000, the eight sales he missed cost you $40,000 in gross profit. You really have no choice but to fire him.

By that same logic, you'd fire any massively underperforming employee. Dreadful accountants, unreliable installers, insubordinate receptionists—anyone who isn't getting the job done.

So why do so many remodeling companies stubbornly clinging to websites that don't work?

My definition of "not working" includes any website that doesn't do what websites are supposed to do: Make prospects fall in love with your company so they call, set appointments, and buy from you. Period.

Actually, I can answer my own question from above. I know the answers because I've asked hundreds and hundreds of remodelers and contractors that very question. Here are some of the most common reasons, with commentary and suggestions:

1. **Don't Realize The Website Is Underperforming:** This is by far the most common situation—the owner of the company has no idea that they are losing prospects in droves because their website lacks power to convert lookers into buyers. The key is to learn the elements of "conversionability" that will be taught in this section.

2. **Just Had The Website Built And Don't Want To Start Over:** This the second most common reason, but the rationale holds no water. This is like holding on to the salesperson at the beginning of the chapter simply because you've already

invested a lot of time and money in him. It's an emotional decision—sometimes a prideful decision—that's not based on logic or facts. It's ALWAYS more expensive to keep an underperforming website (or salesperson!) than it is to bite the bullet, swallow your pride, and do it right.

3. **No Confidence That It Can Be Done Any Better:** This is a cousin to #1 above—it's a belief that all websites will perform about the same as long as they look decent. Also, many business owners have already been through the "website development" ringer with multiple companies over the years, and are convinced that they all suck. While that conclusion is often true, *it's not absolutely true.* You're about to learn how to do it better.

4. **Gets "Lots of Positive Comments" About The Website:** Another cousin to #1 above—it's hard to believe your website is underperforming when you have people tell you it's great. But think about those episodes of American Idol during tryouts where somebody who is AWFUL auditions and genuinely thinks they are terrific. They've been surrounded for years by parents, siblings, and friends who tell them they're great. But when exposed to the scrutiny of professional talent evaluators—or common sense—they're shocked to learn they are unbearably terrible. The same thing happens all the time with websites.

5. **Doesn't Realize The Importance Of The Website:** This is becoming rarer the further we get into the 21st century, but you'd be surprised. There are still some business owners who are convinced that all the repeat and referral business they've gotten the last 40 years is going to continue to sustain them. They also think their website isn't hurting them. Except that's not true. It's exceptionally difficult to see the business you're missing from a crummy website—after all, you don't see (and therefore miss) the people who never call.

Clearly, terrible salespeople are easier to spot and rectify that money-sucking websites. That's why the first step, as they say, is to ***recognize and admit that you have a problem.***

Does yours have a problem? Go to our website at UnlimitedLeadFlow. com/book and request a FREE website checkup. It's really simple; we'll take a look at your website and grade it a 0 to 100 scale based on 18 specific elements.

It's just our opinion, but trust me, if we say your site scores a 32 out of 100, you have a lot of work to do. By the way, the average score is 32 out of 100. Yeah, there is _always_ a lot of work to be done.

If you do discover you're hemorrhaging opportunities, give yourself a break. You're in business, and you're going to make mistakes. Those mistakes are going to cost you money sometimes. It stinks, but it's called life. Just don't continue to knowingly make the same mistake—that's just stupid and unforgivable!

If you think the terrible salesperson in the example costs you a lot of money, it's NOTHING compared to the damage your damaged website is doing to your top and bottom lines. EVERY customer you'll ever sell is going to check out your website. It could literally be costing you hundreds of thousands or millions of dollars a year in sales.

CHAPTER 23
Common Website Mistakes

Aᴛ ꜰɪʀꜱᴛ, I couldn't figure out why Randy, the remodeler on the other end of my phone, sounded so depressed.

Randy: My new website comes up first in Google search and my unique visitors are at an all-time high.

Me: So why are you calling me?

Randy: My old website never came up in search results, but it pulled in five to 10 leads a month. Now I'm getting basically ZERO.

Me (looking at his website): That's not surprising, it's terrible. How much did you spend on this new site?

Randy: $17,000 for the site and one year of SEO services.

Me: Can you get your money back?

Randy: (silence; possibly tears)

I changed his name, but Randy's story is not only absolutely true, it's also, sadly, very common.

Remodelers all over the country are being fleeced by slick web development and SEO companies, and they don't even know it. But, as they say, "an ounce of prevention is worth a pound of cure." Let me help you take a peek below the surface so you can detect—and avoid— some of the most common internet marketing mistakes:

Mistake: Wooing Google Over Humans

Everyone knows their site has to be optimized so Google will find it and rank it high in the search results. But most SEO companies focus so much attention on Google that they forget that HUMANS are the ones who actually, you know, buy stuff.

As a result, they unnaturally STUFF keywords into the website—to the extent that they murder your chances of enticing real humans to read it.

On the next page is the main headline from Randy's site: "Home Windows Installed By Experts In Bridgeport, New Haven, Hartford, Danbury, and Throughout Connecticut & Eastern New York."

Think about it: would you EVER imagine saying <u>that</u> FIRST when you meet a prospect in person? Of course not. It's stupid. When people read this kind of Google-chasing drivel on the first page they see, they immediately click away to find something that answers their REAL question they have when searching: "I need to buy windows, why should I pick THIS company instead of all the others?"

Mistake:"Hey Baby, My Apartment's Around The Corner. Wanna See It?"

Seriously, can you imagine some moron trying that pickup line in a bar? It would never work in a million years. And trust me, you wouldn't want any part of the woman who took that rancid bait.

With that in mind, why are the "web experts" so determined to litter your website with all the little buttons, forms, and offers that say "Get A Price," "Visit Our Showroom," "View Our Special Offers," "Download Our Brochure," and "Sign Up For Our Newsletter"?

Look, I get it. You need a way for prospects to let you know they're interested. But throwing 16 hooks into the water simply isn't necessary when you have a good website. One or two hooks—of course. Five or 10? Too many.

Randy's website is cluttered with exactly <u>SIX</u> of these kinds of offers (including TWO that say "Get A Price") on the top half of the home page of his site alone. The pseudo-guru's logic is simple: Give people a form to fill out for something… then when they do, pounce and sell. You're going to have to trust me on this one: "bait and pounce" is not a good way to sell nowadays.

Think about it: why on earth would somebody want to give you their precious contact information <u>before</u> they even have any CLUE *who you are, what you're about, how you're different, or what they can expect when doing business with you?* Why would they do that? For the most part, they wouldn't. Hence, zero leads, Randy.

If your website actually takes the time to explain all those things, people draw a *natural conclusion* that they should call you—assuming your reasons are compelling—because they trust you. There's no manipulation needed. No "bait." And for Pete's sake, no pouncing.

Again: It's okay to have a "Get A Price" button or form on your website. Just don't make these kinds of forms the MAIN/ONLY thing people see right when they find your site. Trust me, it's a HUGE turn-off.

In Summary: Just Say "No" To Nerds

There are thousands of website and internet-search companies out there. But most of them are run by technical people (i.e., nerds)—not marketing people. And the nerds tend to measure success by misguided standards. Standards that are shortsighted, wrong, and very costly to YOU.

Websites should be designed and written with the goal of <u>converting lookers into buyers</u>—not just looking pretty. Search strategies should be focused on <u>generating high quality leads</u>, not just ranking high on Google.

It costs more to design, write, and build a website this way—our average website cost is $24,000. But assuming the website will last 5 years before it needs to be overhauled, that's only about $400 a month. Trust me, this is not something you want to "save money" on. Not if you're the kind of company trying to get to $10MM in sales.

In the end, remember that internet marketing is still just marketing. The goal is to persuade people to buy from you. And if your website fails to persuade, you lose.

CHAPTER 24

"Conversionability" – Turning Lookers Into Buyers

Now that you know what NOT to do when it comes to a website, let's turn our attention to creating a website that will move the needle. To make that happen, your site has to have what I call "conversionability."

Conversionability is the process of increasing "stickiness" on your website so people will **read it, absorb it, believe it, and act based on it.**

In other words, it's about turning lookers into buyers.

It's not enough to have a beautiful website with lots of cool pictures on it. Lots of your competitors have beautiful websites, too.

The four major elements of conversionability are:

1. Initial Engagement
2. Identity
3. Social Proof
4. Evidence

We've already talked at length about Identity... so let's talk about the other three in detail right now: Initial engagement, social proof, and evidence.

Initial Engagement – The Three Hurdles

Imagine opening the door of a public restroom only to be punched in the face by a horrible, rancid smell. You really have to go, so you decide to enter anyway. But when you flip on the light switch, you see a clogged toilet, a wet floor, and other random nasty stuff strewn about.

If people don't like what they see and the way they feel the split second they land on your site—and the ensuing few seconds after that—they'll run away and look elsewhere. So the first step of "conversionability" is to get people to <u>stay</u> on your site when they first land on it.

To make that happen, you have to help your website visitors clear three major hurdles in the first eight seconds they are on your site. Otherwise, you lose visitors who SHOULD be buying from you.

Here's why: When somebody lands on your website, their subconscious brain goes into hyper-efficient scanner mode. It makes a near-instant decision about whether to continue looking at your site.

If you don't engage the prospect on three different split-second engagement hurdles, you'll lose.

Here are those three hurdles:

Engagement Hurdle #1 (0.5 Seconds): "Is This Website Total Garbage?"

When someone first lands on your site, they immediately start scanning the page for any sign you either ARE or ARE NOT the solution they're looking for.

If the site looks unprofessional, or if loads too slowly, or if it's hard to tell what you sell, or if it's not even for the category they were searching (Example: Searching for siding, but roofing comes up on the page), then they'll bail out in less than one second. **Literally, LESS THAN ONE SECOND.**

Engagement Hurdle #2 (3 Seconds): "Is There Anything Interesting Here?"

Assuming your website wasn't a total train wreck per above, the prospect is now going to take about two or three additional seconds to see if anything on the site is worth looking at more carefully. This is where most websites fail—even reasonably nice-looking sites.

The major transgression is "ME-TOO-itis." In other words, your site looks, feels, smells, and tastes just about like every other website. Don't believe me? Check these out:

All of these sites look "okay" and have a certain level of professionalism. But none of them do anything AT ALL to "stop the prospects in their tracks" and make them want to keep looking through the website. Let me be perfectly clear: I'm not saying these websites can't be successful; I'm just saying they are definitely getting fewer visitors, fewer leads, and fewer sales than they SHOULD be getting.

It's tempting to think if your website is not HURTING you (like those that fail on the first hurdle), that everything is okay. But trust me,

NOT BEING TERRIBLE (clearing the first hurdle) is not even close to the same thing as BEING AWESOME (clearing the second hurdle).

To make it over the second hurdle, your website must give the reader the promise that you offer a superior value and it's worth pursuing further.

This isn't accomplished with design or colors or pictures. It's done with WORDS. Words that capture your identity. Words that explain who you are, how you're different, and what people can expect when doing business with you. Here's a good example of clearing the second hurdle:

137

Promises are made. Expectations are set. Words are used to describe how they're different and how they're better. That's what we call IDENTITY—and it's discernable in just a couple of seconds of a quick scan! It's a heck of a lot better than "Lone Star Roofing of Texas provides roofing and other construction services for both residential and commercial clients." Snore.

Engagement Hurdle #3 (8 Seconds):"Do I Trust These Guys?"

This is where lookers get turned into buyers. Once the prospect reads (again—words!) your headlines and understands that you offer a superior value proposition, they're going to want you to PROVE it. They want to know if they can trust your claims… and in turn, trust you. This is where the elements of testimony, social proof, and evidence come into play.

Testimony means they want to hear what you have to say. If you tell them (like above) that you don't apply sales pressure, play pricing games, and you don't accept down payments, they're going to want to know more about what that means. There had better be additional clarifying information for them to read and absorb.

In other words, you can't just make a claim and the leave it hanging out on the line all by its lonesome. You have to back it up. You have to explain it. You have to give examples. Don't assume people know or believe anything. Use words to give depth and meaning to your headlines.

Social proof means job photos, customer references, and online reviews. Web visitors want to see and believe that other people have used you—large quantities of people, preferably—and actually LIKE you. They want to see pictures of your work and hear others sing your praises. **They want to shortcut their own due diligence by seeing what others think.**

Once they make it over hurdle number two, they're going to spend about five additional seconds SCANNING THE HOMEPAGE to find additional information I just mentioned. If they don't see it readily available, they'll bail out. If they see your claims are empty and not backed up, they'll bail out. If they don't find proof that others know and love you, they'll bail out.

That's eight total seconds. Tick tock.

We'll talk about how to actually provide the information they are looking for—the testimony, the social proof, the evidence—in the next few chapters.

For now, the hurdle is just to allow the web visitor to quickly see that it's available… *at a glance*.

In marketing, seconds matter. Half-seconds matter. Milliseconds matter. Make sure your website is doing everything it should be doing to capture viewers and successfully guiding them over the first three critical hurdles. If you do, you'll see your conversion go up EXPONENTIALLY—and you'll make a ton more money.

CHAPTER 25
Social Proof

Social proof is an easy concept to understand—but the vast majority of contractors still don't take advantage of it.

Simply put, people want to know what other people think about you when forming their own opinion of your company.

If they can rely on the opinions of other people, they won't have to take the time and effort to research you themselves.

Social proof is the most powerful when:

A) The people providing the opinions are as much like the reader as possible (location, gender, race, income level, etc.)

B) The information they are giving is real, unfiltered, and honest, and

C) There is a lot of it.

The great thing about your website is you can put as much social proof on it as you are willing to gather. The more, the better. You never have to worry about having too much because if a given web visitor doesn't want to read through it all, they don't have to. But just seeing that there is a lot available is impressive… and will make them feel warm and fuzzy even if they skip most of it.

In this chapter we'll cover the most important kinds of social proof that you should have on your website, including:

- Online Reviews

- Testimonials

- Case Studies

- Customer References

- Photos (with captions)

Online Reviews

How important are online reviews? On a scale of 1 to 10, I'd put them at about 17.

Think about it. We rely on online reviews for input—REAL INPUT—on lots of different things. Cars, Cancun resorts, iPhone apps… basically everything.

Here's an example. A few years ago, my desk lamp died, so I went on Amazon to find a replacement.

After a few minutes of searching, I found one that appeared to offer everything I thought I wanted in a lamp: The Z-Bar High Power LED Lamp, manufactured by Koncept. The lamp was sleek and modern looking… but more importantly, it pivoted in three places (hence the name "Z-Bar") which allowed it to have a very, very long reach. Perfect.

The only problem was the price tag: $195. Ouch. I was thinking more like $30 to $50.

I kept looking for other less expensive lamps, but I kept coming back to the Z-Bar… it had many features that made it the perfect fit for my lamp needs. I started reading the online reviews—all 23 of them— to see what others thought.

Look, I know that you could probably care less about lamps. But I'd like for you to read the review below to begin to comprehend how important online reviews are for your prospects:

8 of 8 people found the following review helpful

★★★★★ **Great Desk Lamp**, November 19, 2009

By **Jack Safro "J.S."** (St. Petersburg, FL) - See all my reviews

This review is from: **Z-Bar High Power LED Lamp- Silver/Cool Generation 2**

I had some apprehension about such an expensive desk lamp, but I am glad I took the plunge. I was looking for a non-fluorescent articulating desk lamp. Most articulating lamps need constant fiddling/tightening, and don't hold their position very well. The Z-Bar stays right where you put it. No fuss, no tightening or loosening. It also has a tiny footprint. I am using the included desk clamp to attach it to the desktop hole made for wires.

The lamp puts out good light. It doesn't irritate me like fluorescents, and it is almost soothing (I purchased the "Daylight" model). The six individual lights do create a slight six shadow effect. If you can, set the light so that it illuminates from the opposite of your dominate hand (if you are right handed, have it shine from the left so as not to create a shadow from your hand onto your work.

The Z-Bar puts out good light wherever you shine it but it does not cast much ambient light, and the work area is somewhat small (read: if you are looking to light up a room, this is not what you want). You can raise the lamp higher for a broader area.

Bonus: this sucker does not get hot (pretty warm, but not hot). At any time you can touch the lamp without fear. It also uses only 9 watts at full brightness (compared to, say, 60 watts for a normal incandescent).

My only other complaints are niggling. Turning the unit on/off requires 4 presses of either the + or - buttons (though the buttons are of good quality and easily accessible). Also, it is a contemporary looking light. Not my style, but I will accept its function over form. Despite the look, it is fairly non-obtrusive, and it goes with pretty much any modern-day office gear (I got the silver).

This is a great and functional product of high quality. After a childhood of being hit on the head with a burning hot desk lamp that wouldn't stay put, I feel that I am finally beginning to see the light (or is that the result of repeated head trauma? ...). I recommend this product! If you spend a lot of time at work and hate fluorescents, you may wish to spend a bit of scratch on decent lighting. It's a quality of life issue.

(side note: I originally bought the mini-high power led desk lamp. It was nice, but too dinky, so I returned it. I would only recommend that model for a very small work area.)

Help other customers find the most helpful reviews

Was this review helpful to you? [Yes] [No]   Report abuse | Permalink

💬 Comment (1)

After spending an hour reading all 23 reviews (including twelve 5-star reviews, one 4-star, five 3-star, two 2-star, and three 1-star), I shrugged my shoulders and made the purchase.

Why? Because I felt absolutely certain that *I knew what I was getting:*

- The guy writing the review was apprehensive—just like me!

- The Z-Bar lamp stays in place without constant fiddling and tightening

- It has a tiny footprint

- The light is good… but it can create shadows—something to watch out for and be aware of

- It doesn't create a lot of ambient light

- It doesn't get hot

- I saw the problems—minor as they were—of pushing buttons to turn it on (instead of a switch)

Do you think I could have learned all that from the manufacturer's description? Do you think I would have believed them if they DID tell me all that? No and no.

Alas, the power of the online review.

By allowing existing customers to detail their experience, we allow prospects to read believable, granular information about what they can expect. This allows them to effectively "crowd source" their due diligence. If you fail to actively solicit and make available customer reviews, you are losing a huge opportunity.

Think about all the times you've personally used online reviews to make purchasing decisions on everything. I once spent 90 minutes reading reviews for a 99-cent group-texting app. I didn't want to get an app that wasn't exactly right for my needs. It wasn't the 99 cents I was worried about—it was making certain that the app actually did what I needed it to do.

Yet I still find the majority of remodelers don't have very many reviews. It doesn't seem to be a priority.

Online reviews allow your prospects to get real, believable, unfiltered opinions from your past customers!

Read that lamp review again. Does it look canned? Is it full of platitudes? Does it simply say "the lamp is great!"? And most of all—is it believable?

To properly execute online reviews on your website, you've got to be smart. Here are some suggestions:

Don't Try To Manage Reviews Yourself: Some companies will try, in essence, to become their own review service. This means polling/surveying customers and posting the results on their website.

There are lots of problems with this approach, namely:

1. You have now lost the third-party credibility that comes with online reviews (you can "doctor" your results however you like)

2. You have to have somebody manage all this stuff—gathering, sorting, posting—trust me, it will eventually fall through the cracks

3. It's time consuming and expensive.

Ultimately, it usually just doesn't get done.

DO Use A Service To Encourage And Aggregate Reviews: The good news is some companies can gather and post third-party online reviews for you. By third-party reviews, I'm talking about Google, Facebook, Houzz, Angie's List, BBB.... and over 150 others.

It's actually quite easy and inexpensive—usually about $300 a month. That is an absolute bargain compared to the manpower you'd have to expend to get a fraction of the results.

This is actually a service we offer; here's how it works:

First, we put a review button on your website that looks like this:

When somebody clicks on it, they are taken to your review page, where they are given an option to read reviews or leave a review.

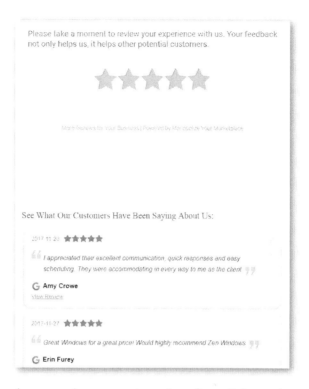

If they choose to leave a review, they first click on the number of stars they want to give you, from one to five. If they choose only one or two stars, they will see this message:

This gives you a chance to "intercept" the bad reviews before they happen, so you can course correct and remedy the problem.

If they choose three, four, or five stars, they then see this screen:

We can customize this page to include whichever review sites you prefer. Several of our clients HATE Yelp (Go to UnlimitedLeadFlow. com/book for keyword "Yelp" to see why) and leave it off. Google is the best review source because it also helps your SEO the most.

The reviews are then left on the respective third-party sites where they will not only be seen by your prospects, but will also dramatically boost your SEO effectiveness.

If you send us your customer list once a month (or once a week, at your discretion), we will send a series of customized, automated emails to your customers to solicit online reviews through this system.

Our system then continuously monitors over 170 review websites and alerts you via email when you get new reviews. We then program your website to show these new reviews ON YOUR SITE as they come in… and we have the ability to only show four- and five-star reviews if you wish.

It's a fantastic system that pays huge dividends. To learn more about it, check out our website.

Another Option – Guild Quality

Another option for online reviews is a company called Guild Quality. They are a well-established player in the remodeling industry and have the added benefit of using telephone follow-up to make sure that your customers actually fill out the surveys they send.

While other online review sites can provide good information, their data often comes from either the happiest and least happy clients. Guild Quality can provide a detailed survey from a larger percentage of the client base, with a more robust sampling of the overall experience that clients are finding. It is an essential process for companies that want to provide a great overall customer experience.

Some important points to remember about Guild Quality:

- They use mail, e-mail, and phone calls to reach an extraordinarily high 70% of clients.

- They send the surveys directly to the contractor in real time upon customer completion.

- They indirectly encourage a company get better by providing the opportunity to celebrate their strengths and work on their weaknesses. This frequent self-review helps grow a culture of quality over time.

- They help companies to evaluate both the overall performance of their business as well as the performance of individual team members.

- They help encourage a sense of ownership among team members as they eagerly await great reviews and take responsibility of less positive ones.

- They provide an extensive review of results through various reports, including comparing a company to others in its industry.

Testimonials

Testimonials are those great little snippets of people saying awesome things about you that companies used to gather and post on their websites. They were kind of like online reviews, except you had supreme control over what they said, and whether or not they got posted at all.

The reason testimonials went out of style is because online reviews are much more authentic and trustworthy—and therefore infinitely more valuable.

But that doesn't mean that you can't use the testimonials you already have.

Here's my advice: If you don't have any testimonials, focus strictly on gathering online reviews. Skip the rest of this section.

If you <u>do</u> have existing testimonials from days gone by, go ahead and post them on your website ALONG with your online reviews. The more testimonials you have, the better. In fact, if you have a lot of testimonials, put ALL OF THEM on your website, and make sure they're all on one single page.

Remember the website we looked at earlier in this book when we were talking about identity? It was a company named Upscale Remodeling. Go to their website (Google it) and go to the Reputation tab on their main navigation, then click on "Testimonials."

Here's what you'll see: A TON of testimonials!

There's something I call "The Law of 3 ½ Scrolls." While it sounds exotic, it really just means it should take a website visitor about 3 ½ scrolls to get to the bottom of a testimonials webpage. The goal is to make the visitor feel like they've been scrolling for a long time.

And while that might sound bad (and exhausting), it's actually a good thing. Here's why: Nobody's going to read all your testimonials. Nobody. But when the prospect sees so many that they had to scroll 3 ½ times (or more) to get to the bottom of the list, they'll be impressed.

Remember, the broad topic here is SOCIAL proof.

On the Upscale Remodeling "Testimonials page," you have to scroll FORTY-ONE times to get to the bottom (at least on my mouse)!

That's fantastic! The reaction I want from the web visitor is "Wow, they have worked for a lot of people... and they all seem happy." Even if they give up after four or five scrolls, they'll be impressed.

A big factor in social proof is just plain-old quantity. Five scrolls are better than three. Forty-one is better than five. This goes for online reviews, as well as case studies, photos, and customer references (which we are about to talk about).

Bottom line: If you have testimonials, use them. If not, let's move on to...

Case Studies

A case study is a way for you to document how you helped your customers achieve a positive result with their project. They are, by definition, more detailed and through than a review or a testimonial. Case studies are not told from the perspective of the customer. Instead, you write it up—and therefore, you control the narrative.

Case studies should focus on specific customers. They should be documented with photographs, along with a descriptive story of what you did for them, what challenges you overcame (if any), and what the final result was. The more detail, the better.

The idea with case studies is to have your prospects say to themselves, "Hey, that's kind of like what I'm trying to do." When they read the case studies, they should be able to see themselves in the stories and imagine the results you will get for them.

The pictures you provide should show, if possible, the customers themselves, along with before, during, and after photographs of the project.

Think in terms of your identity when writing case studies. If your meticulous precision is an important part of your identity, you should showcase that in the case studies. If frequent communication with the client is your calling card, your case studies should highlight that. And so forth.

Since case studies take more time and effort to prepare—and because they are so powerful—you don't need to have a ton of them on your website. Try to get two or three for starters... and grow that number to 10 if you can. Ten good case studies will go a long way toward convincing your prospects that you are everything you claim to be in your marketing.

You can see several good case studies on the Upscale Remodeling website I've already referenced several times.

Customer References

Here's a crazy idea: what if you gave your prospects customer references *on your website?*

What I'm talking about is a list of names, phone numbers, cities, and project types of actual customers. All sitting <u>right there</u> on your website, in plain view.

Like 15 of them. Or 20. Or 30.

Without the prospect having to fill out a form. Or even identifying themselves at all.

No strings. No restrictions. No conditions.

Told you it was a crazy idea! But also one of the best—and definitely under-utilized—ways to improve conversion on your website.

Let's think about this for a minute:

In a court of law, your references are called "witnesses." The jury (your prospects) have the ability to call them up, interview them, solicit their unvarnished opinions, and draw their own conclusions. References are more powerful than reviews because your customer can play attorney and interview the witnesses himself!

If you make these "witnesses" available without prospects having to jump through hoops (like asking for them), that's a supreme show of confidence. It sure beats the heck out of "giving them three references" if and when they ask for them. It's critical that your reference list have NO LESS than 15 names on it—the more the better. You don't want to be perceived as handpicking happy souls and flushing the rest.

IMPORTANT! When you provide the references, also make sure you tell your prospects what kinds of questions they should ask when they DO call. I prefer the following:

- Overall, how satisfied were you with the quality of the work?

- What about the contractor's responsiveness?

- Was there anything about the job that upset you? Or didn't meet your expectations?

- If you had to do the project over again, would you choose this contractor?

You could come up with more, but that's a good start! I've found that if you don't give people questions to ask, they might not call simply because they are unsure what to say. This will help out.

Now, let's handle some common objections I get to this method:

Objection 1: "What if my customers don't want to be on my website?" Then by all means, don't put them on the list! You should get written permission, of course... but you will find this a lot easier to get than you think. As long as your customers are truly happy, many of them will be thrilled to share their experience. After all, how often does somebody ask you your opinion on anything?

Objection 2: "What if they get too many calls?" Take them off the list! Make sure your customers know that they can contact you at any time to request to be taken of the list—either permanently, or just for a rest. A good solution is to have two or three lists, and rotate them periodically—once or twice a month. You will quickly find out that only your most earnestly interested prospects actually take the time to call your list. And most of them actually WAIT until after they've engaged you in conversation to actually pick up the phone. *Note:* If you are a really big company with hundreds of customers and thousands of prospects per month, you may even want to rotate lists DAILY.

Objection 3: "What about my customers' online privacy?" Have your website nerds code the page so that it's not indexed by Google or other search engines. This is easy to do, and it ensures if somebody Googles your customer's name, your webpage (with their name on it) doesn't come up as a search result.

Objection 4: "What if my competitors see this list of my customers?" So what?! What exactly do you think they are going to do with that list? Do you think they will call them up, tell them that you are terrible, and try to make them talk bad about you? Remember, these are your happy customers. Your competitors aren't going to do anything with this list. And even if they did, it wouldn't affect you in any way.

You can see a good example of this at a website called IntegrityHomePro.com. Click on About Us in the main navigation bar, and then look for "Our References." Sure enough, you'll see the list of names and phone numbers… along with the list of questions right there on the site.

If you're not quite that daring, you can get 50% of the bang for the buck by making the list of references available to anyone who fills out a form to request them. This is what Upscale Remodeling does—just click on "References" under "Reputation" and you'll see it.

Photos

Suffice it to say, people are going to want to see photos of jobs you've done—especially in categories where there is an impressive "after" shot compared to the "before." If you do kitchen and bath remodeling… if you do metal roofing or siding… if you are in the shutter or sunroom business, you should add as many photos as possible to your website.

Service companies like HVAC, plumbers, and electric—not so much.

But if you do have pictures on your website, here's a tip for you: To the extent possible, put a caption under the photo to tell the viewer what they should be looking for. A person looking at a photo of a bathroom you remodeled might not notice the intricate mosaic tiles you used to accent the shower. Nobody's going to notice the crown molding or standing seam roofing or lack of seams on your siding unless you tell them to notice it. Remember—point at the showerhead!

Wrap Up

This has been a long chapter—and for good reason. Social proof is one of the most critical elements of your website, and has more potential to affect your "conversionability" than any other aspect. People want to do business with companies they can trust. Publish trustworthy accounts of happy customers who love and recommend you whole-heartedly, and you will convert more lookers into buyers than you do now. That's a promise.

CHAPTER 26
Evidence To Prove Your Case

THE FINAL ELEMENT of conversionability is EVIDENCE. To the extent possible, you have to prove your claims! Here are a few ideas for you:

- **Use Demo Videos:** One of my metal roofing clients once built a potato gun and fired potatoes at over 200 mph at various kinds of roofing materials to back up their claims that their roofing materials were impervious to hail stones. Another client posted videos of a big fat guy stomping on one of their windows to prove that they didn't break easily. Another client hired a couple of muscle-heads from the gym to beat their windows with crowbars, baseball bats, and chains to show that hurricanes couldn't smash them. Another client burned their windows to show how they were fireproof.

- You get the idea. You don't have to go super fancy and high-tech to get your point across. Your iPhone will take HD videos that you can then hire somebody $15 an hour to edit. Do it.

- **Charts and Graphs:** This sounds simple, but it's very effective. If you claim your windows are more energy efficient, create a graph comparing a .21 U-Rating to a 50 mpg hybrid car. People will understand that. If you offer a glass breakage warranty, create a chart with the header "Covered Against" and then pictures of baseballs, footballs, kids throwing rocks, lawn mowers, golf balls, fists, etc. to help people understand. Get creative here.

- **About Us Page:** The About Us page is a throwaway after-thought for most companies. But when done right, it can be a powerful piece of evidence to convert prospects into customers if you use it properly.

Let's look at an example of a terrible About Us page, so you can see what NOT to do:

"For 30 years, the management team at Awesome Windows has been involved in the fenestration industry. Their vast experience covers all phases of the window industry including building our own window systems (which we've been doing since 2001) to consulting, installation, and after care service.

Today we offer to the public TRUE factory direct value. We build a wide variety of products from the most affordable line to our most feature rich energy efficient product system. All designed to "keep out heat, cold, and noise."

People, we can do better. Much better, in fact.

Your About Us page represents a fantastic opportunity to HUMANIZE your company. Tell your prospects what kind of people you really are... so they can connect with you on a HUMAN level... and understand where your identity is coming from.

Nobody wants to read a hollow, truncated history of your company ("We started in 1984..."), a rehashing of all the crap you sell, or a bunch of platitudes about your dedication to customers and service.

Here's a better way: Tell a story.

Make it a personal story that illustrates why you operate the way you do. A story that shows how your mentality and philosophy were molded. A story that helps people know and love the real you.

For a couple more good examples, go to UnlimitedLeadFlow. com/book and look for the Freelite Windows and Upscale remodeling examples. No, seriously. Do it.

If you read the examples, you might be tempted to think there is "too much text" and "nobody is going to read all that."

And you would be wrong.

These pages are designed to seal the deal on getting prospects to want to do business with you. By the time they meander over to your "About Us" page, they've already probably thoroughly absorbed your identity (assuming you have one) and checked out mounds of social proof and evidence (assuming you've provided it).

You should already have them preferring you over other contractors. They should already be wanting to do business with you. And since everything else they've seen on your website has been so interesting, relevant, and engaging, they're going to keep clicking and clicking and clicking.

Until they find your interesting little story that gives a little bit of backstory. In their mind, they're going to pay you tens of thousands of dollars to complete this project for them; trust me, they'll gobble up every delicious morsel of information about yourself you make available.

Let's take the example from above from Freelite. I interviewed the owner, Chip Marvin, to get a feel for him and his company. Here is what I discovered:

- A genuinely nice man who cares about people

- A soft-spoken man who seems like he wouldn't hurt a fly

- A man with a strong aversion to heavy-handed sales techniques

- A man who's passionate about helping his customers make the right choices for their situation

Based on this, I started asking him about his background: How did he start this business? Why is he so put off by sales pressure? What was he like growing up? What did he want to be when he grew up? How do people react to his soft-spoken personality in a sales situation? Like that. And more.

What I found out didn't surprise me based on what I had already divined by just talking to him. A guy with a religious studies degree from Yale with no business experience moved to Tucson in the 1970s to look for opportunity.

If you skipped over the examples above without actually looking at them, you really should go back and study them—in detail—right now. I mean seriously, check out this awesome headline:

If "Type A" Personality Means Somebody Is Driven, Aggressive, And Forceful, You Might Say That My Personality Is "Type Z."

It's not going to get much better—or much more engaging—than that.

Wrap Up

Your website is your single-most important marketing tool because all of your prospects are going to look at it sooner or later.

An effective website not only looks great. It also turns lookers into buyers by having a conspicuous identity and utilizing social proof and evidence to convince people you're the best choice.

Never underestimate the power of a great website—or the damage that an under-leveraged website can do to your business.

I cannot stress enough how important it is to hire the right company to create your website—and how nearly 100% of web companies out there have no idea what an identity is, let alone how to integrate it into your website. They don't know how to gather or present evidence. In fact, the majority of website companies can't go much at all beyond making a site look pretty. They ask you "what do you want to put on your site?" as if you are an expert at writing strong copy. Isn't that their job?

Yes. Yes, it is.

I said it earlier and I'll emphasize it again: Our websites cost more than most. And on the surface, they don't look all that much different from a pretty site that can be half for 25% to 50% of the cost. But think about YOUR business. Do your windows *look* all that different than your cheap competitors'? Does your HVAC system *look* much different? Or you siding or roofs? Just like with your company, it's what's under the hood that makes the difference... and what makes paying more a smart investment with a huge ROI.

Once your website is in place, it's time to move on to generating online leads.

SECTION 4
Online Lead Generation

Most contractors have a love-hate relationship with online lead generation. The leads are usually (but not always) cheap. And they're generally pretty well-well qualified. But they're hard to get in large enough quantity to really blow up your business.

Let's review the 4-Step Formula:

1. **Sell awesome stuff that people genuinely love.**

2. **Charge high prices.**

3. **Master the internet.**

4. **Use radio & TV advertising.**

With a great company and high enough prices to afford more marketing in place… and with your awesome, identity-based website in place, it's time to crack the code and generate large quantities of qualified internet leads. They're often the most responsive kinds of leads—after all, they were actively online looking when they found you.

But they're also a zero-sum game.

Later on, we're going to talk about radio and TV advertising. Part of the idea behind that is to expand the market—to make it bigger. Over time, you can convince people who hadn't really considered replacing their windows that they should really consider it. Or to upgrade to a metal roof. Or replace their heating and cooling system.

But internet leads come from people who are online right now actively looking for somebody to buy from. If you don't get the lead, guess what? That lead will go to your competitor. That's what I mean by "zero sum game." It's you or them. Which means it's a moral imperative that you figure out how to get them to call you instead of them.

CHAPTER 27

Pay Per Click – Instantly Cut To The Front Of The Line

A FEW YEARS AGO, I took my kids to SeaWorld for spring break. Turns out, since the entire state of Texas is on spring break at the same time, this wasn't a terribly original idea. When we arrived at the park and saw the massive lines of people just waiting to get in, I remembered something an old friend had told me years ago:

"If money can solve it, it's not a problem."

I whipped out my credit card and bought the elusive "Fast Pass," which essentially buys you line-cutting privileges over all the suckers who wouldn't/couldn't/didn't pony up for it. The cost was not insignificant; the Fast Passes basically *doubled* the price of admission for my family of eight.

But boy was it worth it.

As we entered the waiting corrals of one of the rides—one where you ride a raft and then plunge down from the top of a Mayan temple into a lagoon—there was a sign posted that said, "Wait from this point: 90 Minutes." There were a couple hundred people waiting in line... BEYOND that point.

But we didn't wait in that line. No, sir. We entered the "Fast Pass" lane... and proceeded to walk right past those hundreds of sweaty, irritated, and exhausted people—in plain sight. We didn't stop until we got to the very front of the line where they were loading people into the rafts.

I felt like a celebrity running amok in my own personal play land. (Though I'm sure a few non-Fast-Pass folk wanted to kill me).

To recap…

The non-Fast Pass people's wait: Close to two hours.

My wait: Less than five minutes, including the time it took to walk past them.

The moral of the story: If money can solve it, it's not a problem.

It's the same with contractors and pay-per-click (PPC). **While SEO can be an agonizingly long wait in line for a ride, PPC is the "Fast Pass" to skip the line and go straight to #1 on Google.**

This is even more important now that Google has changed how they display search results on a page. In the past, there were one or two paid ads at the top, while the rest of the ads showed up on the right-hand side of the page. It was obvious that ads were "second class citizens" and organic results were the "belle of the ball."

Not anymore.

Now, the first organic result doesn't show up until well below the fold (the part of a webpage that you have to scroll down to see) on every single results page.

For example, here are the results that appear above the fold (the part of the page you don't have to scroll down to see) when I search "roofers Detroit":

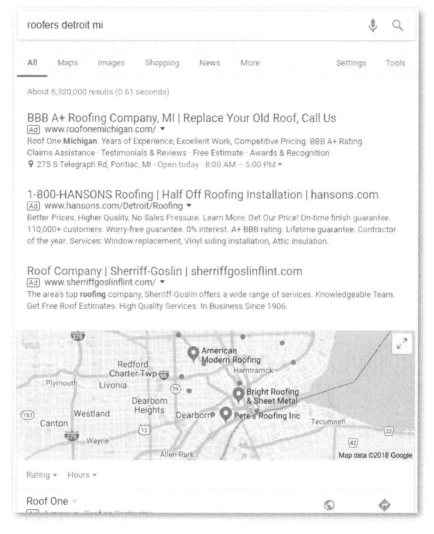

Not an organic result in sight. In fact, I have to zoom out 33% just to fit the first organic result in an image:

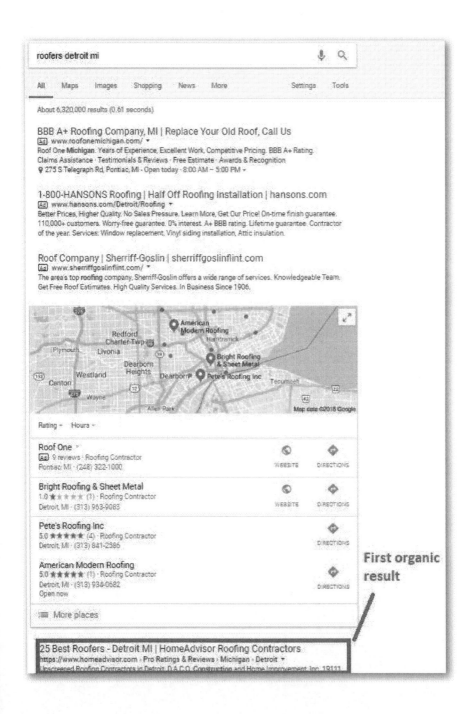

First organic result

To recap the order of the results page:

1. Paid Ads

2. Local Pack (I'll talk about this in the SEO chapters)

3. Organic Results

If you're wondering why Google displays results this way, it's simple: **Follow the money.** Of course it's the money! Just like SeaWorld, Google is going to let the customers who are willing to pay the most cut to the front of the line. It's just that simple.

All of those organic search results don't pay jack squat to Google, so Google has no incentive to reward them. In fact, Google has recently admitted that part of their "algorithm" is to actually give preferential organic search positions to companies who spend money with them on PPC. (Hold that thought. We'll come back to it).

The Organic-Results Monopoly

Look at that last image again and notice the first organic result—it's HomeAdvisor. Google has recently teamed up with HomeAdvisor. When people now search for home improvement services, HomeAdvisor takes the first organic spot most of the time.

To compound the problem, Google also tends to show "aggregate" websites like Yelp and Angie's List on the first page of results. So not only do will you <u>not</u> show up for organic results until halfway down the page, but you also have to compete with ginormous companies that may or may not be in Google's back pocket.

Yeesh.

Here's an example of what I mean. I searched "window replacement Boston," and these are the first organic results:

Best Window Replacement in Boston, MA - Yelp
https://www.yelp.com/search?find_desc=Window+Replacement&find...Boston%2C... ▾
Reviews on window replacement in Boston, MA - Renoviso, A D Construction, Rennovare Construction &
Fine Carpentry, Solo Glass, Jeff Fisher Windows, ...

25 Best Window Replacement Companies - Boston MA | HomeAdvisor
https://www.homeadvisor.com › Pro Ratings & Reviews › Massachusetts › Boston ▾
Hire the best Window Replacement Companies in Boston, MA on HomeAdvisor. We Have 1420
Homeowner Reviews of Top Boston Window Replacement ...

Boston Replacement Windows & Home Exteriors | Champion
https://www.championwindow.com/Boston/ ▾
★★★★⯪ Rating: 4.4 - 124 votes
Champion Windows of Boston | Your Local Window & Home Exterior Expert. Specializing in
Replacement Windows, Custom Sunrooms, Entry & Exterior Doors, ...

New England Replacement Windows | Boston Replacement - NEWPRO
https://www.newpro.com › Windows ▾
★★★★★ Rating: 4.9 - 115 reviews
New England Replacement Windows are offered by the New England Window Replacement experts at
NEWPRO. Contact Today For Your Replacement New ...

Window Replacement in Boston - Renewal By Andersen
https://www.renewalbyandersen.com/window-company/096-boston-ma/retailer ▾
Consultation. Window Replacement in Boston. Renewal by Andersen of Boston, MA is proud to serve
the window replacement and patio door replacement needs of the greater Boston area including
Framingham, Nashua, Plymouth, Shrewsbury, and Worcester.

Top 10 Best Boston MA Window Replacement Installers | Angie's List
https://www.angieslist.com › Local Reviews › MA › Boston ▾
Join for FREE to read real reviews and see ratings for Boston Window Replacement Installers near you
to help pick the right pro Replacement Window.

Window Replacement in Boston, MA at The Home Depot
https://www.homedepot.com/l/services/ma/boston/replacement-windows/ ▾
★★★★★ Rating: 4.9 - 13 reviews
With a variety of window styles available, you can confidently choose The Home Depot to help upgrade

If you want to rank organically on page one for replacement windows in Boston, you have to duke it out with HomeAdvisor, Yelp, and Angie's List. Admittedly, "replacement windows Boston" is a highly competitive keyword. But you'll get the same kinds of results for much smaller markets and locations.

These types of companies have a monopoly on organic home-improvement search results. **But with PPC, you can instantly leap-frog** over the HomeAdvisors, Angie's Lists, and companies that spend millions on advertising.

Bottom Line...

SEO will almost always take a *looonnnggg* time to bear fruit—expect to wait anywhere from six to 12 months just to START seeing results. And the competition is STIFF—all caps required.

Don't get me wrong—SEO isn't dead for independent contractors. It's 100% necessary to master the internet (Step 3 in our 4-Step Formula to get to $10MM). Without a strong SEO strategy, you simply can't do it. I'll discuss why in the SEO chapters of this book. **For now, it's important simply to understand that while SEO takes a while to "kick in," PPC is <u>immediate</u>.**

PPC lets you cut in front of all of your competitors... even the ones who rank first organically after they spent months or YEARS trying to get there. It lets you push past companies that hog the first page of organic results (like HomeAdvisor). **It lets you go from page-seven anonymity to Page-One Rock Star in MINUTES.**

In other words, PPC is your "Fast Pass" to mastering the internet and making the jump to $10MM.

Now that we've established a bird's-eye view of PPC's benefits, let's briefly touch on a different topic: Why PPC is such a sore spot for many contractors.

CHAPTER 28

PPC – Problems, Difficulties... *And Solutions*

HEAR YOU LOUD and clear: "Yeah, yeah, yeah... front of the line. Great. But, newsflash, PPC is not cost effective. It doesn't work. It might even be a scam."

But here are the cold, hard facts taken directly from industry studies:

- PPC ads now get roughly 50% of ALL clicks on results pages

- PPC traffic converts nearly 47% better than organic traffic

- 52% of people who click a company's PPC ad call that company

These stats are, of course, for PPC campaigns done the RIGHT way.

The Fast Pass wouldn't be worth it if it were $1,000 per person. Or if the Fast Pass didn't actually work to get, you know, into the actual ride.

Just about every remodeling contractor in the country has been burned by PPC companies who promise the moon, then deliver the "poo-poo platter."

168

That's mostly why 65% to 70% of remodeling contractors don't do <u>any</u> PPC advertising at all. None. Zero. They've been burned too many times, and they're convinced that it JUST DOES NOT WORK.

Maybe that's you.

And out of the 30% of contractors who DO utilize PPC advertising? Over HALF have no idea if it is working or not. When you ask about results, all the contractors can tell you is how much they spent and how many CLICKS they got.

And out of the 30% of contractors who DO utilize PPC advertising? Over HALF have no idea if it is working or not. When you ask about results, all they can tell you is how much they spent and how many CLICKS they got.

Actual leads? Who knows. (Certainly not them).

The result: 90% of the remodeling PPC leads are being harvested by just 10% of the companies. The big money is going to the companies that figured out how to generate large quantities of real LEADS, while everybody else either quit or is farting around wondering what their cost per click should be.

Cost per <u>click</u> is actually a huge part of the problem. Contractors' lack of success often stems from focusing too much on it. While cost per click is a metric to keep an eye on, it's not THE most important element of PPC. Not by a long shot.

What is? Cost per lead, of course.

Let's break this down a little further…

The Difference Between "Normal PPC" and "PPC Lead Generation"

Most PPC campaigns fail because almost all pay-per-click providers use the old, outdated model of buying clicks. **This is what I call "<u>normal</u>" PPC—getting as many clicks as possible for the lowest cost per click possible in the misguided hope that more clicks equal more leads.**

"Normal" PPC doesn't track actual leads or cost per lead. As such, you don't actually know if your campaign is generating sales. In all honesty, it's probably not. Generating simple clicks is easier than generating clicks from QUALIFIED interested prospects. Most PPC providers make no distinction between the two.

The result: "Normal PPC" campaigns that are Epic Fails... and reason numero uno that most contractors won't touch "normal" PPC with a 10-foot pole.

There is, however, a different type of PPC. One that most contractors don't know exists. But it's hands down the better type of PPC for remodelers, builders, and construction companies.

It's called **PPC Lead Generation**.

PPC Lead Generation still tracks clicks and cost per click. It still requires a monthly budget (except when it doesn't... more on that in a minute!). But PPC Lead Generation uses more sophisticated methods and technology to collect and measure what's *really* important: **ACTUAL LEADS and COST PER LEAD.**

"Wait a second!" you say. "Can't most PPC companies already tell you how many calls you've received?"

Good point—most of them can. But here's the MAJOR problem—the number of calls you get and the number of LEADS you get are two completely different things! That's because all lead-generating campaigns—online or offline—will inevitably generate calls that are not leads.

I mentioned this a second ago. "Normal" PPC can generate clicks and calls. But that's not the issue. What is the issue is that these clicks and calls are not coming from QUALIFIED prospects. You know... the people actively in the market for YOUR specific service.

When you run a typical, click-focused PPC campaign, you'll get calls from toner cartridge salesmen. You'll get calls from people who want you to fix a cracked window. You'll get calls from current customers checking the status of their job. You'll get calls from leads that already called you yesterday.

All of these register as CALLS. But none of them are actually leads. And PPC companies don't distinguish calls from leads. As a result, you basically have to guess which are leads and which are not.

The reason no providers track LEADS is twofold: 1) It takes a lot of time and effort to sort through the calls to determine which ones are actually leads, and 2) they don't want you to know how they're really performing (because trust me, it's not that good).

In terms of tracking leads from phone calls, PPC Lead Generation takes things 10 steps further than "normal" PPC.

I'll explain using our own PPC lead-generation service, which we call "No-Risk PPC" (I'll discuss in more detail in a minute).

We use a technology that places a unique phone number on your Google ad and on your website so that all calls can be tracked. Everything about your website is 100% your website EXCEPT the phone number.

Other PPC companies do this, too. It's actually pretty common, so they can track the calls.

But we don't just track calls. We have a team of admins who transcribe every call and categorize them as either LEADS or what we call "zero calls." A *zero call* is the toner sales guy, your current customers, and people calling to ask about things you don't actually sell. In other words, NOT leads!

But if the caller asks for a quote for what you sell—and gives his name and contact information—that's a lead. A **true** lead.

This tracking system also allows you (i.e., us) to determine the actual cost per LEAD (not click). Take all the money you spend on PPC, divide it by the number of true leads you get—that's your cost per lead.

It's pretty simple. And it allows you to actually know how well your campaign is working. Or if it's working at all.

The Next Big Thing: No-Risk PPC

Like I said, we provide PPC Lead Generation. But we've made some radical changes to make it the easiest, lowest-cost, risk-free way to generate remodeling leads.

I'll tell you why in a second. First let me tell you how we got there.

For the first few years we offered it, our PPC lead-generation service looked and felt much more complex to contractors. Basically, it seemed like the "same ol', same ol'" if you were on the outside looking in.

The result: Even though our PPC services actually WORKED, most contractors still didn't even want to entertain a conversation about pay per click. The term "PPC" was a complete non-starter.

Even for those willing to have the conversation, many often balked at the relatively large cash outlay required to get started. Realistically, you had to bring $5,000 to the table to fund a serious PPC campaign for a market of any size… and with all the negative baggage surrounding PPC, that's too big a risk for many contractors to want to take.

Then there was the **optimization period**, which typically takes 30 to 90 days from launching your campaign. During this time, the PPC provider is testing, refining, and improving your campaign so it works as efficiently and effectively as possible. Optimization includes refining the ad groups, the ads themselves, the keywords and phrases used, the landing pages… and of course the bidding. It's not a project—it's a process that MUST to be implemented to squeeze the most results out of your campaigns.

Honestly, one of the main reasons many PPC companies don't get good results is they aren't sophisticated enough to know HOW to optimize—so the results never get good.

But even in a best-case scenario, there are going to be some choppy waters in the early going—no matter which PPC provider you choose. That means higher click costs, lower conversions… and ultimately, higher lead costs. It used to be that if we started running into $250… $300… or even $400 or $500 costs per lead in the early going… many of our clients would get nervous and bail out. "See! I knew PPC didn't work!" they'd say.

But we know that in almost every single case we can get the lead costs down to a reasonable level once we get through the optimization period.

Bottom Line: Though our PPC lead-generation services worked, there were still enough initial hurdles (namely the up-front money and optimization period) to make it hard to get and keep good PPC clients.

We've since fixed these problems in a BIG way. But before I tell you how, I want to help you understand WHY we were dead set on ensuring PPC was a crucial weapon in all our clients' lead-generation arsenals.

The reason is simple: PPC **works**!

Let me show you the cold, hard proof.

You know how earlier I said 90% of leads go to the 10% of companies that have figured PPC out? The following are examples.

One of my clients spends $250,000 a month on PPC advertising. A quarter million A MONTH! (And yes, they are a very big company).

Another one of my clients spends $80,000 to $100,000 A MONTH on PPC advertising. A MONTH!

They're not spending that kind of money because it doesn't work. They're spending it because it's their number one most reliable and lowest-cost lead generation method.

To get to this point, these companies had to get through the "unstable" optimization period and put up sizeable ad budgets to start seeing results. But once they got past that point, it was all gravy.

We wanted ALL of our clients to experience the amazing results PPC can provide. To achieve this, we knew we had to remove all of the risks and barriers that make contractors apprehensive about starting PPC.

So we pressed "Pause" on our then current PPC lead-generation service. We sat down, put our heads together, and developed a revolutionary type of PPC lead generation—one that contractors could immediately jump into without fear of losing ANY money.

It's called No-Risk PPC. Here's how it works...

We'll pay for your PPC advertising ourselves, out of our pocket, and only charge you for actual leads AFTER they are generated. And here's the kicker: We guarantee the cost per lead will always be $300 or less. (About 5% of the time, the cost per lead can be $400 or less due to extreme competition in some locations and industries).

All you have to do is tell us the number of leads you want, and we deliver them to you for $300 or less per lead—guaranteed.

These aren't toner salesmen, current customers, and service calls. We provide only TRUE leads.

True leads are people who contact you by phone, web chat, or web form and give their contact information and specifically request a quote. The leads come in directly to you, in real time, from your own website. That's completely different than lead generation services like HomeAdvisor or CraftJack who generate leads on THEIR website… then resell them to 10 or 15 contractors at the same time. Nope—the leads we get you are exclusively YOUR leads.

Twice a month, we'll send you a report on your leads along with an invoice; you then have five days to dispute any leads if you feel there is a problem. After that—and only after that—do you pay.

With No-Risk PPC:

- You don't have to worry about running out of money 10 days into your monthly campaign—there is no ad budget!

- You don't have to worry whether clicks are (or are not) turning into leads.

- You don't have to worry about people who called the wrong number, calls outside your service area, or calls for services you don't provide counting as leads.

- All you have to focus on is closing the leads you get. And since PPC leads are usually the hottest of the hot, that shouldn't be a problem.

Here are some answers to questions you might have about No-Risk PPC:

Q: What if the cost per lead comes in above $300?

A: Then you still only pay $300 per lead, and we eat the rest. Just know that we are very good at generating high quality PPC leads for less than $300—you should expect your leads to cost about $130 to $270 each.

Note: The maximum cost per lead is higher ($400) for a few industries and a few locations. For example, metal roofing and basement waterproofing… and highly competitive cities like NYC. For the vast majority of windows, siding, kitchens, HVAC, etc. … the maximum is $300.

Q: What are the requirements for participating in this program?

A: You must be able to handle at least 30 leads a month, both financially and capacity-wise. Part of our "secret sauce" is spending enough money to get a high enough "impression share." That means this program won't work for smaller companies who can't handle 30 additional leads a month.

Q: Is there a monthly management fee?

A: Yes, we charge a $1,000 a month management fee. In some cases, we will discount this fee for the right situation—multiple locations, less competitive scenarios, or—in rare cases—when we just feel the need.

Q: How many leads can I get from you in a month?

A: As many as are available in the market. We will give you an estimate before we start. Naturally, the bigger the market, the more leads that will be available. Also, naturally, the range varies greatly from about 30 on the low end to as many as 500+ a month for some services in some markets.

Q: Are the leads high quality?

A: Yes! Our clients report that the closing ratios from their PPC leads are very similar to their other lead sources.

Q: How is this different from the 742 other PPC programs people have tried to sell me on?

A: Just like the name says, there is no risk. We don't require ad budget money up front… you only pay AFTER you get your leads. And we guarantee that you'll never pay more than $200 for a true lead.

Q: What if I don't like the quality of the leads you send me?

A: Discuss it with us. We can possibly adjust the campaign to fix the problem. Or you can simply quit the program. Either scenario is extremely rare.

Q: How long is the commitment?

A: There is no commitment, but please be aware that it does take 30 to 90 days to optimize your campaign. That means that during the first month or two, your lead costs will be higher (still never more than $300), and you can expect the lead cost to fall over time.

Q: When do I have to pay for my leads?

A: We will invoice twice a month for you leads. You pay via automatic ACH from your checking account. We do not accept credit cards.

Q: How is this different than buying leads from Angie's List, HomeAdvisor, Etc.?

A: These are leads that are coming from YOUR website… so you are the only person who will get the lead. You won't have to beat 10 other contractors to the punch. Also, since the prospect went to YOUR website, they will already know who you are, and why you are the best choice to buy from.

Q: Okay, but your leads are so much more expensive than theirs!

A: That's a false conclusion. First of all, our leads' MAXIMUM guaranteed price is $300, which is a lot different than "our leads are $300." Frequently lead costs are under $200, and occasionally even under $100. And yes, you are correct, even $100 is less than HomeAdvisor's $30 (or $40 or $70 or whatever). But non-competitive, qualified leads that have already seen YOUR website and who have contacted YOU directly are easily worth $150, $200… even $300. The $10MM mindset of not cutting corners and doing things the right way (instead of the cheap/easy way) applies to your marketing, not just the operations of your company!

Q: How do you get such good results (when others always seem to fail)?

A: Two things: Specialization and experience. First, we specialize in contractor marketing—and contractor PPC. We know all the keywords because we've run these kinds of campaigns hundreds of times before. There's no guesswork. Which dovetails into our experience. Like anything else, PPC is a skill that can be mastered if you put in the time and effort. We have a team of skilled PPC gurus who do nothing all day long but worry about your PPC campaign. They know if they don't deliver results (LEADS!), then our company loses money. Other companies, by contrast, usually farm their PPC out to somebody else who does NOT specialize in contractor marketing, who does NOT focus on lead generation, and who is NOT on the hook for your results.

We'll look at the "nuts and bolts" making PPC work in the next chapter. Right now, let's do some number crunching to see how much you can make with No-Risk PPC.

Regardless of your past experience, No-Risk PPC is BY FAR the quickest, easiest, and least expensive way to generate huge quantities of high quality leads.

In fact, PPC can easily bring you enough leads to <u>add $1MM to $3MM in annual sales</u> STARTING TOMORROW.

Don't believe me? **Let's run the numbers:**

Let's say PPC generates 50 leads a month and you close 30%. That's 15 sales. If you average $10,000 per sale, that's $150,000 a month.

That's $1.8MM a year.

Double the lead count from 50 to 100, and now we're talking $3.6MM in new sales per year. That's on top of whatever you're already doing!

Now the gut punch: Remember, it's a zero-sum game. Every lead you DON'T get is 100% for sure going to one of your competitors, and you're simply LOSING the money to them. Your chance of getting that lead some other way (advertising, referral, etc.) is practically zero. ZERO. The customer very likely won't ever even know you exist.

The Smartest Question You Can Ask

Some contractors have asked us what is the MINIMUM number of leads No-Risk PPC can generate.

Honestly, I don't get that. Why would you *want* the minimum?

I know, I know… smaller company, limited capacity, and so on.

But still!

On the other hand, a few smart remodelers have asked us the question that shows they really "get" No-Risk PPC That question is…

"What is the **MAXIMUM** number of leads can you get me?"

Now <u>that's</u> a great question!

Think about it.

If I can really get you high quality LEADS (not clicks) with an absolute guaranteed max cost of $300... why on earth you would NOT want every single lead you could get?

One smart window company in Pennsylvania called me and said "I'll start with 100 a month, then up it as many as you can deliver starting next month."

Another intrepid remodeler in Milwaukee simply said, "I'll take 1,000 a month if you can generate them—but it will take me a few weeks to up my capacity to handle them all."

(No, we cannot deliver THAT many in Milwaukee... but during the busy season, we can deliver about 140 to 180 a month).

And why not? As I've shown, PPC (when done right) is the easiest and most cost-effective way to generate leads and spike sales.

Remember: This book is about making the jump to $10MM. No-Risk PPC is a good way to get you at least one-third of the way there... while also financing the growth the rest of the way to $10MM (I'll get to that in one second).

Not Everybody "Gets" PPC Right Away

Let me tell you a story about that company I mentioned that spends $250,000 a month on PPC.

When I first started working with them, I to their office and met with them for a "kick off" meeting like I always to, where we discuss strategies and budgets.

One of their budget items, of course, was PPC. At the time, the company was doing over $40MM a year in sales and had a marketing budget of roughly $4MM.

I scratched my head when I looked at their PPC number for the previous month. It was $20,000.

"$20,000?" I asked, "Why is this number so LOW?"

They responded that that's just how much they had budgeted. It was $20,000 a month in peak months (seasonal business), and only $10,000 for non-peak months.

Basically, it was an arbitrary number.

As such, I had them pull the records from the previous month and asked them if the $20,000 lasted the whole month, or if they "ran out."

Turns out, they had "run out" of PPC money to spend on the 11th of the month.

In other words, from the 12th to the 31st of the month, they spent NOTHING on PPC. Zero. Nada. Zilch.

They had no budget left. They spent it all.

Then I had them research what their cost per lead had been, and how their conversion of those PPC leads were.

Turns out—it was there absolute _LOWEST cost per lead_ of ANYTHING they were doing, and the conversions were actually HIGHER than average (compared to other lead sources).

Then I found out (to my horror) they were only running the PPC campaigns in fewer than HALF of the geographic areas they serviced. Why? Obviously, *they hadn't allocated enough budget.*

Here's what I said to them, word for word: ***ARE YOU CRAZY!?!! You should spend every possible PENNY you can on PPC… BEFORE you spend a single cent on anything (and I mean ANYTHING) else!***

They got the point. They immediately shifted budget out of less productive things to free it up to "max spend" on PPC.

Over the next six years, their company continued to grow (to well over $100MM), and as their footprint grew, their PPC budget grew as well… all the way up to $250,000 a month.

Honest to goodness, that's a true story.

Here is what you should take from that story:

1. Not everyone "gets" the power of PPC right away—even really smart people running really successful companies. Right now, that might be you… and that's okay.

2. You can "grow into" PPC. Yes, "unlimited" is the best number of leads to buy. But start with 50 or 100 a month—we'll help you grow to as many as exist.

If your entire marketing budget is only $20,000 a month, the thought of spending all or most of it on PPC might be frightening.

But realistically, if you stagger your lead flow (50 the first month, 100 the second month, 150 the third month, etc.), **you can just let the sales from PPC finance the growth of your company.** Sound familiar? I just said it a minute ago!

In other words, instead of having a $20,000 budget and a $2MM company, why not have a $40,000 marketing budget (half in PPC, the other half in whatever you're already doing) and have a $4MM company?

Boom, you're well on your way to $10MM in sales. Or more.

And there's no risk.

CHAPTER 29

PPC - Nuts & Bolts

So what's our secret PPC sauce that allows us to make this amazing no-risk offer?

First, understand that there are two options for getting PPC leads:

1. Continue to pump more and more money into your campaign until you get the number of leads you want. (Not a good plan if you want a good cost per lead and ROI).

2. Out<u>hustle</u>, out<u>smart</u>, and out<u>maneuver</u> your competition, so you don't have to out*spend* them.

Since we use our own dime on our No-Risk PPC clients' ad spends, we do the second option.

Here's the truth: Most contractors doing PPC have zero clue about crafting an effective, lead-generating campaign. They don't know the first thing about bidding, quality score, creating landing pages, and utilizing negative keywords. So instead of focusing on improving the QUALITY of the campaign, they keep increasing the ad spend of their second-rate campaign until they get leads.

This is the "lazy man's" way of doing PPC. And it's a terrible strategy.

Sure, you may be generating 10 more PPC leads per month than your competitor down the street. But if your cost per lead is triple or quadruple that of your competitor's, are those 10 extra leads worth it?

Nope.

This is especially true if the leads are junk. And as mentioned in the last chapter, "junk" leads are most PPC providers' specialty.

That's why most contractors are convinced PPC is nothing but a money pit. They don't take the steps to make PPC work, so they just assume that it doesn't. It would be like buying a gym membership, never going, and then complaining that you're still fat. Remember: The key to PPC is to outhustle, outsmart, and outmaneuver the competition. And that requires putting in the necessary time to get results.

Quality Score

To outhustle, outsmart, and outmaneuver your PPC competition, you need to focus on **Quality Score**.

In a nutshell, Quality Score is how Google rates important aspects of your PPC campaign. Google wants only the most relevant content showing up in their searches, so its uses Quality Score to determine **A)** how often your ads get shown and **B)** how much you pay per click. If Google deems your ads relevant to the users searching specific terms, your ads will show up more often and cost you less money each time someone clicks them.

Quality Score is the code that most PPC providers fail to crack... and it's why most PPC campaigns are go down in flames 10 seconds after liftoff.

The good news is that, while Quality Score encompasses a few factors, it's not splitting-the-atom levels of difficult to figure out.

To prove it's not rocket science—just a little technical—I'll now breakdown the elements you need to achieve a great Quality Score.

Quality Score Component #1: Choosing The Right Keywords

As with search engine optimization (SEO), keywords are critical to your PPC campaign's success. You need to choose keywords that are not only what your target market is searching for, but will get them to take ACTION.

Here's what I mean...

Let's say you're a roofing company in Charlotte, NC. You want to use PPC to generate immediate leads for shingle roof replacement (no repairs).

When selecting keywords for your PPC campaign, **be specific**. This will help you get more qualified prospects, increase your Quality Score, and keep your keyword prices lower.

Let's look at three keywords you could choose for your PPC campaign focusing on your shingle roof replacement services—each with a different level of specificity:

- *"Roofing services."* This is a vague keyword. People searching this term could be looking for dozens of different things. They could be looking shingle repair. Or a metal roof. Or even a roof cleaning service. In other words, you're highly unlikely to get the type of leads that you want—people looking for shingle roof replacement.

- *"Shingle roofing services."* For our intent in this example, this is a better keyword than "roofing services." With this keyword, you'll filter out people looking for a different type of roofing material. Still, this keyword is pretty vague. To be sure, you will get calls for people looking for shingle roof replacement. But you'll also still get calls from people looking for things like roof repair. Whether that's acceptable is up to you. But if you don't do repairs—or find that it's not profitable—you want to go with a more specific keyword.

- *"Shingle roof replacement company Charlotte."* This is more like it. With this keyword, you filter out 98% of the internet searchers you don't want contacting you. You all but eliminate people looking for roof repair... or roof replacement with a different material… or who need their roof cleaned. And since this is a specific keyword, you'll have less competition than you'd have with the general keywords listed above. That means lower keyword price, higher ad placement, and more leads for the service you TRULY want.

Note: When you go with specific keywords like "shingle roof replacement company," you WILL get less website traffic and fewer phone calls than if you use general keywords like "roofing services." But the traffic and calls you DO get will be higher quality.

Think of it this way… would you rather have 300 phone calls and 30 qualified leads, or 120 phone calls and 50 qualified leads?

Negative Keywords

An efficient way to filter out unwanted prospects is to utilize **negative keywords**.

Basically, you tell Google which keywords you DON'T want to show up for when people search. This is an effective tool for our example shingle roof replacement company. If the company absolutely wanted no traffic from people who need roof <u>repair</u>, the company would simply put repair-related keywords on their negative keywords list.

Of course, you need to be careful with negative keywords. If you do too many—or word them a certain way—you could prevent qualified prospects from ever seeing your ads.

Like I said earlier—running a PPC campaign isn't rocket science. But it does take skill and knowledge to pull off effectively.

Branded Keywords

A lot of our clients balk when we tell them to bid on keywords that contain their companies' names. "Why the heck would I pay for what is essentially my own traffic?" they ask.

It's simple. If you don't, one of your competitors will.

As I mentioned earlier, organic results now usually don't show up until almost halfway down the page. Even if you're the first organic result for your company name, you potentially still have four paid results above you, pushing you down well below the fold.

The biggest companies in the world bid on branded keywords:

Budweiser

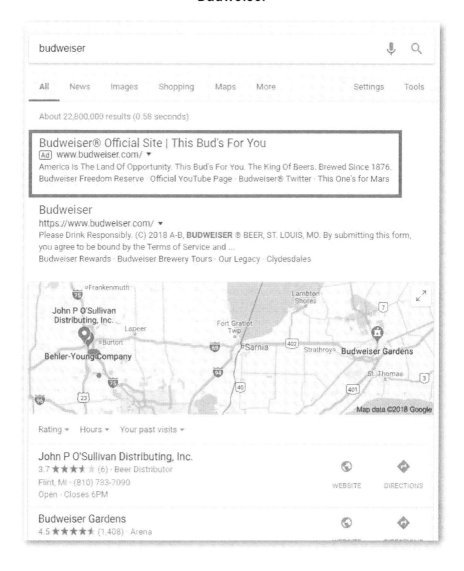

Progressive

progressive   🎤   🔍

All   News   Maps   Shopping   Images   More   Settings   Tools

About 268,000,000 results (0.60 seconds)

Progressive.com | Progressive® Insurance | Official Progressive Website
[Ad] www.progressive.com/ ▾
★★★★☆ Rating for progressive.com: 4.6 - 656 reviews
You Could Save an Average of $668 with **Progressive**. Get Your Free Quote Today! Roadside Assistance.
Good Student Discount. Safe Driver Discount. Accident Forgiveness. Bundle Home & Auto. Guaranteed
Repairs. 80 Years of Service. Online Quoting. 24/7 Customer Service.

Progressive: Ranked One Of The Best Insurance Companies
https://www.progressive.com/ ▾
Get insurance online from **Progressive**. Join today for quality protection that 4 out of 5 would
recommend. Get insurance for just about anything you need.

Contact Us
Contact Progressive Insurance via e-
mail, phone or U.S. mail. Use ...

Find an agent
Contact an agent today and get the
expert guidance you need for a ...

Car Insurance
Get an auto insurance quote online
and find out if you could ...

About Progressive
Progressive began selling auto
insurance in 1937. We're a top ...

Retrieve a quote
Starting fresh? No sweat ... getting a
quote is easy. Start a Quote ...

Progressive Insurance
Even more within reach. From an
insurance ID card as close as ...

More results from progressive.com »

Progressive (@Progressive) · Twitter
https://twitter.com/Progressive 🐦
An overflowing mailbox can alert burglars that you're not at home. Pausing your mail and newspaper
delivery is a simple step you can take before you travel to deter thieves. pgrs.in/2Jv3gyd
1 day ago · Twitter

Hansons

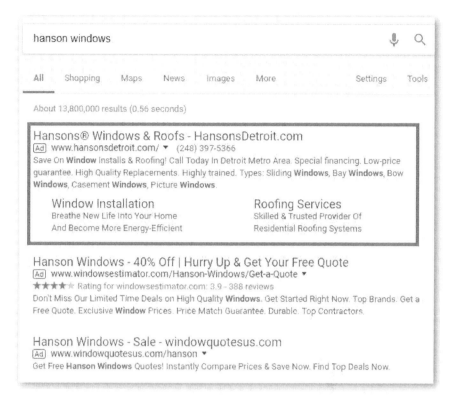

Notice that last image—the one for Hansons. There are ads under the Hanson ad. These are ads from lead aggregators, which I'll get to in upcoming chapters. These ads are designed to siphon some of the direct traffic and leads when someone searches for the Hanson brand name. If Hanson had not used a branded keyword in their PPC campaign, the company would only show up in the organic results—which are BELOW the paid ads.

You might be thinking that people don't click on paid results as much as organic results. That consumers are averse to clicking on a link when the word "Ad" is next to it. But you'd be dead wrong.

Like I said earlier, half of all clicks on results pages go to PPC ads and PPC traffic is shown to convert 50% better than organic traffic. What more… almost half of consumers can't tell the difference between paid results and organic results!

In other words—paid-for results aren't just "on par" with organic results... they're unequivocally BETTER.

The Bidding Process

With PPC, you can't just select any old keyword you want and automatically get results. You have to **bid** on the keywords that will provide the highest ROI.

Since I've already gone over keywords a fair amount, I'll keep this brief. When bidding on keywords, you want to analyze factors like competition and cost. Some keywords have huge search volumes... but they also have huge competition. As a result, the cost to bid on the keyword will be higher than a keyword with a lower search volume.

Fortunately, there are a ton of tools (some even from Google itself) to help you pick the right keywords. Google Keyword Planner shows the historical stats of keywords to provide insight into how those keywords could perform in the future. Google also has Auction Insights that not only tell you how keywords you're considering are performing, but who is already using them!

Quality Score Component #2: Writing Powerful PPC Ads

Let's say you've come up with a list of great keywords for your PPC campaign. The next step is to actually create your PPC ads.

This is tough for contractors without proper copywriting skills. There is very limited space with which to work in PPC ads, and Google is strict about what it does and does not allow in an ad.

For example, here are some things you CANNOT currently do in a PPC ad:

- Have a headline longer than 60 characters (including spaces).

- Have a description line longer than 80 characters (including spaces).

- Use excess capital letters.

- Put a phone number in the ad text.

- Put an exclamation point in the headline.

- Have the words "click here" anywhere in your ad.

Bottom line: You have to create a PPC ad that is powerful enough to get people to click—with very little space and some heavy-duty restrictions.

So, what's the secret to writing persuasive PPC ads?

This is where Section 2 (Identity) of this book becomes a great resource. Once you've mastered how to write powerful copy, you can create influential ads in the smallest of spaces.

In a nutshell, here are the elements of an effective PPC ad:

- Powerful, passionate, precise language. (Against, see Section 2 of this book).

- An enticing limited-time offer.

- A strong call to action.

Let's take a look at a real-life example I found. (This particular example also demonstrates how to outhustle, outsmart, and outmaneuver competitors who have bigger ad budgets).

I searched "Orange County California AC repair." Four PPC ads showed up. But only one of them is what I would call "savage." By that I mean one ad is light years ahead of the others in terms of power, persuasion, and—yep—hustle.

Can you detect the "savage" in this group?

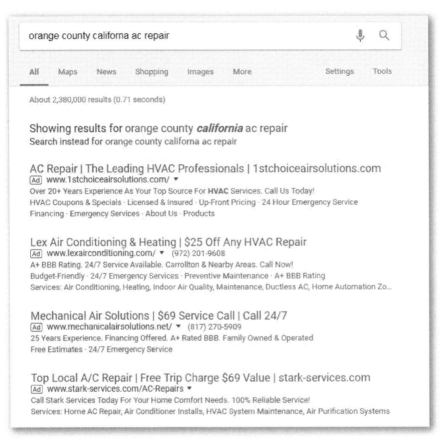

Spotted the savagery?

Here's a hint: Look at the third and fourth ads. Notice the prices in the headlines.

The third ad mentions a $69 service call. The ad directly underneath it mentions a free trip charge worth…

… *drum roll…*

$69.

Stop and think about how awesome that is.

The company with the third ad thinks it has a hook to get people to click. Whoever came up with this ad for the company no doubt thought, "Oh, man… advertising a $69 service call? Genius! How can people NOT click this ad?!"

Then the company with the fourth ad pulls the rug right out from under them. Their response is basically, "Ummm… a $69 service call is a terrible offer. We'll give you a free service call. And BTW, it's worth $69."

Now THAT takes cojones… and acute awareness of what competitors are doing.

In other words: Outhustling. Outsmarting. Outmaneuvering.

And here's the thing…

Stark Services (the savage company in the fourth ad slot) is not only almost certainly getting the best response of these four companies… they are also likely paying less on their PPC campaign because they are in the last spot of paid ads (With PPC, the higher you rank, the more you pay).

It's win-win for savage Stark Services. They're winning the conversion battle… while paying LESS.

Quality Score Component #3: Creating Powerful Landing Pages

Now that you've got your great list of keywords and powerful PPC ads, the next step is to create a landing page that will persuade prospects to contact you.

When creating landing pages for your PPC campaign, the message of your landing pages MUST be consistent with the message of your ad copy.

Does your ad mention a FREE service, doodad, or whatchamacallit? Then your landing page needs to mention a FREE service, doodad, or whatchamacallit in big honking letters above the fold.

Are you a general contractor who specifically mentions window installation in your ad? Then your landing page needs to focus on WINDOWS.

Your PPC landing page shouldn't *just* be your homepage. Or even your website's regular window-installation webpage. It should be custom-built to do the following…

A) Perfectly match the contents of your ad. (Synergize, man!).

B) Have conspicuous strong calls to action even Mr. Magoo could see. (A big phone number, an eye-catching contact form, etc.).

C) Your Identity.

For an example of this, let's go back to those AC companies in the PPC ad example I just showed you.

Here is the webpage that comes up when you click on Stark Services' PPC ad:

Besides the HUGE phone number, what' the first things you notice? Yep—the free trip charge valued at $69.

The huge callout reinforces the same offer that's on the ad. **Consistency between your ad and landing page is massively important to a successful PPC campaign.**

Think about it. When someone clicks on an ad (or, really, ANY page in the search results), they are doing so because the headline and text on the results page convinced them to. They want to learn more about what was promised.

If your landing page is NOT consistent with your ad, guess what? You lose. The visitor will click away within seconds because they did not IMMEDIATELY find the information they were looking for.

In other words—if your ad mentions a free service call worth $69, you better have that offer FRONT AND CENTER on your landing page.

Here's another hustle technique Stark is doing that their competitors are not: **a dynamic offer**.

I clicked on Stark's ad on a Tuesday. Go back and look at the landing page. What does it say in the offer box? *"Call this Tuesday...."*

The "deadline" for the offer is whatever the day happens to be. If you click on the ad on a Thursday, you get an offer that is good only for that Thursday. If you click on a Monday, you get an offer that is good only for that Monday. This is a subtle yet powerful "urgency" technique.

Also, did I mention the HUGE the phone number? And notice the form: "Schedule Service." The calls to action are CLEAR and stand out.

Now, take a look at the landing pages for the HVAC contractors in the first two PPC ad slots:

1st Company:

2ⁿᵈ Company:

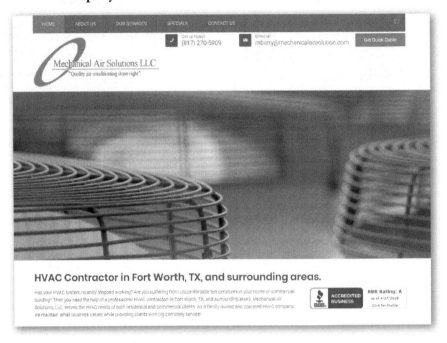

In case you're one of the two companies and you're reading this book, let me put this as delicately as I can: These landing pages STINK.

There's no consistency. There's no callout, contact form, or big honking phone number. There's no enticing offer, specific deadline, or attention grabber.

That offer on the first landing page? It's terrible.

It shows the incentive people get when they purchase a whole new system. AC companies love to promote these kinds of offers because they make all their big money on system installs.

But notice that my original search was for "ac repair." Almost nobody goes online looking for a new system. Instead, they go online because theirs is BROKEN.

In other words, this website is selling something people are not trying to buy. It's like going to a hamburger website and them telling you how great their steaks are.

Now, let's look at the landing page for the third PPC ad—the one that Stark Services' PPC ad calls out directly:

3rd Company:

This page is also pretty lazy, but it's a step up from the pages of the first two companies. There's a service offer… but it's a free service call on any repair over $500, which everyone is desperately hoping isn't them.

They have two places where you can "request" or "schedule" an appointment, but both require a click—neither is just a form. The short form on Stark Services' webpage is much more effective because it reduces the steps a prospect needs to take.

Other Factors To Consider

Here are some other items that determine the success of your PPC campaign—from the efficacy of your ad campaign to the number of leads you generate…

Competitor Analysis

Pay attention to what your competitors are doing. Find out which competitors are running ads, find out their offers, and make yours better.

If the competitor is offering 50% off installation, you offer 60% off installation. If your competitor is offering a $69 service call, you offer a FREE service call worth—that's right—$69.

The Speed Of Your Website

Be aware that certain widgets and applets can slow down your page loading time, which will kill your Quality Score with Google.

Just like your company, Google has a reputation to maintain—they don't want to direct their users to slow-as-molasses websites. Make sure you have a quick, clear, greased path to your website.

Bounce Rate

This is the percentage of people who visit only one page of your website and then leave. When determining Quality Score, Google considers the bounce rate of a website. To keep your bounce rate low—where Google wants it to be—you have to have a site that people find engaging and have a desire to stay on.

Mobile Friendliness

As of this writing, about 60% of internet searches come from mobile devices.

Check everything on mobile to make sure it displays properly on your site… phone numbers, forms, chat widgets, etc. What looks great on desktop may look terrible on mobile. A great mobile website increases user satisfaction, which increases—you guessed it—your Quality Score with Google.

Impression Share

This is the percentage of how many times your ad was shown versus how many times it COULD have shown. Example: If your ad had the potential to be shown 100 times and was actually shown 50, your impression share would be 50%.

You might be thinking: "Uh, why wouldn't my ad show up 100% of the time? I'm spending money here!"

Impression share is affected by a few different factors. If a competitor's ads have a higher Quality Score and Ad Rank than yours, they'll tend to show up more than you. Missed impression in this instance are known as **Search lost IS (rank)**. Likewise, you could also have a low impression share because of a limited budget. This is known as **Search lost IS (budget)**.

Here's the good news: **When you're a No-Risk PPC client, you don't have to worry about impression shares.** We handle that FOR you. All you have to do is pay for the sweet, sweet leads we deliver to your doorstep (for $200 or less per lead!).

Online Chat & Answering Services

PPC leads are the hottest of the hot. If you don't answer your phone when they call or get back with them almost immediately, they'll move on to your competitor down the street.

This is where online chat and a 24/7 phone-answering service are your best friends. They ensure that a lead gets immediate attention, and they can scoop up the leads you or your staff can't get to personally.

One Last Thing You Should Know About PPC...

As you can see, pay per click can be complex. It's not rocket science or splitting the atom... but it is sufficiently complicated that it's best left to the professionals.

Think of these last three chapters covering PPC as a Cliffs Notes overview. You now have a basic understanding of how to make PPC work. If you're not using No-Risk PPC (detailed in the last chapter), then at least draw on the info in this book to help whoever is running your PPC campaign improve your results.

Now let's turn our attention to the internet-marketing method that is ridiculously convoluted and makes contractors want to pull their hair out. (Yes, even more so than PPC!).

I am, of course, talking about SEO.

CHAPTER 30
Search Engine Optimization 101

Note: The following chapters on SEO mostly discuss how to rank well on Google. Google is by far the most-used search engine, so it's where you want to focus most of your effort. I'll talk briefly about other search engines, but know that optimizing for Google is MANDATORY for making the jump to $10MM.

F PAY PER click is a 100-yard dash to the top, search engine optimization (SEO) is a marathon.

There's no quick or easy path to land on that coveted first page. There is no way to buy your way into the top three results. There is no "Fast Pass" that will let you cut to the front of the line. Even with the right strategy, it can take six to nine months just to START seeing results.

SEO is a grind. But you MUST do it if you want to run a successful company in today's digital age.

It might seem like I've downplayed SEO's significance in the PPC chapters. Even though paid results have taken prominence over organic results—and ranking well organically is harder than it used to be—SEO is still a critical, 100%-necessary component of mastering the internet and making the jump to $10MM. Especially with Google's ever-increasing emphasis on the "Local Results Pack" (which I'll get to in a minute).

Here's why SEO is <u>required</u> for success…

Statistics show over 85% of consumers use search engines to find local businesses. In other words—if you're not engaged in SEO, you're reaching only about 15% of your potential market.

Not only that…

You have to be on page one—preferably in the first three organic results—to stand a chance… AND be one of the top three "local business" listings in the Local 3-Pack with the correct star rankings and map (I'll get to that in a second).

Studies show over 90% of searchers don't go beyond the first page of results, and the first three organic results on page one get 30% to 50% of organic clicks, while the top three local business listings get 10% to 17%.

In other words…

Not only is NOT doing SEO NOT an option… but doing it poorly is also NOT an option.

And SEO isn't something you can stop. **You can't quit once you reach page one and expect to stay there.** Nope—you have to do it day in and day out for <u>as long as you're in business</u>. Period.

If you quit at ANY point, your rankings will freefall within as little as two months. Google wants its users to see only the best, most relevant information from what it considers the best, most relevant websites. Not only does Google keep a close eye on this, but because your competitors <u>didn't</u> stop SEO, they will quickly overtake you. Talk about a one-two punch!

Before I jump into how to optimize for Google, let me first set the stage. It's important for you to understand how Google operates, so you can formulate an SEO strategy based on what it *actually* wants from its results.

Google's "Level-5-Classified" Algorithm

Coca-Cola kept their secret formula for Coke in an underground vault for 125 years. Legend has it that only two people have seen the actual paper the formula is printed on. Thousands of soft-drink companies have tried to "crack the code" on the Coke formula… and failed.

With regards to its rankings algorithm, Google has taken this brand-specific-formula secrecy to the next level.

Google's algorithm isn't locked away in some vault. It's not protected by a dozen armed guards and a pack of rabid Rottweilers or anything. And, honestly, I'm not even sure if it's ever been written down on an actual piece of paper. Google keeps its algorithm cloaked in secrecy because it makes changes to said algorithm ALL THE TIME.

I'm not just talking about those big algorithm changes Google rolls out with every few years (Panda, Penguin, Hummingbird, etc.). Google constantly makes small, unannounced modifications to its algorithm—up to a few times per day!

As a result, thousands of companies have tried to figure out Google's search-engine algorithm… and got "Coca-Cola'ed" in the process.

Let me make one thing clear—by the time you're reading this book, some of the information in these SEO chapters will be outdated. That's just the nature of the beast.

That said, I've done my best to provide evergreen tactics that historically have been effective in the past and will likely still work going forward. We might not be able to predict what Google will do… but we can use precise data to get an idea as to what Google wants to see now and *possibly* in the future.

I'll discuss that in the next chapter. For now, let's talk about the undisclosed agenda that Google doesn't want to admit. Once you know this, you'll get why Google is so clandestine about its algorithm.

Exposing Google's Dirty Little Secret…

Google's only goal is to be valuable enough as a search engine to be able to sell PPC ads to businesses.

If Google can return amazing organic search results for users, it can charge for paid ads above those organic results. This is why search engines like Bing, Yahoo, and AOL Search have either died or currently dying a slow death. (Do you remember AOL Search? Neither do I).

The reality is that Google has achieved its goal. Its current algorithm and offering to internet searchers are so good that they can now put PAID ADVERTISING before organic listings—and not a single person searching Google cares. In fact—in most cases—organic results no longer even show above the fold.

Here's the results page when I searched "window installation Detroit":

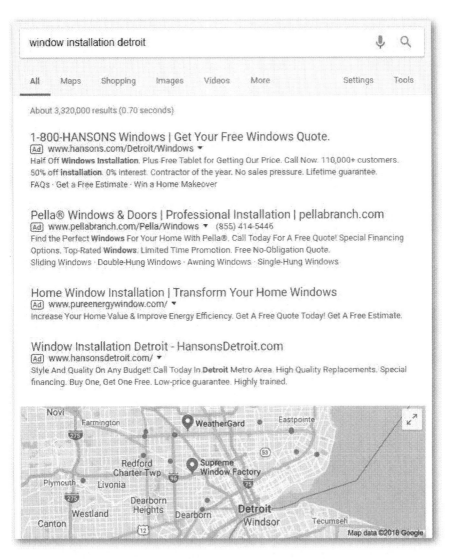

Not an organic result in sight.

Sure, there's that little sliver of the Local 3-Pack map peaking from the bottom of the screen. (I'll talk more about the importance of the Local Pack in a minute). But it's obvious that Google gives the prime real estate to the companies that pay for it.

And therein lies the key to it all: Why Google constantly tinkers with its algorithm, keeps its formula top secret, and insists on ruling the search-engine world with an iron fist.

It's all about the **money**.

Think about it. Organic listings don't make Google any money. The only incentive for Google to improve its search algorithms—and thereby the user experience—is to make money from PPC.

Consider this…

As of this writing, about 70% of Google's $100+ billion yearly revenue comes from their Google Ads (formerly AdWords) PPC service. And every year, that number grows and grows.

This is because PPC—when done right—works tremendously for businesses. So companies back up the Brinks truck at Google's doorstep to get their piece of the pie.

This is why Google changes its algorithm all the time. It doesn't want anyone to "beat the system." If companies figured out Google's algorithm, the user experience would suffer because search results would turn to garbage. This would make Google worthless to internet searchers. And that, in turn, would mean no companies would want to pay Google to advertise.

As a result, Google must stay 10 steps ahead of the thousands of companies trying to "crack" its code; it's the only way Google can retain its value to paying clients.

This means that to continue to have good rankings, companies have to do SEO <u>24/7/365</u>. If you skip even just one month, you could fall WAY behind… even if you are crushing it in the rankings.

Results Come Slow & Steady

Let's go back to that whole SEO-is-a-marathon analogy.

The average time it takes a man to finish a marathon is 4:22:07—or 9:59 a mile.

If you were to start training for a marathon, you would be nowhere close to cracking this time. In fact, it'd probably take you TWICE as long.

But if you continue to put in the necessary work, you'll gradually shave seconds off your time. While it might take you 15 minutes to run a mile that first month, it might take you 14 minutes 30 seconds the second month. Then 13 minutes 45 seconds the third month. Then 12 minutes 50 seconds the fourth month. And so on.

This is how it works with SEO. You can't go from a 15-minute mile to a 10-minute mile within a couple months. You have to chip away at it through hard work and a consistent regimen.

In other words, don't expect to hit page one within a couple months. It won't happen.

In fact, measuring your success by whether you're on page one—especially if you're just starting out—will make you hate SEO and want to quit.

Instead, you have to measure results in smaller chunks... like you would when training for a marathon. Rather than agonizing over hitting the first page of results, look at your progress in three-month increments. If you see a consistent upward trend, your SEO strategy is working.

Measuring results in small chunks is especially important if you're located in a big city with a lot of competition. Basically, the larger the area you're in, the longer it's going to take to get results. If you're in a big city like Los Angeles or Chicago, expect a two-year commitment AT MINIMUM to get good rank results.

Like I said, SEO is a grind—and the exact opposite of "instant-gratification" marketing. (Don't believe those guys that tell you they can get you to page one in 30 days—it's a load of crap I'll expose in the next chapter).

But don't worry. Though I've made SEO sound like a terrifying monster in this chapter, I'm simply trying to set your expectations. To be honest, SEO really isn't as painful as you might think. To prove it, let's look at what it DOES take to get good search-engine results...

CHAPTER 31

SEO – What Does Google REALLY Want?

GOOGLE MIGHT GUARD its algorithm like a momma bear protecting her cub. But there is <u>enough</u> information out there to make an educated guess about what Google likes to see.

It's like how a good doctor treats a bacterial sinus infection. The doctor doesn't know exactly which bacteria is causing the infection or how exactly said bacteria is causing it. But he or she knows enough through years of study and experience which medicine and treatments are most likely to successfully treat it.

With regards to Google, <u>everyone</u> is a like a doctor treating a bacterial sinus infection. No one knows exactly how Google works. But we have sufficient information to get it to do what we want (give us good search-engine rankings) and treat problems as they arise.

With that in mind, let's look at the factors that will play the biggest roles in getting you to rank well.

Keywords & Keyword-Dense Content

Keywords are one of the most important aspects of SEO. They tell Google what your website is all about, so Google can link to your site on the results page when users search for that term.

Since you're a contractor, you're obviously a local business. This means you want to use **geo-targeted keywords** for your SEO campaign. These are keywords like "kitchen remodeling <u>Houston</u>" and "siding installation <u>Plymouth</u>." You want keywords that contain the areas in which you service. This lets Google know where you work, so they can show you in the results page when someone from that area searches for your service.

Note: The bigger the city/town/location in your keyword, the harder it will be to rank well for that keyword. For example, hitting the first page for "bathroom remodeling Chicago" (population: 2.7MM) will be MUCH harder than "bathroom remodeling Elmhurst" (population: 47,000).

While there are many more searches involving keywords with "Chicago" than "Elmhurst," there is also much more competition. A good strategy in this case—actually, in all cases—is to create individual service pages for all of the areas in which you work.

Here's an example...

We Provide Replacement Windows For All Of Central PA

Here Is A List Of Cities & Towns In Which We Work.

We offer window replacement for all of Central Pennsylvania. Below is a comprehensive list of the specific areas in which we service.

• Annville, PA	• Hershey, PA	• Mount Gretna, PA
• Camp Hill, PA	• Hummelstown, PA	• Mt. Joy, PA
• Carlisle, PA	• Lancaster, PA	• New Cumberland, PA
• Chambersburg, PA	• Landisville, PA	• Palmyra, PA
• Dover, PA	• Lebanon, PA	• Pittsburgh, PA
• Elizabethtown, PA	• Lewisberry, PA	• Salunga, PA
• Gettysburg, PA	• Linglestown, PA	• Seven Valleys, PA
• Grantley, PA	• Lititz, PA	• Shippensburg, PA
• Greencastle, PA	• Manheim, PA	• Spring Grove, PA
• Hanover, PA	• Marietta, PA	• Strasburg, PA
• Harrisburg, PA	• Mechanicsburg, PA	• Wyomissing, PA
		• York, PA

When you click on a location, you land on an individual service page for that city:

Welcome To Wyomissing's Refreshingly Different Replacement Window Company

- Firm, No-Pressure Online Quotes
- A TRUE Lifetime Warranty
- No Money Down
- And Much More...

Welcome to Zen Windows. We are one of the leading replacement window companies in Wyomissing, PA. We've earned our reputation by doing several things that are unique to this industry in terms of product quality and the customer experience. We think if you really understand what's important when choosing a window company, you'll agree that Zen Windows beats the competition, hands down:

- **Most Efficient Windows:** Our windows have the best energy ratings, period. Our windows feature a U-Factor of .15, which is the window equivalent of a 50-MPG car. Nobody has a more efficient window.

- **A True "100% For Life" Warranty:** You only pay for your windows once. If something goes wrong, your bill for the repair, including materials, labor, and trip charge will be $0.00. We even cover broken glass! Read more about

When creating individual service-area page, make sure you fill it with relevant keyword-dense content—and enough of it. You want to aim for at least 400 words per service-area page. Also, make sure that none of the service-area pages contain duplicate content!

Semantic Search—Your Keywords' Best Friend

A great feature Google has recently added is semantic search. If someone searches "window installation Dallas," your website can still show up even if your keyword is "replacement windows Dallas." Basically, semantic search doesn't take search inquires as literally.

This is a very good thing for you. Someone might be in the market for the service you offer, but may not search the exact keyword you're optimizing for. Essentially, semantic search broadens the number of people you can reach—without you having to do any extra work.

In order to take full advantage of semantic search, you need to reverse engineer your content appropriately. When slogging through the copywriting aspect of your site for SEO purposes, don't be afraid to use different variations of keyword-dense search terms.

"Nerd Coding"

Nerd coding is all the technical behind-the-scenes stuff that goes into SEO. This is the kind of thing you want to leave to professionals. If you try it yourself, you WILL fail.

I'm not being a jerk—just honest. Here are just SOME of nerd-coding items that must be done it even stand a chance:

- Keyword research and analysis
- Doc type analysis
- Optimization of title tags of all important pages
- Optimization of other meta tags (description, etc.)
- Optimization of header tags H1, H2, and H3
- Analysis of bold tag
- Optimizing JavaScript and CSS codes
- Optimization of non-index able attributes like frames
- Optimizing HTML source code
- Image optimization
- Schema markup
- Optimizing internal linking structure (navigation)
- Optimization of external links
- Broken links analysis & correction
- W3c validation (for home page)
- Creation & optimization of HTML site map
- Website architectural correction
- Content optimization
- Canonicalization error correction
- Blog setup & maintenance
- Google Analytics setup
- Disavowing toxic backlinks

And that's not even the half of it! Do you think you can handle all this yourself? I sure as heck couldn't. That's why I've got a team of SEO coding nerds on staff.

I won't go into detail on these "nerd-code" items listed above—each one could fill its own book. Just know that you have to audit and verify every single item on this list MONTHLY to ensure it is still up to date. And going without them is 100% NOT an option.

Direct Traffic

In a way, ranking well on Google is a popularity contest. Google loves, loves, LOVES websites that get a lot of direct traffic—people who visit your website by typing your site's URL into the address bar on their browsers. The more "popular" your website, the more Google likes it.

I know… you thought you left awful popularity contests behind in high school. But there's a good reason Google checks a website's direct traffic when deciding where to rank it. In Google's eyes, direct traffic legitimizes a website. It demonstrates authority and that your site is a place people want to visit.

There is no limit as to how to drive direct traffic to your website. Radio, TV, direct mail, internet ads, billboards, truck wraps… all of it works.

This actually dovetails nicely with Step 4 of our 4-Step Formula for getting to $10MM: TV advertising. TV advertising is a must to make the jump to the next level, and I'll talk about it more in the next section of this book. But for our purposes right now, know that TV (along with the other marketing methods I mentioned) is a great way to build brand awareness WHILE driving direct traffic to your website.

Bottom line: You can do all the right "things" to SEO optimize your site, but if you aren't getting direct traffic (and a lot of it) from other sources than search, your site will likely never rank that well organically. Google just isn't in the business of helping the underdog—period.

Consistent Great Content

A common question contractors ask is, "How often do I need to post content?"

Unfortunately, there isn't a set answer. Every situation is different, and multiple factors go into how often you should post—what keywords you're targeting, your geographic location, the type of business you have, and so on. Google also updates results with varying frequencies, depending on the audience/market you serve. For example, content from news websites will get ranked faster than content on a local business's website.

Google uses three mechanisms to sort and rank websites—Googlebot, Crawling, and Indexing. Googlebot is the software that finds and collects data for Google to add to its searchable index. The Googlebot "crawls" websites to find new information to report to Google. Quality information and content gathered from the crawling is then processed and added to Google's searchable index.

This is why when you type "Best Sushi Dallas" into Google, the results come up in literally .026 seconds. Google has already crawled, indexed, and stored the results based on its algorithm. All it really has to do to provide your result is pull from its "storage space," so to speak.

How often does Google crawl? As with most Google-related questions, the answer is the same—it depends. That said, **shoot for at least one high-quality, search-engine-optimized blog post per week.** Google "crawls" websites more frequently when they are consistently updated with quality content. Four great posts per month (at least 500 words each) is more effective than 10 mediocre posts that are wafer-thin on content. Remember: Google wants to show the best of the best results, so it can make money with its paid ads.

What's "wafer-thin"? Any blog post that is so keyword stuffed that it doesn't have any readability to it. Google tracks things like time spent on page, links clicked, and even where your mouse cursor sits and moves on a page. If your blog posts or weekly content updates get zero traffic, Google gives you a gold star for effort... but you'll still be sent to the back of the line.

Videos

Putting videos on your website is also a great way to boost search-engine rankings. Video is becoming more and more prominent with each passing year.

Why?

- They captivate prospects' attention and keep their eyes glued to your website for a longer period of time, which Google tracks (and loves).

- They reduce your website's bounce rate (very helpful for SEO).

- They relay information in a way that's easy for your prospects to understand (the visuals help this greatly).

- Google indexes the spoken words in a video to written words, which increases your keyword density and makes your site more "valuable."

I would STRONGLY recommend uploading videos to YouTube and then embedding them on your website. Believe it or not, YouTube is the second-largest search engine. Having engaging, optimized videos on YouTube will help you show up in both Google <u>and</u> YouTube's results.

And guess what? **Google owns YouTube!** Do you think Google might show a tiny bit more favoritism toward YouTube-optimized videos than non-YouTube-optimized videos?

Gee, I wonder….

Types Of Videos You Can Use

Fortunately, you don't have to be the next Spielberg to create effective videos. And you don't have to have expensive recording equipment—the cameras on smartphones are now so sophisticated that Hollywood is shooting major movies with them. In fact, YOU don't need to create your videos at all—there are plenty of services that will write, film, and produce videos for you.

Here are a few types of videos that work well for SEO and user engagement…

- **Demonstration Videos:** One great use of video is to dramatically demonstrate what your products can do. Think the glass on your windows is strong? Hit it with baseball bats, crow bars, and chains. Is your siding fireproof? Set it ablaze and see what happens. Want to show that metal roofing stands up to hail? Shoot a potato cannon at it so people can see what happens.

- **Video Testimonials:** Social proof is one of most effective marketing methods. Put real, genuine video testimonials from customers on your website and watch your user engagement spike.

- **Commercials:** These are always a good way to capture and hold people's attention. Throw them on your website if you've got 'em!

- **Whiteboard Videos:** These are the cool videos where a hand draws an image relating to the subject that the voiceover is speaking. These are highly engaging because they can get really creative.

Pay Per Click's Influence On Organic SEO

After years of speculation, Google finally admitted that their PPC clients get preferential treatment when it comes to organic search. Everybody always THOUGHT this was true. But with Google coming right out and saying it, it's now indisputable that PPC has to be a part of your SEO strategy.

Think about it. **Why <u>wouldn't</u> Google show a little more love to the companies that give them thousands of dollars per month?** It's kind of like slipping the host at a restaurant a $20 bill to "magically" reduce your wait time. It's not EXACTLY bribery. But you get under-the-table preferred treatment for flashing a little green.

Is it fair? Not really. Is it necessary to get the best rankings? Yes.

The good news is that PPC also helps your SEO in a number of other ways. It drives more traffic to your website, which is a plus for your organic rankings. PPC's extensive reporting gives you key insight into which of your keywords are working, allowing you select the best ones for SEO. And if you come up multiple times on the search-results page (for paid <u>and</u> organic listings), you appear more legitimate in the eyes of your prospects.

Links

When another website links to your website, it's called a **backlink (or an inbound link)**. Google is a big fan of quality backlinks. <u>Quality backlinks are when good, popular websites relative to your keywords link to yours.</u> Google sees this and says, "If this popular website is linking to this other website, this other website must also be high quality."

Which sites link to yours determines the quality of the backlinks. For example, if Houzz or a major remodeling-related website links to your website, Google will determine that backlink higher quality than a backlink you'd get from your buddy's Wix-made movie-review blog that only you and two other people have visited.

But getting quality backlinks is only part of your SEO strategy. You must also **disavow toxic backlinks** on a regular basis. Toxic backlinks are things like link wheels, paid links, and any other type of spammy links that try to game the system. If Google finds that you have a surplus of toxic backlinks pointing at your website, it will penalize your rankings.

The thing about toxic backlinks is that you don't know your site has them until you look. (Unless you're the one inserting the toxic backlinks—but <u>you</u> wouldn't do that!). You can view and remove toxic

213

backlinks yourself through Google Webmaster Tools or hire a company to remove the toxic backlinks for you.

I'd strongly suggest hiring a professional to do it for you. Identifying and removing toxic backlinks is an ongoing process—you can't perform any sort of action that will make them go away once and for all. As such, it should be done on a WEEKLY basis.

Lastly, you'll want to have strong **outbound links**. These are the opposite of backlinks—instead of other websites linking to yours, your site links to others. Linking to other websites with relevant content helps Google understand YOUR niche, thereby boosting your site's legitimacy and authority. Google works under the assumption that your website doesn't hold all the answers to people's questions. So when you have quality outbound links, you increase your website's "usefulness."

As with other aspects of optimizing for Google, you have to be smart and fastidious about outbound links. You can't stuff a page with 157 links to popular websites and expect good Google juju.

In fact, just the opposite.

Link-stuffing your website can provide a temporary rankings boost... but only until Google catches you (and it WILL catch you). Then you don't just go back to where you were before... you get pushed into a search-ranking black hole where no one will ever find you.

Consider this: shady spam sites like Canadian pharmacies, gambling, and porn use outbound-link-stuffing to get traffic. Do YOU want Google to associate your website with these guys?

Independent Third-Party Reviews

Online reviews are not only an important form of social proof, but also a good way to enhance your SEO.

Here's why:

1. 92% of people read reviews before making a buying decision, and 84% of people trust online reviews as much as recommendations from their friends. When you post your reviews on your website, people WILL read them. As a result, they spend

more time on your website, which boosts your site's credibility and authority in Google's eyes.

2. Having reviews on your website increases keyword density naturally. This can help increase your rankings when people search for your keywords.

3. Backlinks from high-value websites (Facebook, Google, the BBB, etc.) are always good for SEO. (See the "Links" section above).

So, how do you link directly to your online reviews from your website? There are plenty of widgets (website apps that perform different functions) that can link your different online review accounts to your website. We do this for clients—take a look:

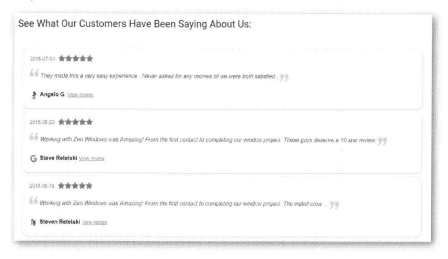

Bounce Rate & User Engagement

At the end of the day, Google wants to showcase websites that people like visiting. To do this, Google measures everything about your website related to user engagement—from how long people stay on your site to how many pages they click on to how quickly your website loads. One aspect Google takes a long, hard look at is **bounce rate**— the percentage of people that land on your website, view only one page, and then leave.

When Google sees a site has a high bounce rate, it assumes that people don't find the content on that site interesting. As a result, Google ranks the site lower.

The general rule of thumb is that a bounce rate between 25% to 40% is great, 41% to 56% is average, and 57% and up is high. But these aren't metrics you want to live and die by—bounce rates differ depending on the industry and TYPE of website.

Retail websites like Amazon have an average bounce rate of 20% to 40%, since people tend to view more than one product while browsing the site. Blog websites—a food-recipe site, for example—have a bounce rate of 70% to 90%.

While that seems like a drastic disparity, comparing a food blog to a retail site is apples and cantaloupes. People don't use sites like Amazon the same way they do blog sites. With Amazon, users virtually "browse the aisles" and look at multiple products and pages. With blog sites, people tend to read one post and leave. They printed the recipe for "Grandma's Old-Fashioned Apple Pie," so they got what they came for.

Bounce rates for lead-generation websites (i.e., what YOU have as a contractor) are 30% to 55%—basically right in that rule-of-thumb sweet spot. Landing pages with big, honking calls to action have a bounce rate similar to blog websites: 70% to 90%. That's because the goal of a landing page is to get the user to take action ASAP—fill out a quote form, download a report, and so on. As a result, people are more likely to visit just that one page.

Does Google factor in the type of a site and the industry when analyzing bounce rates? Yes. You don't need to have a bounce rate of 25% like Amazon to rank well with your remodeling website. Google is sophisticated enough to know how people view and use these websites.

Mobile Optimization

As of this writing, around 60% of internet searches are done on mobile devices. That number will only increase as mobile devices continue their inevitable march toward world domination. [Insert Evil Laugh Here].

What's that mean for you, the contractor? You better offer up a dang good mobile website experience.

Google has a separate search index for mobile-related searches. That means if you rank first for a certain keyword on a desktop, you will NOT automatically rank first for that keyword on a mobile device. Google crawls desktop and mobile websites differently because people view mobile and "desktop" sites differently. It's now thought that a mobile-first approach is best. This means you should focus more time and energy ensuring the experience and SEO for your mobile website is properly optimized.

The Rise Of Local SEO

Many of Google's algorithm updates are designed to stop under-handed companies from cheating the system. Google has in recent years, however, updated its algorithm a few times not to prevent the bad stuff, but to improve the good. In fact, a few major updates in the last year or two have focused solely on how to improve <u>local search</u> results.

It makes sense. Since 85% of consumers use search engines to find local businesses, Google naturally wants to provide the most relevant results for its users. (So it can, like I said, make more and more money with its PPC services). In other words, the "closest and best" results get shown.

As a result, Google has done a number of things to improve search results for users looking for local companies. One of the biggest is the Google Business Local 3-Pack.

Why You NEED To Be In The Local 3-Pack

Even though the Local 3-Pack has been around for a few years, it's a relatively recent addition.

You've no doubt seen the Local 3-Pack before...

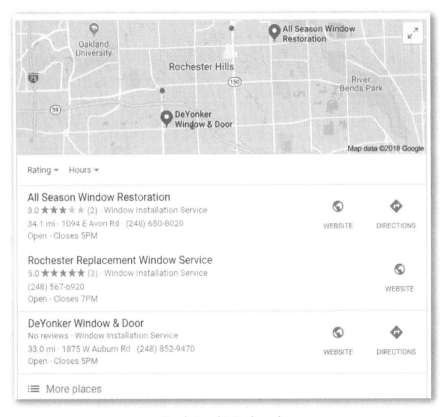

Google Local 3-Pack result.

Along with paid ads, the Local Pack typically pushes down the "blue-link" organic results below the fold. The Local Pack doesn't always appear in the search results, but it's becoming more and more common. And when the Local Pack does show up, it gets anywhere from 10% to 60% of clicks, depending on the search term and industry.

The Local Pack used to show five to seven businesses on the results page. A few years ago, Google decided to shrink that number to three. It's consequently a lot harder to squeeze into the Local Pack than it used to be. There is no foolproof formula to get into the Local 3-Pack, but here is what will give you the best shot...

- **Having a consistent Name/Address/Phone Number (NAP) across all websites, directories, and local-listing sites.** This will help you show up when someone in your vicinity searches for the service you provide.

- **Making sure your website is mobile optimized.** People now search more on their mobile devices than desktops, and the trend toward mobile search will only continue. Having a strong mobile site will increase the chance of ending up in the Local Pack.

- **Optimize your Google My Business profile.** Google tends to favor companies that use their services. ::wink, wink::

- **Have a strong website.** At the end of the day, Google wants to provide the best results. Part of determining whether you're worthy of a Local 3-Pack spot is how much traffic your website is getting, how long users stay on your site, and whether it's catered to what Google users are searching for.

- **Be in the right location.** This one you can't control. Whether you show up in the Local 3-Pack depends on how close you are to the searcher's location. If your physical address is 25 miles from where someone is searching, you probably won't show up in the Local 3-Pack (especially if you have a lot of competition). Your physical location is determined by the address used on your Google Business Page and your website. (Tip: Don't lie—Google will know. Google sees all).

Like I said, there is no guaranteed way to wedge yourself into the Local 3-Pack. But the steps above can help.

Schema Markup

Schema markup is a powerful yet underutilized search-engine tool. Basically, schema markup provides internet searchers with more information about your company on the actual results page.

Here is what schema markup looks like:

1-800-HANSONS: Replacement Windows, Roofing & Siding
https://www.hansons.com/ ▾
1-800-**HANSONS** offers **windows**, roofing & siding in Michigan, Ohio, Colorado, Nebraska, Iowa, Utah and South Dakota.

Replacement Windows
Do you need new replacement windows for your home, but don ...

Grand Rapids, Michigan
1-800-HANSONS of Grand Rapids, Michigan uses the ...

Vinyl Siding
Does your home need vinyl siding? Let your imagination run wild ...

The Hansons Story
The 1-800-HANSONS Story. It Was Time for College. I remember ...

Contact Us
Call Us. For specific questions concerning your order status ...

Window Options
1-800-HANSONS window options are available on all of our ...

More results from hansons.com »

As you can see, there is A LOT more info for a result that takes advantages of schema markup. Searchers can learn much more about the company and click individual pages right from the results page. The outcome? More traffic to your website, more leads, and better search rankings.

Schema markup is complicated and technical to implement. But it's a must-have to stand out to both internet searchers and Google. Period.

What To Do About Bing

Optimizing for Bing isn't mandatory if you want to succeed—you can completely ignore it and still make the jump to $10MM.

That said, Bing <u>does</u> account for 21% of internet searches. Not only that, but Bing also powers Yahoo's search engine, which makes up around 12% of all internet searches.

So, in all, Bing/Yahoo make up 33% of the search-engine market share.

In other words, Bing isn't necessarily the ghost town it's made out to be. People do use it, so optimizing for it won't hurt. (Unless, of course, it cuts into the time and expenses of optimizing for Google).

The good news is that there is a fair amount of overlap between what Google and Bing look for when deciding what to put on page one. Both focus on keywords, quality backlinks, and strong content, so many of the SEO practices you perform to court favor with Google will also help with your Bing results.

That said, there are a few differences between Google's and Bing's algorithms.

Both searches engines reward strong content. But while Google emphasizes new and fresh content, Bing likes content that has been posted for a while. Bing's rationale is that content that has been online for a certain period of time is more authoritative than newer content.

Another key difference is that Bing more often includes social media posts in its results. This means one of your tweets or Facebook posts could show up on page one of Bing's results. Google, on the other hand, has been pretty hush-hush about how much social media affects rankings.

So how do you optimize for Google <u>and</u> Bing with such differences? Despite how it appears, you don't have to choose one over the other.

With regards to new versus old content, it's simple. Consistently create strong content, and you'll win with both search engines. Google will pick up the new stuff you create, while your older content percolates for Bing.

As for social media, it doesn't matter how much or little it affects search-engine rankings—you should be engaged in social media, period. Social media is a powerful tool to reach your audience, build your brand, and increase business. (I'll talk more about that in Chapter 32).

Paying The Price For "Level 10" SEO

Good SEO for an average-sized company in an average-sized market with average-sized competition runs anywhere $3,000 to $5,000 per month. Large markets could be more than that.

I know what you're thinking… **"$3,000 to $5,000 per MONTH for SEO?! That's a lot of money!**

I'm going to assume that you are legitimately trying to make the jump to $10MM. If that's the case, then you cannot tolerate sub-par SEO. The cost—measured in terms of lost leads and business—is simply too high.

If you're paying a reputable company somewhere in the $1,000 to $2,500 per month right now, simply put, they are not doing what you need done. It's impossible. There are just too many things that need to be done by competent people (read: not some dude in India making $4/hr). At that price range, you're going to get Level 5 SEO. Maybe level 6 or 7 if you're lucky.

With these companies you don't have to worry so much about spammy SEO; **instead, you have to worry about what they are NOT doing (leaving out) in order to save money so they can sell their services and still make money.**

This is kind of like a reputable competitor of yours who is "good enough" but still not nearly as good as you are. You KNOW for a fact that they are leaving things out that you do great in order to sell that job for 30% to 50% less than you do. This is the same thing.

You want to make sure that <u>everything that can be done</u> is getting done on your behalf. Cutting corners to save money does you no favors whatsoever.

If you're sweating from the mere thought of spending $3,000 to $5,000 per month on quality Level 10 SEO, look at it this way: How many leads are you LOSING by not doing everything right? And more importantly, how much is that costing you?

Let's say your typical lead cost is $250, and you are currently paying $1,500 for Level 6 or 7 SEO. And let's say that Level 10 SEO for your market will cost you $3,500. That means you'll have to pay an extra $2,000 a month to get what you actually need—which is only 8 extra leads a month!

Let's be honest—that's more than reasonable. Especially considering that Level 10 SEO takes care of EVERYTHING for you...

- Keywords
- Content
- Nerd coding

- On-page and off-page optimization
- Backlinks
- Monthly maintenance
- Schema markup
- Reporting
- Reputation Protection
- Algorithm Alerts
- And everything else I mentioned in the last two chapters

Considering that **A)** "Level 10" SEO is 100% mandatory for contractors to make the jump to $10MM, **B)** you only need to generate 6 to 10 extra leads a month from your efforts, and C) there is NO WAY you could handle it all by yourself, paying an extra $2,000 or so a month for Level 10 SEO is a no-brainer.

Also think of it this way:

- If you budget 10% marketing cost against sales, then you only need to net $30,000 to $50,000 in monthly sales for SEO to be a winner. Level 10 SEO will account for a lot more than that.

- What about the leads and sales you might MISS from using cut-rate SEO? You could save $1,000 a month and miss $100,000 in sales without even realizing it. Make the jump to the $10MM mindset—raise your prices if necessary so you can afford to do things right.

Three "Magic SEO Pills" That Are Actually Search-Engine Cyanide

Ever notice how there are approximately 129,347 different diets, programs, pills, products, and scams for weight loss?

Heck, you probably have someone on your Facebook friend list who's become a "representative" for some multi-level-marketing company and the latest fat-loss fad product (stomach wraps, magical diet pills, etc.) they're hocking.

Even though 99.9% of these flash-in-the-pan remedies don't work, people buy them up by the millions. The thought of getting a killer beach bod while exerting zero effort is just too tempting to pass up.

Deep down, though, everyone knows—but won't admit to themselves—that there's really just one simple three-step process to losing weight:

1. Lay off the Big Macs.

2. Hop on the treadmill.

3. Repeat steps 1 and 2 until you get the result you want.

This method is **GUARANTEED to work, but it takes time and energy. That's why everyone always flocks to the latest bogus "solution" that promises instant results.**

It's the same with SEO.

Contractors don't want to put forth the required time and effort to get good results. As a result, they fall for all the gurus promising magic solutions that launch your site to the top of Google Mountain with no effort or time.

It's a load of bull.

Like I've mentioned 37 times already, the ONLY company that knows Google's search algorithm is Google. And Google changes it constantly specifically to stop "cheaters" from gaming the system.

For proof, take a look at some of the biggest algorithm changes over the years:

- **Panda (February 2011):** This update penalized sites for duplicate, plagiarized, or thin content, as well as keyword stuffing.

- **Penguin (April 2012):** Penalized websites that had spammy and irrelevant links.

- **Hummingbird (September 2013):** Another change that focused on keyword stuffing and poor content.

- **Fred (March 2017):** Weirdly not named after an animal, this change penalized sites with low-quality blog posts designed only to generate ad revenue.

Let's look at three of the biggest "no-no's" when trying to rank for Google... the types of practices most of the $300-SEO companies use.

224

#1: Keyword Stuffing

- **What It Is:** Putting a bunch of keywords for either your products or the geographic locations that you service into your web copy. Like "vinyl siding" or "replacement windows"... except for something like 16 times on a page. Or listing 13 cities you service in the first paragraph of your text. Or both.

- **What You Think Will Happen:** Google will index your page and surmise that your content is really super-duper relevant to those keywords and locations... and therefore Google will rank you high in the search results.

- **What Will Really Happen:** Google might indeed rank you high—for a little while. But when Google sees that nobody is staying on your page for more than a few seconds <u>because the content STINKS</u> for humans to read, it will push your site lower and lower and lower. This is like a fad diet that helps you lose 10 pounds in the first month, but then you gain it all back plus five pounds the next month. Don't do this!

#2: Duplicate Content

- **What It Is:** Content on your website (or a web page) that can be found elsewhere on the internet. It doesn't matter where the company is that has the same content... and it doesn't matter who had the content first. Google absolutely positively HATES duplicate content and will assign "duplicate content penalties" accordingly.

- **What You Think Will Happen:** Well, it depends. If you are stealing somebody else's content because it's easier than thinking up original content, you're just lazy and a thief. You might as well back a truck up to somebody's house while they're on vacation and take their furniture. Or maybe you hired a company to build your site and they are lazy so they just use the same content over and over for multiple clients. Not good.

- **What Will Really Happen:** Google will slap you like the proverbial red-headed step child. You should check your site for duplicate content at least once a month and force any thieves to stop using your stuff.

#3: Spammy Links

- **What It Is:** It sounds like the worst breakfast meat ever, but what I'm talking about are links that originate outside your website to your website… but that come from questionable, irrelevant, stupid websites. In other words, toxic backlinks, which I mentioned earlier.

- **What You Think Will Happen:** Google will see this huge quantity of links coming into your site and say, "Wow, look at all these links! This must be a really popular website!"

- **What Will Really Happen:** Google says, "Wow, look at all these spammy links! What a freaking loser. Let's push this jack wagon to the 39th page!"

One Last Thought On SEO…

Your head is probably spinning with info-overload from these last two chapters. But even if you don't remember the difference between schema markup and a toxic backlink, here's the only thing you need to know: **In today's digital age, you need an effective SEO strategy running 24/7 to master the internet and climb your way to $10MM… and there is no way you can do it by yourself.**

The question then becomes who, exactly, you should partner with to ensure you have strong SEO.

Since you're a contractor, you want to stick with SEO companies that work within your industry. There are specific SEO and marketing strategies that are effective in the remodeling/home-improvement sector that don't work for other industries. An SEO "generalist" (i.e., a company that uses the same exact SEO strategies for ALL types of businesses) won't typically utilize the strategies you need to get the best results.

On the other hand, SEO companies with extensive experience in the remodeling industry know exactly what both Google <u>and</u> your target market wants. As a result, they can craft an effective SEO campaign that will have a MUCH greater chance of getting you not only on the *first page*, but in the ***top three organic results***—which is where you NEED to be to succeed.

To quote Will Ferrell's character Ricky Bobby from *Talladega Nights*: "If you ain't first, you're last."

CHAPTER 32
Third-Party Lead Sources

WHAT ABOUT BUYING leads from lead-generation companies like HomeAdvisor, Quinn Street, and CraftJack? Will it help you cross the $10MM mark?

No… I can't say it will.

In fact, my advice is to stay away from these companies. Far, far away.

I'll explain why using one of the biggest third-party lead companies—HomeAdvisor—as an example.

In my decade-plus long career in marketing in the remodeling industry, I've yet to find a single business owner who claims to actually like the company. Almost all contractors actually HATE them. Some do tolerate them—but they don't like them.

In fact, HomeAdvisor used to be called Service Magic, but they changed their name in 2012. They say it was to "update their branding." If you believe that, I've got a bridge you may be interested in buying.

The problem contractors have with HomeAdvisor—and companies like it—stems from the company's tendency to sell the same internet-generated lead to potentially dozens of competing contractors at the same time.

This makes lead generation essentially a remodeling contractor version of *The Hunger Games*—it's a savage battle to be the last contractor standing to claim the lead.

Third-party lead sites don't even try to hide it. This is taken from HomeAdvisor's FAQ page (text in bold is my emphasis):

Q. How does HomeAdvisor work?

A. First we find homeowners looking for help completing home projects and collect information about their project. Our patented ProFinder technology then identifies relevant professionals, taking into account our pros' availability, service type and location preferences. ***When we have a match, we send the homeowner's information to the matched pro instantly so that he/she can win the job.***

So even though you get the lead, you don't really get the lead. As HomeAdvisor says, you have to "win" the job once they throw the lead your way.

Yikes.

Like I said, there are a brave few companies who have learned to tolerate HomeAdvisor. But most contractors have the kind of hatred for the company that is normally reserved for the DMV, 6 am flights, and Justin Bieber.

And it's not just HomeAdvisor, either. It's any company that wants to sell you leads that they generate FOR you off the internet.

The general name we can assign to all these kinds of companies is "**lead aggregators**." In other words, they exist to aggregate leads from the interwebs and sell them... to you. There are lots of them, and they're all about the same: Quinn Street, Contractor.com, Get Service Leads, CraftJack, and Renovation Experts, just to name a few. (Some may have gone out of business since this was written—they come and go all the time).

My Little Experiment With Lead Aggregators

To prove how unpleasant dealing with lead aggregators can be for contractors and homeowners, I ran a small experiment. I put myself in the shoes of the average homeowner in need of replacement windows.

I began by searching "CertainTeed Windows" on Google. I figured CertainTeed was a popular brand, so why not.

A lead aggregator called Window Quotes popped up in the results page (notice the time is 4:40 pm):

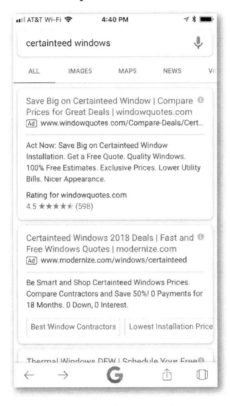

Since I was playing the part of the naïve homeowner, I naturally clicked on the ad for the Window Quotes website. And why wouldn't I?

- Four-and-a-half-star rating.

- Free quotes.

- Apparently "big savings."

What's not to like?

Well, once I clicked through to the site, input my contact info, and hit "Submit"… *EVERYTHING.*

Within SIX MINUTES, my phone had blown up with calls from SIX different local window companies—all looking to set in-home appointments.

Here's a look at my call history immediately after I filled out the online quote form… starting at 4:42 pm… just two minutes after I found the ad, and another minute filling out the form:

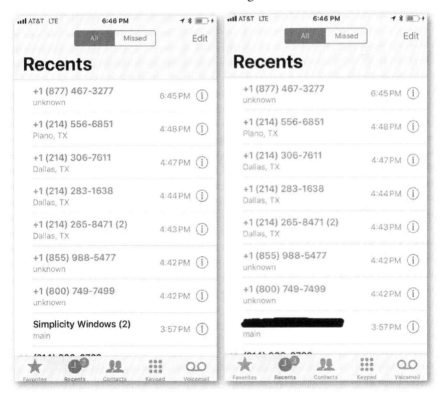

Things only got worse over the weekend. **By the following Monday (four days after I input my info online), I had received 33 phone calls—nine from the same company!—and four emails.**

I felt like a fresh bucket of chum thrown into a kiddy pool filled with ravenous sharks.

Why was I getting so many calls?

The homeowner (me, in this case) THINKS they are contacting CertainTeed, when in fact, they are putting their information into a lead aggregator. They then turn around and send that information—instantly—to the DOZENS of contractors who have paid them for leads.

Yikes!

I don't blame the contractors in this situation. Like I said, lead aggregators turn lead generation into a bloody battle of Last Contractor Standing. If you're not vigilant (i.e., a ravenous shark), you lose.

But is all this worth it?

Is it worth fighting 10 other contractors for what is *maybe* a qualified lead?

Is it worth blowing up an unsuspecting homeowner's phone to try to set an appointment, when all they want is a little information?

My answer is no. There are much better ways—for both you and the homeowner—to acquire online leads. Ways that don't involve competing with a dozen other contractors for the same job.

But alas, the purpose of this chapter is to discover the goodness to be found in lead aggregators—if any. So here is my advice to you, dear contractor, as you consider whether or not to delve into the world of lead aggregators:

Advice 1: Don't do it. It's not worth it.

Advice 2: If you insist on it, bring your A+ game and get ready for a dogfight.

Don't worry, I won't leave you hanging there. Let's delve into the details for both pieces of advice:

Reasons To Avoid Online Lead Aggregators

Too Much Competition: I think I've made this point clear by now. The HomeAdvisors and CraftJacks of the world sell the same leads to three to 20 other contractors. The unsuspecting homeowner who uses these sites will get incessant calls and dozens of emails… and they'll regret the moment they ever clicked "Submit" on that online lead form. You've got better things to do with your life than trying to out-elbow 17 other guys to pay a dollar for a kiss from an ugly girl. You're better than that.

The Leads, By Definition, Are Price Shoppers: The reason the girl in the last sentence is ugly (it's an analogy, play along) is that online lead generators screw you over by promising to get you "multiple quotes" from prescreened pros. Take a look:

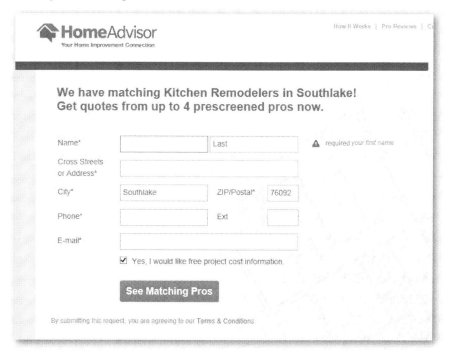

The very first expectation prospects are going to have from you is LOW PRICE. I don't know about you, but I don't offer the lowest prices, and I'm not interested in doing so. It's completely antithetical to everything we've talked about in this book. But that's who's going to answer the phone if a miracle occurs and you do actually get through to a prospect.

Spend That Money To Generate That Lead Yourself: Let's say you spend $50 per lead and get 20 leads. Chances are high you'll only actually get in touch with one to two of them, which means you really paid $500 to $1,000 for a lead. What else could you do with that money? Lots of things! You could buy No-Risk PPC leads, for starters. Then those same prospects will see YOUR website, benefit from your price conditioning, and fill out your form on your site. Then you can have that lead all to yourself.

One of our clients had given $2,500 to CraftJack for 50 window leads at $50 a lead. After completely wasting their time trying to get in touch with the first 30 leads—with only two set appointments—our client called CraftJack to quit. When informed that there was a strict no-refund policy, the client actually told CraftJack to just keep the money. They'd rather take the financial loss than double their losses by wasting time chasing non-responsive leads.

Yes, it's that bad.

Advice For People Who Insist On Jumping Into The Shark-Infested Waters Anyway

Some of you simply can't resist the siren's song, so you insist on participating in the feeding frenzy despite the warnings. And that's okay. The truth is that you CAN mine some gold out of these leads, but you have to have strictly disciplined systems in place to make it happen:

React Quickly: And by quickly, I mean you've got like nanoseconds. You need to route the leads to somebody who has no other purpose in life besides dialing that phone and getting through to that lead the instant it arrives. Because you can bet your life that many of the other contractors who also just bought that lead are going to be right on top of it.

The statistics on this topic are staggering: If you fail to contact an internet lead within FIVE MINUTES, that lead is 100 times less likely to be contactable. Read that again. If you've ever bought an internet lead, called on it an hour after it came in, and were disappointed to find you couldn't get in touch with anyone, now you know why. You should be shooting for one to five SECONDS to call the prospect. If you can't play in that league, don't play at all.

By the way, this is good advice for YOU, too… with ALL your leads. Even your PPC leads. Faster is ALWAYS better.

Be Persistent: This one seems antithetical to what I just said. I just told you that if you miss the first five-second window, you're dead meat.

But not necessarily. See, when that lead first comes in, the prospect is going to get slammed by contractors for two minutes to 24 hours. But then the calls will subside… which leaves an open to call 24 to 36 hours after the lead came in. You can still find interested people—you just have to wait out the initial rush. Persistence pays, but it is a massive pain in the butt. Whoever is tasked with this job is going to hate it—be ready for that.

Get Great Software To Automate Follow Up: Immediately subscribe to remodeler-specific customer relationship management (CRM) software like MarketSharp, so you can manage all this automatically. It's a great program that will take the leads FOR you and allow you to do any or all of the following: route the lead to somebody's cell phone via text message; send an email or text message instantly to the prospect; set reminders for follow-ups; generate mailers with personalized URLs. And more.

Most companies I know that have success with lead aggregators are large and put a lot of resources into follow-up. In other words, they have the systems in place to handle this type of lead generation.

Bottom line: Lead aggregators aren't for everyone. But you CAN see success with them. You just have to fight tooth and nail for every single lead.

SECTION 5
Radio & TV Advertising – To Infinity, And Beyond!

A FEW MONTHS AGO I got a phone call from an old client who was on the verge of nervous breakdown.

Years before, I had helped him put together a website, write some direct mail pieces, and create some home show materials for his window company. Things had been going well back then—he was chugging along at about $4M a year and experiencing slow but steady growth.

But now he was getting killed.

A new, well-funded competitor had entered the market—and was gobbling up all the window leads by (among other things) spending $1M a year on radio advertising. To make things worse, they were using cutthroat "buy 2, get one free" offers to make the phone ring, then using high-pressure sales tactics to get people to buy.

This was in stark contrast to my old customer's high-integrity approach that relied on no-gimmicks pricing, no sales pressure, and an extremely patient, 2-appointment closing method.

"It's just not fair!" was all my ex-client could muster as he finished telling me the story.

Except… it is fair.

It's fair because my client—and everyone reading this book—has the exact same opportunity and ability to monopolize their marketplace by gobbling up all the leads, too.

You may not have the ability to spend a million dollars on advertising right now. And your offers and sales procedures may differ from the new competitor in the story above.

But you can compete—if you know how. And you'd better start NOW.

The question is: Are you going to wait for big, bad competitors to come in and bully you around (if they're not, already), or are you going to go on offense RIGHT NOW and grow yourself a money tree that will nourish and protect your business and your family for years—even decades—to come?

This section is about playing with the big boys, then becoming a big boy.

Everything we've talked about up till now has been foundational. You have to have the right mindset. You have to build a great, identity-based website that converts lookers into buyers. You have to dominate the online lead generation game. And you have to handle your leads properly.

But all those things put together won't get you to the next level—which is to dominate your market—if you don't have enough leads. All of that is a solid foundation that you can now build your castle on.

To become a dominant force in your market, you have to generate more leads. To accomplish that, you have to do more than simply spend the money. To get the lion's share of the leads, you have to find a way to get a huge percentage of the people in your area to know who you are. They have to understand your value proposition—your identity. They have to know that you're the best option to call, even if they don't currently need what you sell... so that when they *are* ready, they automatically think to call *you*.

Here's the bad news: Even if you've been in business for 30 years and have completed thousands of jobs for thrilled clients—the sad truth is that the vast majority of people in your area have never heard of your company.

Let's review the 4-Step Formula

1. Sell awesome stuff that people genuinely love.
2. Charge high prices.
3. Master the internet.
4. Use radio & TV advertising.

Here's the good news: You can change that by participating in and then mastering media advertising. I'm talking about radio and TV.

Everything up to this point has been appetizers.

Now to the main course.

Let's talk about how to *really* make the jump to $10MM.

CHAPTER 33
A Lesson From A Billboard Marketing Masterpiece

N 2005, MY wife and I found the courage to embark on a 4,975-mile cross-country trip in our silver 15-passenger van with our six kids—at the time aged 9 months to 12 years.

Looking back, I'm surprised we even survived.

The first part of the trip was from Texas to Idaho for to visit the in-laws. Then on the way home we thought it would be fun to stop in Yellowstone Park and Mount Rushmore.

Quick synopsis: The kids thought Yellowstone was boring and stinky; the highlight was a buffalo taking a dump right outside our van. Mt. Rushmore wasn't much better for the kids—we have an infamous family photo featuring the presidents' heads in the background and 5 of my 6 kids either crying, shielding the sun from their eyes, and/or looking like death-row inmates. My ever-happy oldest daughter, 9 at the time, was smiling, oblivious to it all.

The next day we slept in late, grabbed lunch at Wendy's, and hit the highway with a destination of Sioux Falls, SD—about 5 hours due east on Interstate 90. Basically, we were about to drive through 400 miles of middle-of-nowhere nothing.

But as soon as we hit the open road, we realized that there actually was something interesting out there in the middle of the South Dakota badlands.

Wall Drug.

At first, I couldn't figure out exactly what Wall Drug was.

According to the several billboards we passed, Wall Drug had an odd assortment of curiosities, including wood carvings, ice cream cones, and dinosaurs.

They also had Black Hills gold, homemade pie, and a shootin' gallery.

And that was just the beginning.

For the next 50 miles, we were hit with a broken dam's worth of billboards unlike anything I've ever experienced.

Free Coffee and Donuts for Newlyweds—Wall Drug.

Homemade Lunch Specials—Wall Drug.

Western Wear—Wall Drug.

5 Cent Coffee—Wall Drug.

Traveler's Chapel—Wall Drug.

Silver Dollar Display—Wall Drug.

Real Americana—Wall Drug.

New T-Rex—Wall Drug.

Wall Drug, it turns out, is one of the most extraordinary—and successful—tourist traps of all time.

Apparently Wall Drug was actually a drug store dating back to the depression, but over the years it morphed into a gargantuan gas station, convenience store, and kiddie playland despite being located in a pinprick-on-the-map town named Wall. And now they manage to pull in an astonishing 20,000 visitors a day during the summer months.

And it's those billboards—those genius billboards—that make all the difference in the world.

In the 30-minute, 50-mile stretch of I-90 between Rapid City and Wall, I conservatively estimate that we passed a staggering 80 (yes, eighty—think about that before proceeding—EIGHTY) billboards promoting Wall Drug.

Black Hills Gold—Wall Drug.

British Petroleum—Wall Drug.

Old Glory Fireworks—Wall Drug.

Cowboy Up!—Wall Drug.

Homemade Donuts—Wall Drug.

It's a Blast!—Wall Drug.

Sheriff on Duty—Wall Drug!

Some of the billboards were big. Some were small. Some were old and worn. Some were freshly painted and new. Most sat right on the freeway. Some were off in the distance. Sometimes you could see two or three at a time.

And all of them were provocative—even for people who don't list marketing as a favorite hobby. I've put photos of many of them on my website at UnlimitedLeadFlow.com/book if you're interested to see.

Unfortunately, since we had departed right after lunch, our two littlest ones were completely zonked out by the time we reached the Wall Drug exit—and my wife forbade me from pulling over to take a look. Trust me on this one—never wake a child up who has two hours of nap left to go… or argue with you wife in the middle of a 5,000 mile road trip.

We were, however, able to steal a glance of the 80-foot T-Rex as we whizzed by—but that was about the extent of our Wall Drug experience. A few hundred miles later when we finally landed in Sioux Falls for the night, I fired up my laptop and did some online research on this phenomenon called Wall Drug.

You know how I said that 20,000 people a day visit Wall Drug? That's because their billboards persuade an astounding 70% of all cars to stop and look.

Seventy Percent!

Seven out of every ten drivers can't resist the siren's song and convince themselves that, Starbucks be damned, they've got to have a cup of five-cent coffee… or at least check out the extensive collection of wood carvings. Wall Drug's 20,000 visitors <u>a day</u> in the summer is nearly as many as Mt. Rushmore—which has the built-in advantage of being, you know, a national monument.

But Wall Drug has those billboards!

So as you ponder the miracle of the Wall Drug billboards… and as we begin our discussion of radio and TV advertising, ask yourself these questions:

- Do you think there's a positive correlation between the number of billboards (80+) and the conversion ratio (70%)? Of course! That one was easy.
- What if the number of billboards was lowered over that 50-mile stretch from 80 to just 50? Would that make a difference in the conversion ratio? Probably by a little, but not much. After all, 50 is still a lot.
- What if the number was just 10 billboards over 50 miles— one every 5 miles? Would the conversion ratio drop? Almost certainly.
- What if there were just 2 billboards? Would anyone even notice the place?
- What if there were NO billboards? Chances are, people would whiz by at 90-miles an hour while wondering why there was a giant T-Rex staring at them from the side of the road.

As effective as Wall Drug is at getting people to stop, this section of the book isn't about billboard advertising. But it is about putting your message in front of somebody's face enough times—and in a cost-effective enough way—to move the needle on getting people to take action.

We've spent a lot of time in this book talking about internet marketing—and rightfully so. Making sure your company shows up when somebody is searching is a critical part of your success equation.

You know what's even better than showing up first in search?

Showing up first in peoples' *mental searches* when they think about who they should call to buy something… so they don't even have to go to Google for a recommendation in the first place. They already know who to call!

Here's what I've found over and over and over again in marketing—companies simply don't get their messages out therewith enough **consistency and frequency**. There are literally thousands of home improvement and service companies that have been in business for DECADES that are virtually unknown to the majority of citizens in their towns.

After all, how often does the average person need to fix their heater or air conditioner?

Not very often.

And how often does somebody replace their windows or roof?

Even less frequently.

To take your business to the next level, you're going to have to Wall Drug 'em.

The most effective and cost efficient way to accomplish that is not billboards—that was just an example to illustrate the need for consistency and frequency.

The most effective and efficient way to get your business to the next level is radio and TV.

To understand why, all you have to do is follow the money.

CHAPTER 34

Why Traditional Mass Media Still Makes Sense

Most people's first reaction to the idea of advertising on radio and TV is "nobody listens to radio or watches TV anymore." Bottom line: That's simply not true.

Yes, it's true that people spend a ton of time on the internet now. And there are plenty of ways to listen to music from digital sources instead of the traditional radio. Then when you consider podcasts, audiobooks, and XM radio, and it's easy to see why it might SEEM like nobody's paying attention any more.

Same thing goes for TV when you consider YouTube, Facebook, Twitter, and 1,000 other sites people spend their time on.

But the number of commercial radio stations has actually gone UP since the advent of the internet... from 9,915 in 1993 to 11,358 in 2016. And those stations brought in a combined $14 billion in revenue.

The truth is, radio reaches 93% of all Americans every month, including 54% that listen every day. TV is right behind at 88%. Compare that to smartphone use of 83% and you start to get an idea of how popular these "old school" media actually still are.

The two major reasons radio and TV are going to become the most important part of your $10MM+ marketing plan are simple—reach and cost.

Radio and TV are the only reliable and cost-effective way to make your company—your brand—become a household name. Where else are you going to reach literally HALF of the people you hope to sell to for mere pennies per year each?

A good buy on the right station for your company will cost somewhere between $2 and $12 per thousand listeners/viewers (counting only those 18 years and older).

That's as little as ONE-FIFTH OF A PENNY for each person reached. Or on the high end, as much as 1.2 pennies.

If you buy a year-long schedule (my recommendation) that reaches the average listener 3 times a week (which is aggressive), you will pay between 31 cents and $1.87 PER YEAR to reach that person.

Read that last paragraph again, put the book down, and think about it for a minute.

I'm talking about 30 cents to just under 2 dollars to reach a person over 150 times in a year.

Let's say a given station has 20,000 listeners. That's $6,200 to $37,400 per year to talk to ALL OF THEM an average of about 150 times each.

Harnessing this high reach/low media is how you grow to over $10MM in sales.

Here's how easy the radio/TV formula is:

1. Buy as many stations as you can afford, and add more over time as your sales grow.

2. Run 3 to 6 compelling, identity-based ads at a time, and change them up every couple of months so they don't get stale.

3. Wait for people to need what you sell.

4. Capture the lion's share of the business, because people will know to call you.

Even if the prospect still goes online FIRST before calling (and they will), when they see your name in the search results (they *will* see your name, right?!?), they will say "Oh, I know these guys; I'll call them" instead of "these guys look okay, I guess."

The reason is simple: The "Wall Drug" effect on them will produce automatic, involuntary recall of your company and its value proposition. You will own their hearts and minds—and they won't even know it until they decide they want replacement windows or need a new air conditioner.

As briefly stated earlier, there are two major keys to making it work: Consistency and frequency.

Consistency, meaning that your ads are being seen/heard by prospects consistently over time. Not in spurts. Not once in a while. But like Wall Drug—they had billboards all along the entire 50 mile stretch between Rapid City and Wall… a few bunched around Rapid City and a few more bunched right before Wall.

Frequency has to do with how often your ads are running. Rule of thumb: The higher the frequency, the better. 20 billboards in 50 miles is a good frequency. 80 billboards in 50 miles offers four times the frequency… and exponentially raises recognition and responses.

Consistency and frequency are achievable at a very reasonable cost using radio and TV, especially compared to other media. Think about it—how much frequency can you hit people with using the ValPak or home shows? What about direct mail? Or canvassing? Or billboards (in a normal, city situation)? Not much.

But radio and TV allow you to literally bombard people with your message at a very reasonable price… which is why broadcast media is going to be at the heart of your plan to *really* grow to $10MM or more.

CHAPTER 35
Hunting vs. Farming

"*B*UT WE'VE TRIED *radio (or TV) in the past… and it didn't work!!!*" Still, I mostly hit brick walls when discussing this with contractors. If I had the proverbial NICKEL for every contractor that's told me that, I'd have thousands of nickels.

Usually, the bad radio experience goes something like this:

(Note: I'm talking about radio in this example but we could just as easily substitute the word TV).

- Contractor contacts stations and negotiates "great rates" on "popular" station.

- Contractor "writes awesome ads" and has them "professionally" produced.

- Ads run for a period of 2 weeks to 2 months and almost no calls come in.

- Contractor gets frustrated, proclaims "radio doesn't work," and spends ad dollars elsewhere.

- Contractor gets hostile when I even bring up the topic of radio.

Which is approximately like the following:

- Guy goes and buys expensive golf clubs that are reputed to work great, even for novices.

- Guy chooses a beautiful golf course that's reasonably priced near his home.

- Guy plays golf once a week for 2 weeks to 2 months and never breaks 130.

- Guy gets frustrated, proclaims "these golf clubs don't work" and spends his time doing other things.

- Guy gets hostile when I even bring up the topic of golf.

Look—radio (and TV) isn't broke… just like those golf clubs aren't broke.

Instead, look in the mirror: It's the way <u>you think about radio and TV, and the way you execute radio and TV</u> that's broken.

And that's why I'm here—to coach you to radio and TV success so you can grow your business to $10MM+ in sales. It can happen, but it's going to take a <u>change of heart and mind</u> on your part.

The first thing you've got to understand is the difference between HUNTING and FARMING:

There are two main types of advertising efforts: "direct response" and "branding."

Direct response means you place an ad and expect immediate responses that allow you to sell enough to make a profit on the ad.

Branding means you place many ads over time with an expectation that prospects will hear you enough times to know who you are and what you're all about (your Identity) so they just "know" to call you when they need what you sell.

To make these concepts easier to understand, think about them like HUNTING (direct response) and FARMING (branding).

Most contractors start their businesses with a HUNTING mindset—and it's easy to see why.

When you're new in business, you HAVE to find ways to generate cash RIGHT NOW or else you starve to death and go out of business. In the old days (10-15 years ago), it was relatively easy to get all the business you could stand from HUNTING—show up at the home show, place ads in the newspaper or Clipper Magazine. Back then, even the radio worked pretty well for HUNTING.

But the internet totally changed the dynamic of direct response advertising.

Now, because the internet is instantly available anywhere and everywhere (think: phone, tablet, laptop, etc.), people tend to look stuff up online the INSTANT they get the glimmer of a thought to buy something—remember Kevin Bacon!?!

Then by the time your ad appears in the Clipper Magazine $3,000 and 2 weeks later, that prospect has already taken action. They don't need to see your ad—they've already done something. The "itch" has been "scratched." This means fewer leads from the ads you do run.

I'm not saying that direct response advertising can't work and won't work—clearly there is a place for it... and I'll discuss a program we innovated called "No Risk Radio & TV" at the end of this section. It might be a good fit for you, especially if you're new or small.

But the changes discussed above to place an obvious importance on mastering internet marketing—which I have covered extensively earlier in this book.

But to make the jump to $10MM, you are going to have to shift your mindset from HUNTING to FARMING.

The winners of the advertising wars now won't be the guy who spends the most in the Clipper Magazine or in Val Pak, although those may still be useful. The winner will be the one who creates a LONG-TERM strategy to continuously indoctrinate prospects through advertising over the course of time—so that the prospect calls them first... and never has to even look in the Clipper Magazine or on Google.

If you've tried a 2 week or 2 month run on radio or TV in the past (like in the example above), it's almost guaranteed it didn't (and won't) work. The setup is all wrong.

Radio and TV should be thought of as a great place for farming. Contractors should be thinking in terms of reaching prospects OVER AND OVER AND OVER again so that prospects know exactly who to call when they have need of whatever it is you sell.

You know, consistency and frequency.

Plant the seeds, nurture the ground, wait the requisite amount of time, then (and only then!) harvest your crops.FARMING.

It's not an endeavor for the impatient. Or for the starving. But it's the best long-term strategy for serious contractors who want to start nurturing NEXT YEAR'S sales (and the next 5, 10, 20 years) RIGHT NOW.

Let's review:

- Wall Drug gives us an easy-to-understand example of how hitting somebody with a ton of messages causes them to want to buy.

- Radio and TV are super inexpensive on a cost per thousand basis (CPM), which makes them a great wat to reach a lot of people for relatively little money.

- Consistency and frequency are the keys to making it work.

- Think of media advertising like farming—planting seeds and nurturing crops—instead of hunting, which requires finding food today to avoid starving.

The rest of this section will show you how to approach this kind of advertising, including where to start, how to find stations, how to negotiate, how to write ads that work, and more. There is definitely a right and wrong way to go about it… if you mess up and do it wrong, you could quickly lose tens of thousands of dollars.

But if you do it the right way… you could be on your way to $10MM in sales.

Let's go!

CHAPTER 36
Start With Radio

'M GOING TO suggest you start with radio, then progress into TV later. There are some exceptions to this, but they're rare.

If you remember to the beginning of the book, my $44MM (at the time) HVAC client wasn't doing ANY radio or TV; they had built their business using direct mail and newspaper... but had maxed out and were looking for ways to grow. They had tried both (radio and TV) before but were disheartened by both the lack of immediate results and their inability to precisely track leads.

But after showing them the tremendous upside, the excellent cost efficiency (remember, $2 to $12 per thousand!), and pointing out that there really was NO OTHER WAY to get where they were trying to go, they relented and gave me a budget to start.

One million dollars.

That first year, all one million of those dollars went to radio. Here's why:

Reason #1: Radio Is An Excellent Way To Reach Prospects With Astonishing Consistency: People who listen to the radio do so with dumbfounding predictability and regularity. Humans are creatures of habit—they tend to get up at the same time every day. And shower at the same time every day. And drive to work at the same time every day. And eat lunch at the same time every day. Sure, sometimes their routines get out of whack—but on average, people are pretty darn predictable.

Radio takes advantage of this kind of slavish routine in a way that no other media can—not even television.

If you're on board with the concept of FARMING, then you'll realize that you have to nurture EVERY plant consistently from the time it's planted until it's time to harvest. If a given radio station has 5,000 listeners on weekday mornings between 7 and 8 am, there's a good chance that the 5,000 people who are listening today will be pretty much the same 5,000 who listen tomorrow. And the next day. And the next day.

Yes, there will be some turnover—it won't be the EXACT same 5,000 every single day. But over the course of a month... and a year... and several years... you will hit the same people over and over and over again with your message—which is exactly what you're trying to accomplish.

By the end of one year—not to mention multiple years—you start to own the hearts and minds of those 5,000 listeners. If you create the right messaging with a strong identity, those people will know who you are, why you're different and better, and what they can expect when doing business with you. When they finally have a need for (a new kitchen, replacement windows, a new HVAC system, etc.) they will already firmly KNOW who to call—you. They won't even have to go online to find you. They'll already know you and WANT to do business with you.

Reason #2: Radio Makes It Super Easy To Precisely Target Your Market: You know how everyone's always talking about there being hundreds of TV stations? Well, it's true. With cable & satellite, viewers (read: prospects) do have access to literally hundreds of choices, which makes it hard for you to choose where to spend your precious dollars. And generally speaking, people watch *programs* not *channels*. Think about that for a second.

Radio offers people far fewer choices, and that's good. On the FM dial, the frequencies go from about 88 to 107, and only on odd decimal points (88.7, 89.1, 89.3, etc.) That's it. In a major market, there might only be 20 to 25 stations of consequence, and perhaps HALF that in smaller markets.

If there are 25 stations in a major market, you can automatically ELMINATE a huge percentage of them because they don't cater to your target market.

See, young people tend to listen to young people stations. Hispanics tend to listen to Hispanic stations. Black people tend to listen to "Urban" stations. Men tend to listen to sports stations. Women tend to listen to light rock stations. And so forth.

Yes, some women listen to sports radio. And some white people listen to "Urban" or "Hispanic" stations. And it's a matter of fact that many men listen to "Adult Contemporary" stations. But at the end of the day, we have to look at the statistics. And the statistics clearly show that YOUR target market (whoever it may be) are very likely to listen to 3 to 6 stations AT THE MOST. And an individual listener within that target market spends 90% of his or her listening time on 3 or fewer stations.

This makes it exceptionally easy to figure out where to spend your money. I'll give you more details on this topic (choosing stations) in Chapter 39… but for now, just know that it's really easy to target your market.

If you want to reach affluent homeowners, you start your evaluation with adult contemporary (AC), news talk, and news stations. If you want older affluent adults, then you look into oldies (note: there are multiple flavors of oldies these days—details in chapter 39). If your target market is women, lean toward the AC. Men? News talk and sports generally deliver well.

To keep the FARMING analogy going, here's the result: If you want to grow wheat, you can easily grow wheat. If you want to grow potatoes, you can easily grow potatoes. Some goes for peas, tomatoes, corn, or whatever else you want to cultivate. Radio is the king of self-selecting media. You might think the internet is better—but it introduces the problem of too much choice. Sure, there are THOUSANDS of sites that cater to young men… or to affluent women… or middle-class men. Which means your dollars have to spread thin (even thinner than TV) to reach them. But there are only a few stations that cater to any given crowd on the radio dial.

Note: Facebook and YouTube are two of a handful of exceptions; I'll talk about them in a later, in Section Six of this book.

Reason #3: Radio Allows You To Speak With High Emotion: It's hard to capture emotion and feeling in print. Why? Because you're limited to font sizes & styles, colors, emphasis tools (**bold**, <u>underline</u>, ALL CAPS, *italics,* and punctuation) to make the reader "hear" your voice.

On radio, on the other hand, the listener can "hear" your voice because they're actually HEARING A VOICE! All the subtle changes in tone, pacing, pausing, volume, and timbre communicate TONS about what the meaning of a sentence is. Emotion comes through loud and clear. Prospects can judge how authentic the voice is. All of this is good—if it's executed properly.

Obviously, TV gives you the ability to communicate with emotion, too. But based on the other factors listed in this chapter, radio is still probably the better place to *start.*

Reason #4: Radio Commercials Are Cheap and Easy To Produce & Keep Fresh: Have you ever produced a TV commercial? It can be an exhausting, expensive, and time consuming endeavor. Print ads require pre-planning and careful reviews and revisions that can be a pain.

Radio commercials, on the other hand, can be produced quickly, easily, and inexpensively. We usually suggest that EITHER the company owner OR a professional voice talent be the voice of the company… and that 3 to 5 new commercials be cut every 2 to 3 months for the first 12 months. After that you can start to mix in some of the old ads with new ones, but the idea is to keep the commercials fresh and new and interesting.

The average cost to produce a good, professional radio commercial is about $150 to $300, and it takes about 1 day, maybe 2 to turn them around. Easy & cheap!

By contrast, TV can take weeks (or months) of planning, lots of legwork to actually shoot, and several days or weeks to edit into an actual commercial. Each spot will cost a minimum of $1,500... and depending on several factors, can run upwards of $20,000 per spot.

These obstacles can be overcome, and are definitely worth the effort and expense—but they do tip the scales, usually, in deciding to *start* with radio instead of TV.

Reason #5: Radio Is Comparatively Inexpensive To Get Started On: In most cases, you can get started on radio for far less than it will cost you to be on TV. Not always—but usually. To paint a clear picture of why this is the case, I want to explain how we normally buy TV so you can have a comparative frame of reference.

For TV, we almost always recommend using **local network news programming** because:

1. Almost nobody DVR's the local news, and I'm deathly afraid of DVR's. You should be, too.

2. News has a consistent audience, day in, day out. It's the most "radio-like" TV program there is in terms of people tuning in at the same time and same channel. People seem to choose their favorite news anchors and stick with them for years.

3. News tends to deliver an older viewer with more financial resources—good for selling remodeling and home services.

4. There are only 4 major stations to choose from—not hundreds of stations like with general programming.

That last point is important to understand because it's also the reason we <u>almost always</u> start with radio instead of TV.

Since there are only 4 competing news stations (ABC, CBS, FOX, and NBC), their audiences tend to be quite large. That means that even though the CPM (cost per thousand) can be very reasonable, the total amount of investment can still be big.

Think about it this way: If you are paying $5 per thousand listeners for a radio station with 15,000 listeners, that's $75 a spot—you could buy 30 spots in a week for just $2,250.

But if you are paying $5 per thousand for a TV news program that has 60,000 viewers, you are going to pay $300 a spot. That same budget of $2,250 a week will only allow you to buy 11 spots a week.

Then consider large stations in major markets may have over 350,000 viewers, and you can start to appreciate the problem. The problem is frequency: If you're buying very few spots on big-audience stations, it's harder to have an ongoing conversation.

Let me put it this way: would you rather talk to 1,000 people 20 times…or 20,000 people one time (assuming the same cost)? For our purposes—building a relationship of trust with listeners over time—we'd rather have the consistency and the frequency. When your budget grows and you can afford to talk to the 20,000 people 20 times, fine. But for now, let's start with smaller audiences (usually on radio) that require smaller budgets.

Getting Started

I recommend that you allocate 10% of your overall marketing budget to farming-based radio to get started. If your budget is $5,000 a month, then commit $500. If it's $50,000 a month, allocate $5,000. I'll give you some strategies in an upcoming chapter about how to negotiate and buy… but for now, just know this: it doesn't matter how big or how small your budget is. The important thing is to start NOW.

But you have to keep in mind the concept of FARMING when you start. Remember, you're hoping to generate some immediate leads—but your bigger concern is generating leads for the next 2 to 20 *years*. That means that in the short term, you're just planting seeds… and you're still a long way from harvest time. You need to count on this 10% of your budget producing NOTHING.

To be clear: that doesn't mean it <u>will</u> produce absolutely nothing in the short term—but you'd better plan that way just in case. I've seen dozens of campaigns killed off after 2 or 3 months when nervous business owners blinked and quit. Just think if the farmer quit two months after planting!

As your sales grow and your marketing budget grows, then you can steadily grow your radio (and overall FARMING) budget to as much as 50% to 75% of your total marketing budget. It's true—the big do get bigger, and the reason is that they are willing to INVEST their profits back into FARMING advertising activities that will produce even BIGGER PROFITS for them in the future.

If you're unwilling to go this route, then next year and the year after that, you'll still be turning over rocks looking for food. The smart move is to start FARMING right now. And the smartest place to start farming is the RADIO.

The client I mentioned at the beginning of this chapter gave me a $1MM budget to start... and I put all of it on radio. 100%.

Why?

Because in the market we were buying, to get a "full buy" (defined later) on CBS and NBC, it was going to take $500,000 to $600,000 (per station) for a year. ABC, the most popular station, averaged over 350,000 viewers for its highest rated news programs... and was going to require at least $900,000 for a full buy.

In addition, this client wanted to produce very high-end TV commercials that ultimately cost $100,000 to produce five spots... and took 3 painstaking months of planning, filming, and editing.

By contrast, we were able to buy 7 radio stations that first year, and the spots were recorded <u>for free</u> by one of the stations in about 90 minutes... and were edited and ready to go within 2 days.

That worked so well in year one that the broadcast advertising was raised to $3MM for the next year, and nearly all of the additional money was spent on TV. They were ready.

But radio was first... and likely will be for you, too. At least for starters.

CHAPTER 37
Avoiding Common Radio Pitfalls

I N CHAPTERS 39 and 40 I'm going to teach you how to negotiate a great radio buy. I'll show you how to determine which stations you should choose, what to ask the sales rep for, how to evaluate what they show you, and how to pit stations against one another to really get a killer deal.

But first, I want to show you how to do it wrong. I want to expose common pitfalls and help you understand exactly how dangerous this can be.

Pitfall #1: Trying To Negotiate Media Yourself

Here's the problem: Radio has its own set of jargon, and if you're not fluent in it, you can't possibly negotiate effectively. Don't' worry, I'll teach you the basics in the next chapter. Most business owners are good negotiators—it comes with the entrepreneurial territory. You negotiate things like salaries, leases, equipment prices, and selling prices with customers all the time. So the natural inclination is to assume that you can walk into a meeting with a radio rep and negotiate effectively.

But you can't.

Here's how a typical negotiation between a contractor—who is normally a good negotiator—and a professional radio sales rep goes:

Radio Rep: This schedule is $5,000 a month; it includes 10 spots a day during prime day parts (7 am to 7 pm), 10 spots a day during evenings and overnights (7 pm to 7 am), and 5 spots each on Saturday and Sunday. In addition, we'll give you 250,000 impressions a month on our website if you sign a six-month contract.

Contractor: (acting outraged, incredulous) What?!? $5,000? There is no way on earth that is going to happen. My entire advertising budget is only $8,000 a month, and $7,000 of that is already committed to other stuff. MAYBE I could allocate $2,000 a month, but not a penny more!

Radio Rep: My manager will kill me, but I could come down to $3,500, but I need a 12 month contract.

Contractor: (defiant) I'd do $3,000, but I'm going to need 12 spots during the day instead of 10, 15 spots at night, 10 spots each day on the weekends… and I need you do DOUBLE the online impressions. And I'm NOT signing one year contract. You can forget that.

Radio Rep: I'll have to check with the station manager… I can't approve that myself. But I tell you what… if you commit to 6 months, I will get that pushed through. I'll take the heat— do we have a deal?

Contractor: (triumphantly) I'll commit to three months, not a day more. If you get that, I'll sign today.

Radio Rep: (looking defeated but secretly beaming inside) Okay, I guess we can do that. But I'm going to get killed by my boss.

The problem with the scenario is the contractor has no idea what he just bought. His negotiation was based on the points that he could quantify—the number of spots, the dollars, and the length of contract—but with no real understanding of how much those spots are worth. This is the crux of the problem.

Pitfall #2: Obsessing Over A Fake 15% Agency Discount

Here's something I hear all the time... and I do mean ALL THE TIME: "I negotiate directly with the stations and they give me the 15% agency discount."

The implication is that they are getting an awesome deal, and paying somebody like ME to do it will cost them their big 15% discount they are supposedly getting.

This is major league bull hockey. Of course they will "give you a 15% discount" when they are charging you 50% to 4,000% more than a skilled negotiator will get for you!!

Let me set you straight, using the example in the previous section:

What you think happened: You negotiated a $5,000 buy with a 15% "agency discount" and paid $4,250—and therefore saved $750. You think you're a genius.

What actually happened: You paid $4,250 for a schedule worth $1,000 to $3,000, and as a result overpaid by $1,250 to $3,250. You got snookered.

Stubbornly clinging to an imaginary 15% discount has cost lots of contractors tens or hundreds of thousands of dollars a year. I will prove that to you below.

When negotiating radio, you've got to understand, FLUENTLY, an entirely new language. You have to become intimately familiar with things like Net Reach, Frequency, Gross Impressions, AQH, Gross Rating Points, CPM, and CPP. On top of that, you have to understand exactly what demographic is being discussed, and judge the numbers being presented against that. We'll get to all that in the next chapter.

Pitfall #3: Buying Airtime Based On Spot Prices

This is the single-biggest rookie mistake I encounter with business owners when buying radio or TV. They become obsessed with "Cost Per Spot" without any real understanding of what that spot is worth. This then leads to a mentality of "buying as many spots as possible" because, the thinking goes, more is better. I've heard many contractors brag about buying 250 spots for $2,000 or something similar.

This is about the dumbest way imaginable to think about radio.

That's about like a friend telling you he's going to buy a house for $300,000. When you press him for details about the house, all he can tell you is the town it's located in, and that it's a 2-story home. But it's impossible to know if a house is worth $300,000 without knowing exactly which neighborhood it's in, how many square feet, how many bedrooms and bathrooms, how big the lot is, how old the house is, what level of finish out is in the house, etc. It's simply impossible to know if the house is a good value without knowing those details.

Yet business owners glibly pronounce that they got an awesome deal on XXX spots for $Y,YYY all the time.

When it comes to radio it's all about how many TARGETED people actually hear your ad, not the raw number of spots that run or how many dollars each those spots cost. But again, per our discussion of negotiation above, if you don't understand the nomenclature, you're losing before you ever start.

To get this right, you MUST learn to speak the language. Fortunately for you, I'll teach you in the very next chapter of this book.

Pitfall #4: The Sales Reps Will Lie To You And Trick You (On Purpose)

Here are a couple of hard-to-swallow truths:

- Most reps are going to completely avoid showing you any of the data that actually matters unless you explicitly ask for it.

- If you do ask for it, many of them will send you data that makes the buy look better than it actually is by altering minor details that they hope you won't notice... but that actually make a huge difference.

Don't get me wrong—there are a lot of great sales reps out there, and they can be very helpful in many situations. I work with many of them and have a lot of respect for them.

But there are a lot of reps—A LOT—who will try to serve you the poo-poo plater if they get even a whiff that you don't know how to properly interpret the numbers. I'm a highly experienced buyer—having bought well over $100MM of media in my career, and they STILL try to sneak stuff past me. All the time.

On the other hand, an experienced professional media buyer will know how to keep the sales reps in check, control the situation, and get a truly great buy for you.

I'll give you a detailed case study to illustrate this at the end of Chapter 40. But first, before you can fully understand the case study, let's learn to speak the language of media buying.

CHAPTER 38
Speaking The Language

A s you can tell from the preceding chapters, if you want to have a prayer of making a good buy, the very first thing you have to do is become fluent in the language of mass media.

How fluent?

When I was 19 years old, I spent two years in Taiwan as a missionary. Actually, I spent the first two months in a classroom in Provo, Utah learning the basics of Mandarin Chinese. Then I went to Taiwan where I didn't receive any more formal classroom training, but spent about 10 hours a day talking to native speakers in every imaginable situation. By the time I had lived in Taiwan for four months (and six total months of language training), I considered myself FLUENT in Mandarin.

Fluent didn't mean that I could say and understand *everything*, it simply meant that I could get by in almost any given situation. If somebody said something I didn't understand, I could stop them and ask them to say it again or explain what it meant. And if I needed to say a word I hadn't learned or couldn't remember, I could talk around it and explain it so the person could figure it out.

Similarly, you don't need to know *every single thing* about media buying to be "fluent;" you just need to know enough to a) understand the actual terms of the deal, so you can b) avoid being taken advantage of, and c) negotiate a *good* deal. You need to be able to ask for the right things and correctly interpret the numbers they give you.

WARNING: A lot of readers might consider this to be a boring chapter, full of unfamiliar language and weird technical terms. You might be tempted to skip over it and just "leave it to the experts." If you're going to be involved in media advertising (and I'm guessing you are if you've read this far) I'm going to strongly recommend you at least take a few minutes to familiarize yourself with this information.

I'm not asking you to take six months to become fluent in the language... but I am asking you to invest a few minutes to understanding the foundational building blocks of it.

So here we go:

- **TAPSCAN:** TAPSCAN is what the radio stations call the sheet they give you that has all of the data on it you will need to evaluate them (and to compare stations and negotiate). TAPSCAN was the name of a company that made the software that generates sales proposals until it was bought out by Nielsen (as in Nielsen ratings). It is still used by most radio stations in the country: if you call them and say "I need a TAPSCAN with X, Y, Z demo" they will know exactly what you mean. TV stations do not use TAPSCAN; instead, just ask them for a schedule.

  If you contact a radio station as a business owner (and not an agency), the sales rep will almost NEVER voluntarily send you a TAPSCAN because a) they don't want you to know the facts about what you are buying (see previous chapter), and b) they know you probably won't be able to interpret what you are seeing anyway. This chapter is designed to help you intelligently read a TAPSCAN.

- **Demo:** Your demo simply indicates the "demographics" of who you want to target. Your demo can be defined by many factors, but the most important ones are age, gender, income, and ethnicity. See below for info on each of these.

- **Age:** You can define your target market by age. In both radio and TV, the ages are represented in the following ranges: all people (every single listener regardless of age), 18+ (all people over 18), 25-29, 30-34, 35-39, 40-44, 45-49, 50-54, 55-59, 60-64, and 65+.

You are not limited to just these narrow ranges; you can choose any range you want as long as you use a combination of these numbers. For instance: 25-44, or 35-49, or 40-65+.

Most of my contractor clients are most interested in the age ranges 40-64 simply because people with money tend to be older. One of my clients loves senior citizen clients, so we frequently target 65+. What about you?

- **Gender:** In media buying, there three genders: Men, Women, and People. People simply means both men and women. So for example, if you are interested in checking the numbers for all people 18 and over, you would say P18+. If you wanted to check the numbers for women between 40 and 60 years old, you would say "Women 40-59."

  Most of my contractor clients don't care if they are reaching men or women—although I do have some who say that a higher percentage of the people who actually CALL them are women, so they want to target them. Adjust according to your target market needs.

- **Qualitative Data:** Age and gender are considered "quantitative" data—meaning you are measuring the quantity of people in those categories. Qualitative data measures the nature and characteristics of those people, including things like income, home value, education level, ethnicity, and so forth.

  For your purposes, the most important qualitative factor will probably be INCOME—again, reaching people with money is important. Income is usually reported in $25,000 increments starting at $50,000. So for instance, you can ask for schedules with P18+ (or whatever gender/age you want) with incomes over $75,000 (or over $125,000... or whatever). For contractors, depending on the market, we are usually looking for incomes over $75,000 or $100,000. These are rules of thumb that are subject to situational change.

- **CPM (Cost Per Thousand):** This is the most important piece of lingo, by far, that you need to understand. This is a measure of how much it will cost you to reach 1,000 people of a given demo. This is why I covered the demo information above first—so you know what demo to ask for when checking the CPM.

  The reason CPM is so important is that it allows you to REALLY evaluate the cost of a station... and easily compare the cost of one station against another, even across different media. In other words, once I define my demo, I can ask a station for a TAPSCAN that will show me what the CPM is. I can then reliably compare that CPM against other radio or TV stations—as long as they have the EXACT same demos.

  The important thing—*and the thing you have to watch out for*—is making sure that you are always comparing <u>precisely the same demos</u>. You might see a CPM that's $3 cheaper for a given station and get super excited... until you realize the demo is completely (or even slightly) different. Be careful!!

- **CPP (Cost Per Point):** This refers to rating points. You've heard radio and TV stations talk about "ratings," right? I'm not going to bother you with any details about understanding how rating points work because my advice is to use CPM to compare prices and stations instead of CPP. I am simply bringing it up here because you will see CPP and points on TAPSCANS so you'll need to know what it is—and in many cases, know to ask for CMP instead of CPP.

- **Frequency:** This is a number that represents the average number of times a person in the designated demo will hear your ad during the duration of the schedule. To keep things consistent and comparable, you will ALWAYS want to ask for weekly schedules so you can see what the frequency is PER WEEK.

  A (weekly) frequency of anything LESS than 2.0 is too low— people won't hear the spot enough to effectively "Wall Drug" them. A frequency of 2.5 is a good; 3.0 is great; anything above 3.0 is probably too much and will lead to "diminishing returns" (like putting up more than 50 billboards in a 50-mile stretch—at some point, more exposure won't move the needle enough to justify the extra cost).

- **AQH (Average Quarter Hour):** This is a measurement of how many people are listening to a station during a given 15 minute window (hence, quarter hour) on the station. This number will change throughout the day based on listenership. If a 15-minute period has an AQH of 10,000, that means that 10,000 people were listening.

- **Cume:** This is the number of DIFFERENT people in a demo who listen to a station for at least 5 minutes during a given period of time—usually a week or a month. If somebody says a station has a weekly CUME of 22,000, that means that 22,000 different people tuned into the station during the week. But like everything else, you need to make sure you know what DEMO is being discussed—the cume of all listeners will certainly be higher than the cume of W35-54. See what I mean?

- **Gross Impressions (aka GI's or just "impressions"):** This is the total number of times your ads will be seen/heard over the course of a schedule. If 10,000 people heard your ad 3 times each, that would be 30,000 gross impressions. CPM is calculated by dividing the number of gross impressions by the cost of the schedule.

  Important note about gross impressions: Not all gross impressions are created equal. If you run a 5 second ad, that's one gross impression for every person who was listening. If you run a 30 or 60 second ad—it's still just one GI for every person listening. Clearly a 60-second ad is more valuable and impactful than a 5-second ad, but they count exactly the same. I'll give you some more advice relevant to this in the next chapter.

- **Daypart:** The time segments a day is divided by for the purpose of selling advertising time. Primary dayparts are morning (6a to 10a; also known as AM drive), midday (10a to 3p), afternoon (3p to 7p; also known as PM drive), evenings (7p to midnight), and overnights (midnight to 6a).

Generally speaking, AM drive and PM drive are going to have the most listeners, and therefore be the most expensive. There are definitely exceptions though, so ask to see the AQH and GI's for each daypart you are considering.

- **Rotator:** Rotators are spots that the station can run anytime they want during a defined window—as opposed to during a specified daypart. Since rotators allow the station more flexibility of when the spots run, they are willing to give you a lower price.

  For instance, a given station might charge $250 for a 60-second spot during AM drive, $210 during midday, and $280 during PM drive. They might be willing to sell you a rotator that airs anywhere from 7a to 7p for $220.

  Like everything else we've discussed, BE CAREFUL when dealing with sales reps! If you ask for a "rotator" you might get a favorable price while assuming the time limits are 7a to 7p... when in fact it's listed as 5a to 8p. As a rule, the *wider* the time window, the less expensive. Sometimes you will even see 12a-12a rotators... which means they can run the spot anytime between midnight and midnight—in other words, LITERALLY ANY TIME!

- **Length:** This is the length of the spot. For radio, it's usually 60 or 30 seconds, but shorter spots are also available—5, 10, and 15 seconds. Generally speaking, the longer the length, the better the value. In other words, 30 second spots are rarely 50% of the cost of a 60 second spot; instead, the price will usually be 60% to 80%.

  Here's my rule of thumb: When I put a client on a new station, I try to make all of the spots 60 seconds long. That's because the listeners are not familiar with this company yet, and it takes time to effectively communicate their identity. After a client has been on a station for 1 or 2 years, I'll start to move up to 50% of the spots to 30 seconds... but only if the price make sense. If the 30-second spots are 60% of the cost of a 60-second spot, I'll consider that. 80%? No way.

Similarly, I generally only ad shorter spots (5, 10, 15 seconds) if they are added in near the end of the negotiation process and are extremely inexpensive or free. I'll talk more about this in the next chapter.

There are definitely more factors involved that what I've listed above, but this will give you a good baseline familiarity with the lingo, and prepare you to have an intelligent conversation with sales reps—and avoid blindly buying whatever they happen to throw at you. Everything here also applies to TV, too.

The next step is to gather information on the stations, evaluate that information, then negotiate like a pro.

CHAPTER 39
Choosing The Right Stations

PROPER SELECTION OF *stations* for radio (and *programs* for TV) is one of the most important factors in creating a winning media strategy. After all, if you learn all the lingo (last chapter) and negotiate like a pro (next chapter), you're not going to like the results if you're on the wrong station!

Quick reminder: As previously stated, when buying radio you want to look at *stations*—that's because radio stations tend to have the same type of programming all day long, which makes for loyal listeners who rarely change the station. TV, on the other hand, is primarily *program* driven—meaning that people could care less what channel something is on... the programs they like tend to be scattered over multiple channels.

Choosing The Right Station For Radio

Since I've encouraged you to start with radio, I'll show you how to choose radio stations first. Before you can do that, though, you need to understand what kind of stations are available to choose from—and what kind of demographics you can typically expect from each kind of station.

There are actually dozens of different formats... many of which are specialized derivatives of larger formats. That means that you will find some overlap in some formats in terms of music played and demographics served. For our purposes, I'll keep the discussion fairly general.

- **Adult Contemporary (AC):** Plays a wide variety of familiar hits that are soft enough for office listening. AC DJ's add fun, topical content without getting in the way of the music. Expect to hear a combination of older artists like Elton John, Maria Carey, Billy Joel, and Cher... as well as more contemporary acts like Adele, Kelly Clarkson. AC tends to skew toward females in the 35 to 55 range, making it a great place to reach working women who make many home improvement buying decisions.

- **Hot AC:** Same as AC, except is caters to a younger crowd— typically in the 25 to 45 range. Hot AC is a music-intensive, Top 40 radio for adults, without rap and hard rock. It features contemporary, upbeat tempo and a relatable and entertaining DJ presentation and large-scale promotions. Core artists would include artists like Adele, Maroon 5, Katy Perry, Train, Pink, Taylor Swift, and Bruno Mars. For Home Improvement companies, we generally tend to steer away from Hot AC to older-skewing stations. But it is worth checking into.

- **Contemporary Hit Radio (CHR, Top 40):** Plays music that caters to younger listeners from teenagers to mid-20's. It's cool, new music that most adults aren't that interested in. CHR stations will generally play a small rotation of extremely current music, and drop songs as new ones become popular and displace them. This is not a good format to reach homeowners and people with higher incomes.

- **News Talk:** There are two flavors of news talk stations: local and national syndications. Local news talk stations, as the name suggests, hires local personalities to discuss news and politics, and tend to draw a very loyal crowd of conservative-leaning listeners. National syndication stations run conservative programming such as Hannity, Rush Limbaugh, Mark Levin, and Ben Shapiro. Either format is a good way to reach higher income homeowners who purchase home improvement and services. Tends to skew toward men.

- **News:** News stations focus on national and local news, and are similar to local broadcast TV news programs. They tend to be light on commentary and heavy on facts and details, and as a result lean neither left nor right. They also provide local weather and traffic. Many news programs will scatter commercials throughout the program in ones and twos to keep listeners engaged. News stations are an excellent choice for reaching home improvement and services buyers.

- **Sports:** Obviously focuses on sports—although you will want to check to see if the programming features local personalities or nationally syndicated. Local stations tend to draw loyal listeners if the local sports teams are popular. Sports stations are a great way to reach men—although you will want to check with individual stations to see what age ranges they cater to.

- **Country:** There are multiple varieties of country stations, including mainstream country, hot country, and classic country. In my experience, country stations are hit-and-miss. They can cater to men or women (or both) and to a wide variety of ages and incomes. Always check the demographic rankings carefully before buying country. If you find the right audience, however, country can be an important part of your radio mix.

- **Rock:** Like country, rock comes in many flavors—modern, classic, and alternative, to name a few. The main difference is that rock tends to skew heavily to men, and income demographics tend to be less than average. Like with country, check carefully with each station you are considering to determine the audience profile.

- **Oldies:** Surprise, oldies isn't what it was when you were growing up—which was music from doo-wop music from the 1950's. Now there are different varieties of oldies that cater to different decades and types of music. If you are in your 40's or older, chances are some of you favorite music can be found on an oldies station. Check each station's listener profile carefully and you may find some good fits.

- **Urban/R&B:** These are stations that cater to black audiences. Like other formats, Urban has many sub-categories that are tailored to different age ranges. Check any stations you are interested in against your demographic profile to see if they are fit.

- **Public Radio:** Public radio (NPR) generally has a highly-educated, high income crowd, which is obviously good. But it also comes with a major downside, which is they impose massive restrictions on what you can actually say in your ads. As a rule, they allow absolutely no comparisons or selling—only general descriptions of what you sell. That means you can't use any identity points in your ads, which is why we generally (but now always) shy away from public radio stations. Proceed with caution.

- **Religious:** Religious stations come in two major varieties... music-oriented, and preaching-oriented. The major advantage of religious programming is that listeners tend to be extremely loyal, which means you can get high frequencies without spending a ton of money. The major disadvantage is that many religious stations are NOT Arbitron rated—which means they don't pay the fee to Arbitron required to be included in their ranking process. That means you frequently will have NO IDEA what you are actually buying... you're flying blind. That being said, I have still frequently bought religious programming for clients because the demographic of the listeners is a good match, and the stations are inexpensive in terms of raw dollars. For example, one of my clients spends about $2,000 a month out of an $80,000 budget. That's a small enough slice of the pie that I can live with the inexact metrics.

Now that you have a good idea of what kinds of stations exist, and which ones are likely to be best for your company, it's time to research the stations that are available in your market.

Go to www.StationRatings.com and click on your state, then choose your market. The site may ask you to become a subscriber—don't' worry it's free, and it only takes a few seconds to get signed up.

When you get to your market, you will see some information about the market at the top, then a list of the stations, ranked from highest to lowest. It will look something like this:

Tulsa Rank: 65							
12+ Population: 822,700 Ethnic Composition: Black - 8.9% Hispanic - 9% Market Swept: 4x/year							Back
Station	Format	Owner/LMA	SU17	FA17	WI18	SP18	SU18
KJSR-FM	Classic Rock	Cox Media Group	6.2	5.6	5.6	5.5	6.7
KRMG-FM / KRMG-AM	News/Talk	Cox Media Group	6.6	7.0	9.4	7.4	6.6
KHTT-FM	CHR	GRIFFIN COMMUNICATIONS	6.2	5.5	5.6	6.8	6.6
KWEN-FM	Country	Cox Media Group	7.4	6.5	6.0	6.4	5.9
KXBL-FM	Classic Country	GRIFFIN COMMUNICATIONS	5.8	5.4	4.3	5.2	5.9
KMOD-FM	Rock	iHeartMedia, Inc.	6.6	6.8	5.8	5.3	5.6
KBAV-FM	Hot AC	Cox Media Group	5.5	4.7	6.1	4.9	5.1
KVOO-FM	Country	GRIFFIN COMMUNICATIONS	5.1	3.8	3.8	4.9	4.5
KTBT-FM	CHR	iHeartMedia, Inc	3.5	3.4	3.4	3.4	3.9
KTGX-FM	Country	iHeartMedia, Inc	3.2	3.9	3.8	3.7	3.6
KBEZ-FM	Classic Hits	GRIFFIN COMMUNICATIONS	4.0	4.2	3.5	4.0	3.2
KFAQ-AM	Talk	GRIFFIN COMMUNICATIONS	1.1	2.0	1.4	1.6	1.6
KIZS-FM	Spanish Oldies	iHeartMedia, Inc.	0.6	0.7	0.0	0.3	0.8
KTGX-HD2	Classic Rock	iHeartMedia, Inc	3.2	2.3	0.8	0.1	0.8
KTBZ-AM	Sports	iHeartMedia, Inc.	0.0	0.0	0.0	0.2	0.6
KWEN-HD2	Rock	Cox Media Group	7.4	0.7	0.0	0.7	0.5
KAKC-AM	Sports	iHeartMedia, Inc	0.0	0.0	0.0	0.1	0.1

* +Audience estimates are derived in part using Nielsen Audio's Persons 12+, Monday-Sunday, 6 am-12 Midnight estimates, under license. Copyright (c) 2018 Nielsen Audio. All rights reserved.
Nielsen Audio no longer releases audience estimates for stations that do not subscribe to their services. Therefore, the audience estimates on this website include ONLY those stations that pay Nielsen Audio for this data. This website may not include all the radio stations that serve each market.

Tulsa is a relatively small market, so there are only 17 stations listed. Bigger markets might have as many as 30 or 40 stations; smaller markets might have closer to ten.

Note: If you scroll down the page further, you will see a list of "Other Stations Located In Market," which are stations that do not pay Arbitron for their ranking services. These are generally smaller stations, and like I said above in the description of Religious Stations, there is no real way to know what you're paying for with these stations. As a rule of thumb, stick to rated stations.

Back to the list of ranked stations: They are listed in order of market share. In the example above, look at the column on the far right—that shows each station's rating for the most recent period. Don't get too hung up on these numbers because a station that ranks very high overall may rank terribly for you target market. In fact, you don't really need to worry about how stations rank at all—do you know why based on what you've read so far? It's because you are going to evaluate stations based on the cost per thousand listeners (CPM), not based on how many people listen.

Think of it this way, in the context of our farming analogy:

Each station is a piece of land that you are farming. Some of those pieces of land are very large (lots of listeners), and some are very small (relatively few listeners). Some of the pieces of land are ideal for growing certain kinds of crops (demographics)—some are not.

Just because a piece of land (station) is small, does not mean it's not a good place to farm. In fact, you may find that small stations are actually better in some cases, because listeners to lower-ranked stations are just as likely to be loyal to that station as any listener of any station.

As an example, I had an employee several years ago who had a 45-minute commute each way to and from work. He told me that he listened to a certain talk station—KLIF—every single minute of that commute every single day. That station consistently ranks about 30th in the Dallas Ft. Worth market, with a share of only 0.4. But the people who listen to it absolutely LOVE it.

Your goal with advertising is to cultivate prospects into buyers over time. You want ongoing conversations. Lower-ranked stations can accomplish this for you—and often at much lower rates than their higher-ranked brethren.

Radio ads are sold on a supply and demand basis... there is only so much airtime that can be allocated to ads. Higher ranked stations tend to be bought more readily by big advertisers—especially national ones—who are hungry to get in front of as many people as possible... so their inventory is often tighter and their spots more expensive (on a CPM basis) than their lower-ranked brethren.

Don't be afraid to explore the lower-rated stations; you might be pleasantly surprised that you can consistently reach a good number of target prospects for relatively little money.

Determine Which Stations Might Be A Good Fit

Look over the list of stations in your market and throw out any that are obviously not a fit for your company. To learn more about a station, just click on their call letters which are linked to each station's website.

You can also find contact information for a station on their websites; you will normally have to scroll to the BOTTOM of the page and look for something like "Advertise with us" or "business office."

Warning: In my experience, stations are not always very prompt at getting back to you—so I recommend calling *and* emailing them. You'd think they'd be anxious to sick a sales person on you, but for some reason, I frequently have to badger them for attention at first. Don't worry, once the right person gets in touch with you, they'll do everything in their power to get you to buy.

Look at your station list from StationRatings.com; under the "Owner" column, you will notice that there are usually multiple stations that are owned by the same company. In fact, in the example above, you can see that all the rated stations are owned by just three companies. In most cases, you can work with just one rep per company for all the stations they own, which will make your job a lot easier and more efficient.

Now that you know which stations might be a fit, it's time to contact them to gather information, then negotiate.

What To Say When You Reach Out To Stations

Call the station and say "I would like to speak to somebody about advertising on your station." Usually they will put you through to what turns out to be a voice mail. If so, say this when you leave a message:

"I am gathering some information for my boss; we are a (window, HVAC, etc. company) that is looking to get on the radio in this market. I need you to call me back so we can discuss. My company name is (your company name) and my name is (your name). My number is (give number). Again, my name is (name) and my number is (number). You can also email me at (email); that's (email)."

The reason you are gathering information "for your boss" is so they don't try to start negotiating with you. If you the boss and this makes you uncomfortable, have somebody who works for you do this instead.

If you get them on the phone (either when you first call, or they call you back), after introducing yourself, say this: "My boss has asked me to research the market and gather information on specific stations we feel might be a good fit. I would like to send you an email that describes exactly what we are looking for. Are you the rep that we would actually be dealing with, or is that somebody else? (if somebody else, get the name; Once you have the name of the right person, continue): Can I get your email address and phone number please, so I can send that over?

Then send them this email:

Hi (name),

Thanks for your help. Here is what I need you to provide me at your earliest convenience—my deadline is (two days from today).

- Ranker Reports for the market, showing how your station ranks in the following demos:
  - o Adults 35-64
  - o Adults 35-64, HH income $100k plus
  - o Women 35-54
- Qualitative information on your station (Scarborough or equivalent) that shows at least education, household income, home value, gender, etc.
- TAPSCAN (or equivalent) for your station for an 18+ demo:
  - o 60 second spots only
  - o Show a 3.0 frequency
  - o Rotators 6a-7p, M-F only—no weekends

- o Show the CPP and CPM

- o Show AQH

- o Gross numbers, please

- o Note: We are not necessarily going to purchase a 3.0 frequency; we are using this as a baseline to check pricing

- o Timeframe: Starting in (when you want to start, at least a month away)

- o Once you generate that TAPSCAN, please run it again with P35-64 demo and the Women 35-64 demo—leave the number and types of spots the same, everything else will change/update accordingly, including frequency)

Please email the above information to me; my contact information is in my signature if you have any questions. Please note that that I am passing this information off to my boss to evaluate, and I don't know how long he will need to do so.

Thanks!

(name, signature)

If you are ready, you can do the same thing for TV with a slightly different email.

Go online and Google the contact information for four local affiliates for CBS, ABC, NBC, and FOX .

Repeat everything above; the only difference is the specific requirements that you need to ask them for, which would be (use the exact same email except change the blue part to this):

- • Ranker Reports for the market, showing how your station ranks in the following demos:

- • Adults 35-64

- • Adults 35-64, HH income $100k plus

- • Women 35-54

- Qualitative information on your station that shows at least education, household income, home value, gender, etc.

- Schedules for your station for your station for an 18+ demo:

- 30 second spots only

- One spot per LOCAL news program between 4:30 am and 11 pm, Monday through Thursday only

- Also show me the national morning program (if applicable— Good Morning America, Today, etc.). Same thing, Monday through Thursdays only.

- Show the CPP and CPM

- Show the frequency

- Gross numbers, please

- Timeframe: (your time frame)

- Once you generate that schedule, please run it again with P35-64 demo and the Women 35-64 demo —leave the number and types of spots the same, everything else will change/update accordingly, including frequency)

That's it; it seems like a lot, but you are getting the exact same info from all the stations… so it's a lot of cutting and pasting and following up.

What To Do With The Data Your Gather

Once you get the information, one of the tricky things is making sure that they actually gave you what you asked for. You would think that would be easy and obvious—and you would be wrong. You need to check all the schedules to make sure they gave you the EXACT demos, spot lengths, rotator windows, frequencies, etc. that you asked for.

Pull out the P18+ TAPSCAN/schedule for each station and make note of the Cost Per Thousand (CPM) and the total cost. These are going to be your measuring sticks, and are going to allow you to estimate how much it will cost you to get a "full buy" on each station.

Determining A "Full Buy"

I cannot emphasize enough the need to make sure that your schedules actually have what you asked for. If one station is quoting you a 2.7 frequency and another is quoting a 3.0 frequency (what you asked for), your comparisons will be off. You must have IDENTICAL schedules to proceed!

A "full buy" is the amount of money it will take to get a 3.0 frequency on a station for P18+ demo using M-F 6a to 7p, 60-second spots for a given station. We usually don't actually make a full buy—but it is an important measuring stick that allows us to estimate the answer to this question: "How much would it cost to be on every station I want to be on... as much as I want to be on them?"

The reason this is important is that this now becomes your goal! If there are 7 good radio stations to be on and 4 good TV stations to be on—you want to know right now, up front, about how much it will cost you someday to be on all of them. That's when you will be absolutely dominating your market—so I think it's important to know what you are shooting for.

In other words, you need to know what the entire farm looks like... then you can pick a small parcel of land and start farming!

Here's a formula for estimating a "full buy" on a station:

Step 1: Weekly Full Buy (WFB) - Multiply your weekly cost to reach a 3.0 frequency (from the TAPSCAN) by 0.65.

If a station gives you a schedule that says it will cost $4,500 to reach a 3.0 frequency, we multiply that by .65 and get $2,925. The reason we then multiply by .65 is to compensate for money that we will save by negotiating a better deal (remember, this was their opening offer, not the final one!) and by possibly buying LESS than a 3.0 frequency. **This is our weekly full buy number.**

Two important notes:

1. **Gross vs Net Numbers:** Stations traditionally give gross numbers to agencies and net numbers to individual advertisers. The gross numbers are 15% higher, which represents

the traditional agency markup we talked about earlier. It really doesn't matter if you're dealing with gross or net numbers—but it's super critical that you know *which it is* so you know how much you are actually going to pay.

2. **Cost Per Thousand (CPM):** You also need to know your Weekly Full Buy number's CPM. This is going to help you determine which stations offer the best buys. If Station A's WFB number is $3,000 at a $3.25 CPM, and Station B's WFB number is $3,000 at $5.80 CPM, which station do you think is the better buy? This is critical!

Step 2: Monthly Full Buy (MFB) – Next, multiply your WFB x 4 to give you a Monthly Full Buy number. Since most companies set their marketing budgets by the month, it's important to know what a station will cost you for a month. Yes, I know that months are not exactly 4 weeks long, but this quick and easy formula will suffice for our purposes. From our example, we get $2,925 x 4 weeks = $11,700.

Step 2: Annual Full Buy (AFB) – Next, multiply your MFB number by 12 months. Yes, I realize that 4 weeks x 12 months = 48 weeks, not 52. Actually, that works perfectly because we're usually going to negotiate 4 free weeks a year with an annual buy, and we need to know what the station will cost for a full year. In this example, that leaves us with a number of $140,400 ($11,700 per month x 12 months) that represents an **"Annual Full Buy" on this station.**

Then you simply add up all the stations' AFB numbers to know what you will have to invest into farming the entire market.

These numbers will not be 100% accurate, of course. You won't always negotiate exactly 35% off the starting numbers. And you won't always get 4 weeks free in your negotiations. But if you do this for both radio and TV, you will be getting a good idea of what the entire farm looks like from 30,000 feet in the air.

Remember, all you have done so far is gather information. Now it's time to really negotiate.

CHAPTER 40

How To Negotiate And Buy Like A Pro

EVERYTHING UP TO this point has been foundation building—now it's time to erect the house.

Let's review what you've learned so far:

- You determined that farming is a necessary move, and the consistency and frequency are of utmost importance

- You received a quick education on radio terminology and radio station types

- You learned how to find the stations in your market that are probably a good fit

- You learned how to contact the stations to gather the pertinent data

- You learned how to determine a "full buy" for each station and for the entire market

Now it's go time!

Before you start, compare your monthly budget against the Monthly Full Buy numbers for each market. If your starting radio and TV budget is $6,000 a month (remember our 5% rule from earlier to determine this), and a certain highly ranked TV station is going to cost $80,000 a month for a full buy… well, that station is not an option.

A good rule of thumb is this: If a station's WFB number is <u>twice or more</u> than your available radio and TV budget, you're going to want to put it in a file labeled "try later when you have more budget available," and start with stations that cost less.

Once you have a list of stations that are within your budget, reach out to each of them by sending this email (I prefer email, but phone works, too):

Let's use the station from above that had a Monthly Full Buy number of $11,700 and an annual number of $140,400.

Then do this: **Offer them 50% of the Annual Full Buy price for an annual buy.**

Here's the email:

Hello,

We are entering the market with a very limited budget, and we only have enough money to buy 1 or 2 stations. We do, however, want to commit to an entire year so that we can get the very best deal possible. Here is what I would like to propose to you—if it's not a good fit, just let me know—no hard feelings.

I would like to get the schedule that you sent over earlier for 52 weeks $70,000.

Note: the actual number would be $70,200, but I prefer to make the number sound more rounded because it sounds more like it is coming from your budget.

You need to keep in mind that they were asking $4,500 a week for this schedule—so you are essentially asking for $234,000 of radio for $70,000. We already lowered their number by 35% to get our "full buy" number… then we asked for 4 weeks free AND another 50% off.

This is called your opening ask. **If your number is not outrageous, you are doing it wrong.**

You will get responses that range from "Are you insane?" to "I don't think so but let me ask" to "I don't know… let me check."

What you have really done is given yourself a lot of room to negotiate back up and get a price you can live with while still giving the station a win.

Quid Pro Quo Negotiating

As the negotiations progress, keep in mind a "quid pro quo" mindset—this for that. You always want to be getting something in return for giving something.

In your opening ask, you have already offered two major concessions in return for your outrageously low price—did you notice what they were? First, you offered an annual contract—that's no small thing, because it allows the sales rep to count on a steady, monthly income from you. Second, you offered to let them be one of the very few stations you will even be on for that entire year. In other words, you've let them know that ONLY ONE STATION (or two) will get your business, and everybody else will get nothing. That's a huge incentive for them to make sure you buy their station.

Here are some examples of things you can ask for as you slowly, reluctantly raise your price:

- Placing your ads first in the commercial breaks
- Free or heavily discounted spots in off-peak times (evenings, overnights, weekends)
- Promotional giveaways (booths at events, tie-ins to station promotions, etc.)
- Free exposure on their station website
- Exclusivity in your product category
- Weather and/or traffic sponsorships
- Live mentions by DJs or on-air personalities

Negotiation is an art. I won't go into all the details of how to get the best deal… suffice it to say the information just shared is a trade secret that will get you well on your way.

Case Study: How I Negotiated A Deal 4,500% Better Than My Client

With that background, let me show you how I negotiated a great deal for a client… and more importantly, I want you to see how these reps will do everything in their power to trick you into worse deals— without you even knowing it.

A few years ago I started working with a window and siding company in the Midwest. They had become interested in radio and TV recently, and started trying to negotiate a buy themselves. They were smart business people, but didn't know beans about negotiating radio and TV. The result was they thought they were buying ocean-front property in Maui and ended up getting stuck with swampland in Florida.

Here's what they bought:

Summary

About Your Commercial Schedule:

Elizabeth will endorse HomeSealed, recording one unique commercial each week.

- 24 weeks
- Weekly Commercials: 20
- Total Commercials: 480

Added Value:

Mike Mason Half Hour Sponsorship

Nothing's more engaging than a good old-fashioned brain-buster! Every weekday afternoon at 4pm, Mike Mason puts a new-fashioned spin on an old favorite with the Half-Hour Question. Cool questions with just enough spin to "drive ya nuts" and only a half-hour to call in with the correct answer. It's a great way to keep your business top-a-mind with a totally engaged audience!

"Mike Mason's Half-Hour Question, coming up at 4. Brought to you by HomeSealed Exteriors"

Lead Generator 103.7 KISS FM

- 2 weeks
- 18x On Air Commercials (:15) Mon-Sat 6a-7p
- 18x Internet Radio Commercials (Streaming)
- 2x E-Mails to 25,000
- Custom Sweepstakes Page
- Campaign Analytics including Email Address opt-ins
- Answers for up to 3 Survey Questions
- Bounce Back with Coupon/Incentive

Total Weekly Investment: 26 weeks
Week of 8/1 - 8/29 (5 weeks) $800 net per week
Week of 9/5 – 1/23 (21 Weeks) $750 net perk week
Prize for Lead Generation program
*$200 net talent fee per week or $5,200 total

Authorized Signature: _____ Date: _____

This is swampland, pure and simple. Let me explain:

1. After we researched the market, we determined that this is actually the 4th or 5th best radio station for them to be on. That might be okay if the DEAL was so good that they just couldn't pass it up, but....

2. They have no way of knowing how good this buy is based on this document. It states that they will get 20 spots a week for 24 weeks for $800 a week. Is that good? Unless you know HOW MANY PEOPLE will hear those spots, it is 100% impossible to judge.

3. The Endorsement by "Elizabeth" (on-air personality) is way overvalued—it's 20% of the budget. We found out she endorses FOUR companies simultaneously—that's too many!

4. The sponsorship on the left and the list of stuff on the right is FILLER GARBAGE that is worth almost nothing. If you don't know that, it's a problem.

Let me put this even more simply: Anytime you are presented with a summary sheet or PowerPoint slide that shows the total number of spots and the total cost... along with some "freebies"... you are getting a bad deal. 100% of the time. This is how they pray on people who don't know what they are doing.

I actually don't mind, because all the people out there paying too much in the name of "getting a 15% agency discount" are making the station so much money that they can afford to give *me* exactly what I want.

When I called the station and had them send me the numbers on this buy (which the client never saw or even thought to ask for—again, by design of the station), here's what I got:

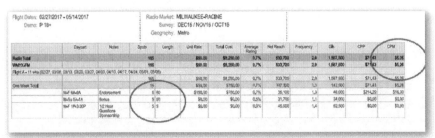

The Cost per Thousand (CPM) looks pretty good at $5.26. Let's stop right there. Before you read this book, did you even know what the "good" range for CPM was? Or more fundamentally, did you even know what a CPM was in the first place? If not, you're making progress!

Back to our story. The CPM looks good at $5.26… but when you factor in that the station is padding this with a bunch of GARBAGE (circled above—look at those "Bonus" rotator spots from 5A to 1A— they can run those spots essentially anytime they want!) and it's not so good. In fact, it's terrible.

It's like going to the store and getting 4 pounds of bananas… 1 pound is fresh and ripe and good to eat, but the other 3 pounds are old and moldy and useless. But all you know is you paid a reasonable price for 4 pounds of bananas.

Let's ask them to take 3 pounds of moldy bananas out, and just sell us the 1 pound of GOOD bananas.

I did exactly that; I asked them to remove the garbage, which exposed what a bad deal this really was:

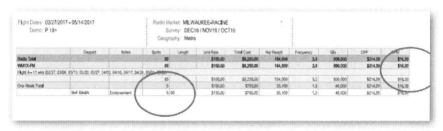

Boom, the price (THE REAL PRICE!) just MORE THAN TRIPLED to $16.30 (CPM).

When I told her I wanted a lower CPM, she pulled a fast one on me—trying to trick me:

Okay, look, the price is down to $9.99—a big reduction. Except she used 30-second spots instead of 60-second spots to artificially lower the price. Important note: <u>She did this without telling me she was going to do it—she simply hoped I wouldn't notice</u>. I'm not making this up.

If you don't know what you're doing, *they will pull this garbage on you all day long.*

I went back and asked to price it out for 60 second spots:

Okay, now the schedule is right, but the price is terrible. I would NEVER pay $14.04 CPM for radio for my clients.

Would you? Would you even know?

I sent this "lower the boom" email; note that I am asking for a price almost 2/3 less than what she had offered:

Hi Tricia,

Thanks for getting this schedule over to me. This CPM is a lot higher than I can pay; I was expecting something a lot closer to about $5. I know you are a highly ranked station, so maybe you just don't have a lot of inventory, and if so, that is understandable. I have a limited budget and am really only going to be able to buy probably one station right now. I want it to be a great buy—and I am able/willing to make it an annual commitment (at least 45 weeks per year).

Let me know if you can get me down into the $5 range... if not, unfortunately, we are going to have to opt out.

Thanks!

Rich

Three hours later, I had this offer in my inbox:

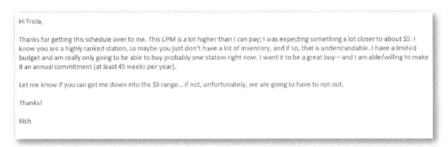

$9.99... the same price she had previously offered me for 30-second spots, but now for 60-second spots. That's a huge reduction with just one ask. I am sure I could get 20% to 35% more off... but since I don't really want this station anyway, I decide not to put the thumbscrews on her.

Instead, I focused on getting a better price from a better station, and I was able to get prices of $8.00 CMP and $7.56 CPM from two stations I like better...

Then I started to negotiate with TV stations, using the formula I gave you earlier in this chapter.

Long story short, I negotiated with one of the best stations in the entire market to get on for $3.50 CPM. Not "moldy bananas," either.

The original deal my client had negotiated on their own was $16.30. I ended up with a better price on a *better* station on TV—for just $3.50.

That's media buying like a boss.

That's how I negotiate deals that are literally 4,500% better than what my clients were getting.

If you think your AGENCY is doing a better job than you could, you're probably right.

If you think your AGENCY is doing a better job than I would, you're almost certainly WRONG.

The problem with agencies is that they almost always leave the negotiation to a junior-level wannabe who isn't experienced enough at buying media.

When I took over one of my clients' $1MM radio and TV budget in 2015, I was able to negotiate deals 20% to 30% better than what they had been paying. This was coming from one of the most respected agencies in their city.

If all this seems like a lot of detail, it is.

That's because it's important for you to understand exactly how critical this kind of negotiating for media buying is. If you unknowingly pay 4,500% too much for your media buy, you just chopped your buying power by 4 ½ times! That means 4 ½ times fewer leads, which means 4 ½ times less sales.

And the bigger your budgets get, the more the errors in negation hurt you. Think about it... the client with the $1MM media budget mentioned a few paragraphs ago. The deals I negotiated them for $1MM would have cost them $1,250,000 the year before. Let that sink in.

So yea, it might seem a little heavy on details. My goal isn't to make you an expert so you can negotiate your own media. I just want you to have a good enough working knowledge that you can have an intelligent opinion when you are presented with media buys from your agency or from the stations.

With that said, now let's move on to creating ads that will move the needle.

CHAPTER 41
Creating Effective Radio & TV Ads

Okay, so you've decided to advertise on the radio. You've picked and negotiated your stations, and you've committed to at least 6 or 12 months to give your ads some time to speak to your target market and nurture them along. Now comes the hard part—writing great ads that will move the needle.

So how do you write an effective advertisement? What elements need to be present—and what should you avoid?

Here are my top pieces of advice for writing great radio ads:

Start With Identity

A common mistake is to make your radio ad a "menu board" style ad. Think about a menu—it shows what's for sale and how much it costs. This leads to ads that say things like "We're a locally owned company that can help you with whatever remodeling projects you have… from energy-saving windows to durable siding to award winning roofing."

Instead, focus on your core selling points—your identity. What makes you different and better than the competitors? Why should somebody choose you? What can they expect if they do go with you?

Each company's identity is unique, so I can't tell you what, specifically, to focus on.

Remember, your identity can be thought of like a court case: If your business were on trial—and your prospects were the jury—what would you say to convince them you are the best choice? Your "case" will probably be built on one or two MAJOR points, and few SECONDARY points, and a handful of TERTIARY points. That brings us to point #2…

Limit Yourself To One Main Theme Per Ad

Remember, with radio advertising, your main objective is to build an ongoing relationship with the listener… starting NOW and extending to many YEARS in the future. There is absolutely NO NEED to try to pile every last ounce of information about your company (or you Identity, for that matter) into a single radio ad.

Instead, focus each ad on one single selling point. Look at the "case" you've outlined (per above) and decide how much weight you want to give to each selling point, then create a schedule that assigns the proper weight to a given topic over the course of a year.

For instance, let's say your main case points are as follows (point, weight):

- Fanatical Attention To Detail – material choices; installations, etc. (40%)

- Respect For Customers – No sales pressure, no pricing games, appearance, etc. (30%)

- Strength of Warranty (15%)

- Other Elements (15%)

If you cut 5 new ads every two to three months (my recommendation), then you would cut 20 to 30 ads in a year—let's say 25. Multiply 25 by the percentages above and you'd get 10 ads about "Attention to Detail," 7 or 8 ads about "Respect," and 3 or 4 ads each for "Warranty" and "Other".

This doesn't mean that you can't MENTION other things in a given ad; it means that you should FOCUS each ad on one major point.

Decide Which Products To Focus On

A lot of people ask me if they should focus on one product (i.e. windows) or is it okay to cover multiple products (windows, siding, and roofing, etc.). The answer is—it depends.

If ONE product is 90% or more of your sales (and you intend to keep it that way), then your Identity should focus on that product, and your ads should focus on your identity as it relates to those products.

If, however, you sell MULTIPLE products, it's probably a good idea to focus your case (and ads) on what I call "bedside manner" types of topics. The way you treat customers. Warranty issues. Customer service issues. Things that apply to all the different products you sell. Then you can MENTION in your ads that you sell windows, siding, and roofing... but the prospect will hear and know that you do all these wonderful "bedside manner" things.

So is it okay, if you sell multiple products, to create an ad that just focuses on, say, windows? Of course it is. But I still would like you to think in terms of "campaigning," or in other words, think of how that one single ad fits into an entire year's worth of advertising. Maybe there's a special promotion. Maybe you need to sell a lot of windows for some reason. Maybe it's seasonal. Just think through all these issues before writing.

Power, Precision, Passion

We talked about this extensively earlier in this book, but this is where the rubber meets the road—and it's the hardest thing to teach others. Your ads MUST communicate with a high level of power, precision, and passion to really have the impact you want. Most ads, unfortunately, are filled with PLATITUDES... words and phrases that are drearily commonplace and predictable, that lack power to evoke interest through overuse and repetition.

The problem with platitudes is that prospects EXPECT advertisers to use them. Do you really believe, literally, that Papa John's Pizza has "Better Ingredients?" or "Better Pizza?" Of course not. It's just puffery; the kind of stuff that we've all heard a zillion times, and therefore lacks power. We can do better.

Here are a couple of examples:

Platitude: *Our sales meetings are short, pleasant, and informative!*

PPP: *If you're a real glutton for punishment… or if you just don't like yourself very much, here's a fun activity to try: Call a bunch of replacement window companies and have them come over for an "in-home demonstration." Trust me—you'll get crushed.*

Platitude: *Vinyl windows are a poor investment because they will warp and bend with the weather, and fail prematurely.*

PPP: *Listen up; I want to keep you from making a HUGE mistake… which is buying and installing flimsy VINYL windows. Yea, they're super cheap… but come on! You're going to get exactly what you pay for. Vinyl windows <u>will</u> warp and bend with the weather, and fail before they're supposed to. They're a terrible investment.*

Don't get hung up on these examples debating me how long a sales presentation should be, or if vinyl of fiberglass windows are better— or even the aggressive tone. Those things are completely beside the point. The point is to use powerful, precise, and passionate language to engage and compel the listener.

It's Okay To Be Negative

Many business owners I deal with HATE the idea of bringing up negative points on radio ads. They say they'd rather remain positive, focus on the good things their company does, and avoid the appearance of disparaging the competition.

That's understandable, but only if you don't know how to use negativity the RIGHT WAY.

The underlying problem is that many prospects can't appreciate the GOOD YOU DO because they have no frame of reference for how badly things might go if they buy elsewhere. If you say you offer a "lifetime warranty" without explaining that other companies SAY they have a lifetime warranty, but they are frequently filled with loopholes, exceptions, and exclusions, the customer can't appreciate it. How would they? How could they possible know that?

Answer: you have to tell them.

This isn't about calling out specific competitors. It's not about bad-mouthing anyone. It's about giving prospects enough information to really UNDERSTAND and APPRECIATE how good you really are.

Here's an example: *If you've been needing to remodel your bathroom, but you've been putting it off because you're concerned about the mess it will cause, the hassle it will be, how much it will cost, and how long it will take… then I'd like to talk to you… We've all heard the horror stories of remodeling jobs that take way too long and go way over budget. I know your name isn't Trump and you don't want to be living with a sawdust infested remodeling crew for three solid months. That's why REBATH has innovated a process that streamlines everything and ensures that the job finishes WITHIN THREE DAYS, with a minimal amount of mess and inconvenience, and always with a fixed price that's guaranteed in writing before we start.*

Tell A Story

I recommend that a good portion of your ads use stories, anecdotes, and metaphors to make the points come alive and easy to understand. Not ALL of your ads, mind you… but a good portion of them. Stories engage listeners and make them want to hear the entire ad. Metaphors take something unfamiliar and compare it to something familiar so it's easier to understand.

Example 1: *What's the best word to describe your bathroom? Outdated? Let's try a little harder. How about "archaic, ancient, extremely experienced… or maybe just plain OLD. Let's put it this* *way... when Noah got off the arc and was looking for a nice, hot shower, he took it in YOUR bathroom. It's THAT OLD!*

Example 2: *The other day my wife and I were looking at pictures of our 19-year-old son from when he was a little kid. There's this one particular picture—you know what I'm talking about—where he was 7 years old and he just looked so small and cute and innocent. Now he's moved out of the house, he's bigger than I am, and can grow a full beard in a week. It seems like FOREVER ago that he was that sweet little boy in the picture. Think about it—12 years. That's a long time. (Ad goes on to talk about this company's 12-year warranties).*

Example 3: *I was a boy scout when I was a kid; we'd go camping a lot, and when we'd pack up to leave, our scout master would always remind us: "Leave it cleaner than you found it." We'd hunt for bottle caps, and pull tabs and bread ties—stuff we hadn't put there—but stuff we were willing to find and haul out so we could fulfill our duty to "leave it cleaner than we found it." And you know what? That philosophy has stuck with me.*

Example 4: *Let's say you needed heart surgery, and the doctor walked in with a sharp knife, some gauze, and a copy of "Heart Surgery for Dummies." Would you care? Of course you would! Installing siding on your home may not be life or death, but trust me: the last thing you want is a guy who just got hired 4 days ago and has no idea what he is doing. 75% of the efficiency and durability of your siding comes from proper installation.*

Warning: So-called experts will tell you that this type of advertising is wrong and bad and harmful. These experts are idiots and should not be paid any attention. To read a story about a time when I had to nuke a conference call full of experts, go to UnlimitedLeadFlow.com/book.

Think Authenticity

Nothing is worse in a radio commercial than "announcer voice." It's that voice that sounds like, well, an announcer is making it. What you want is a REAL voice. One with good inflection, emphasis, and tone. It should be conversational. Like you're talking to a friend. You want the listener to believe that the person voicing the ad really cares. The word you're looking for is AUTHENTIC. Like everything else, there are exceptions. Listen to the spots below and you'll find several conversational spots and one that is decidedly NOT.

Choose A Voice

I cannot overstate the importance of the voice you choose for your radio ads. One of the main reasons to be on the radio in the first place is that it allows you to convey EMOTION through the use of tone, pacing, pausing, timbre, and volume. Choosing the wrong voice can crush this important element before you ever start.

One major problem is what I call ANNOUNCER VOICE. It's very official. It's very "radio-like." And it sounds like garbage. There's no authenticity at all—just a professional announcer.

That doesn't mean you can't hire a professional announcer to get the job done. It just means that you should be going for warmth, friendly, authentic, and REAL.

Don't let the station produce your ad with whatever random voice talent they can find. You want to make sure it sounds exactly right.

Use the same voice for all your ads… you want your listeners to start to recognize the voice… like an old friend. I don't recommend using station DJs because you risk them leaving the station (or worse, getting fired for doing something stupid) and taking all the credibility you've built up with them with them.

I do recommend using the owner of the company UNLESS he or she can't read the ad and still sound authentic. It happens. I've seen dozens of otherwise-capable-and-confident business owners freeze when a microphone was shoved in their face. Not good. That being said, my biggest successes have been with business owner spokespeople. To read more about the pros and cons of starring in your own ads, go to UnlimitedLeadFlow.com/book and read the article there. (Article 8).

You want your voice to be distinctive without being obnoxious, weird, or cartoonish. You want the tone of the voice to match your identity, and mirror the way you feel about your business. Don't take this lightly—spend some time to GET IT RIGHT.

Professional voice talent and production will cost you anywhere from $150 to $300 per spot. That's dirt cheap, my friends. And it can usually be turned around within 1 to 2 days. That's fast, my friends.

Different Kinds of Offers

Since our goal is nurturing large quantities of prospects over long periods of time, there's no need to go crazy with offers in your ads. There are two kinds of offers you can make—information offers and incentive offers—and both have their place. Let's discuss:

> **Incentive Offers:** This is the most common kind of offer; one where you offer a discount (dollars or percent) or any other incentive for calling now. Incentive offers are the calling card of the direct response ad, so I don't really like to feature them prominently in identity-based radio ads. By "not prominently," I mean I don't like an entire ad to be dedicated to incentive offers. If you DO constantly promote various incentive offers as the main thrust of your message, it changes the relationship between you and the listener from "friendly, consultative voice" to "salesman." You become that annoying friend who only likes you because you might buy Amway from him.

> Of course the listener knows that you are selling something anyway, but if you spend TIME and ENERGY helping them understand your identity… and you do it with power, passion, and precision… and you tell stories and use metaphors… after a while you'll develop a bond with them. Not so with the constant "30% off sale" that's so common. Instead, tuck your monthly incentive offer at the end of the spot so it's more of an afterthought than a main focus. Those who are ready to buy will appreciate it; those who aren't won't be turned off by it. It is appropriate to feature incentive offers periodically—just don't overdo it.

> That being said, it can be very effective to mix in incentive offers for short bursts. I have a client that runs mostly identity-based

ads, but then runs a "Christmas In July" promotion every year for a full month that blows the doors off their sales. Then, in August, they go back to identity ads. When people know who you really are from your identity ads, they respond to incentive offers (in short bursts) more enthusiastically. They trust you.

We also use incentive offers extensively in our No-Risk Radio & TV program that is covered in the next chapter.

Information Offers: This is when you give the listener an offer to get additional information that can help facilitate his decision making process when it comes to the products you sell. Maybe you provide an "energy efficiency comparison guide" for windows. Or a report called "12 Major Gutter Protection Systems Compared." Or a "Kitchen Design Portfolio with pictures of 44 of the coolest jobs we've ever done." These kinds of offers nudge prospects who are close—BUT NOT YET READY—to action, which allows you to capture their contact info and proactively market to them in the future. You can make information offers that push people to your website, or to simply call you on the phone.

Okay, so there you have it—my top 9 points for writing radio ads. To see and hear examples of tons of ads that we've written and produced, go to UnlimitedLeadFlow.com/book and click on the link that's associated with this chapter. I know you'll enjoy them as much as our clients have enjoyed how well they've worked!

CHAPTER 42

Advertising on YouTube and Facebook

ARLIER I PROMISED I'd give a little bit of information about advertising on YouTube and Facebook... so here we go.

To be clear, just because YouTube and Facebook are social media platforms, advertising on them is NOT the same as social media marketing, which will covered in Section 6, near the end of this book. It's just plain old advertising—where you pay money to place an in a place where a lot of people will see it.

The first thing to ask yourself when considering these platforms is: Is your objective hunting or farming?

It's an important question because there is a lot of "noise" out there about advertising on social media sites, particularly Facebook. Most of that noise is coming from people talking about direct response lead generation—aka hunting. As in, "Facebook is a dirt cheap way to reach tons of people who can be targeted by geography, age, income... and more importantly, interests."

There is a lot of truth in that—both YouTube and Facebook are a fantastic way to target narrow groups of people. If I were to create a series of coffee mugs based on the album artwork of various classic rock bands, I could place ads on Facebook selectively targeting people who have explicitly said they are fans of bands like Van Halen, Rush, Pink

Floyd, and Led Zeppelin. That's a level of targeting that's unavailable pretty much anywhere else, and very much worth testing out.

But how many people are "fans" of kitchen remodeling, replacing a furnace, reroofing their house, or replacement windows? Not that many.

So for my clients, I like to use YouTube and Facebook as an extension of their radio and TV campaigns. In other words, I like to use them for farming—not for hunting. **Just think of YouTube and Facebook as alternative TV stations.**

The advantage is that these "stations" give you a tremendous amount of flexibility to segment by location, age, gender, and income.

When our clients advertise on YouTube, the first thing we do is run a list of the top producing zip codes for our client. A given area might have 100 zip codes—but if you can see that only 20 of them produce $100,000 or more in sales per year, that tells you a lot about where your best customers live.

Age is great because most of our clients cater to older customers. With a click of a mouse we can filter out the younger people. Boom— they're gone.

If we want to focus more on women, we can. Or men. Or both.

Then we can shoot for whatever level of income I feel best represents my customers. In many cases, we'll only target homeowners in our best zip codes with household incomes of $75,000+ or $100,000+.

Assuming you have a limited advertising budget, this kind of precision targeting allows you to focus your dollars on your most likely buyers, with very little waste.

It does cost more than TV to reach people with this kind of pinpointed targeting—but not by too much. We can usually expect CPMs to be in the $8 to $15 range. Compare that to the typical $4 to $8 CPM for radio and TV and you'll see it's pretty reasonable for that level of pinpoint targeting.

For YouTube, there are two major kinds of ads you can run. The first are called "Bumper Ads" by YouTube—they are 6-second ads that run before the person's chosen video plays. These ads are not skippable, but the tradeoff is they are very short. The idea is to hit the viewer with a hyper-specific identity point that will hopefully stick in their brain after seeing it a few times. Think of 6-second ads like billboards. Your job is to Wall Drug them.

Will people take action and actually click through to your website from these tiny, billboard-like ads?

Actually, yes. Here are some stats from a couple of recent campaigns:

- **Company Type:** HVAC

- **Ad Message:** We always send clean-cut technicians

- **Target Market:** Selected zip codes, men and women aged 35 to 64, income in the top 40%

- **Budget Spent:** $900

- **Impressions:** 169,000

- **CPM:** $5.32

- **Clicks:** 764

- **Cost Per Click:** $1.18

- **Company Type:** Bathroom Remodeling

- **Ad Message:** Master craftsmen, get a free estimate

- **Target Market:** Selected zip codes, men and women aged 35 to 64, income in the top 40%

- **Budget Spent:** $1,870

- **Impressions:** 260,000

- **CPM:** $7.19

- **Clicks:** 282

- **Cost Per Click:** $6.63

As you can see, the CPMs are actually pretty darn good, and the number of people who have clicked through is pretty impressive. It's easy to look at these two sets of data and assume that the bathroom remodeling company is doing poorly because they are paying $6.63 per click while the HVAC company is only paying $1.18 per click.

This is the last chapter of the book! Use what you've learned to come up with a more accurate thought.

First of all, how often do you use an HVAC company versus how often do you remodel your bathroom? There's a reason a lot more people click through—it's a more frequently used service.

Next, if you were the owner of the bathroom remodeling company, you would want to compare your stats against your other advertising options (and results), not against stats from a company in another industry!

If this bathroom company spent that same $1,870 on Fox TV, they would be paying $4.61 CPM, which is lower than the $7.19 on YouTube. But here are the differences:

- The Fox TV ad will theoretically be seen by 405,000 people, more than the 260,000 on YouTube.

- BUT, we know that nearly ALL 260,000 YouTube viewers actually saw the ad, because they clicked on a video right before the ad started playing, and only had to watch for 6 seconds to get to their video.

- The Fox TV viewers may have gone to the bathroom, changed channels, or looked at their cell phone instead of watching the commercial.

- The YouTube viewers were a precise geographic and demographic match for this company; The Fox viewers were literally all over the place in terms of location and demographics.

- The Fox viewers did not even have an option to click and find out more. They had to put more effort into calling a phone number or finding the company online themselves.

This isn't to say that YouTube is better or worse than Fox TV. This is to point out that there are definite advantages that are worth considering.

The other kind of ad you can buy on YouTube is 30-second ads, which is a bit of a misnomer, because they can actually be much longer than 30 seconds. These are the ads that show up before a video that are skippable by the viewer after 5 seconds—you know, you can skip this ad in 5, 4, 3, 2… 1.

The great thing about these ads is that you only get charged by YouTube if the viewer watches the video for at least 30 seconds. If they choose to skip after 5 or 10 or 29 seconds, you don't get charged.

- **Company Type:** HVAC
- **Ad Message:** You'll feel safe and comfortable around our technicians
- **Target Market:** Selected zip codes, men and women aged 35 to 64, income in the top 40%
- **Budget Spent:** $955
- **Impressions:** 59,000
- **CPM:** $16.19
- **Clicks:** 41
- **Cost Per Click:** $23.29

Your initial reaction to this might be, "why would I spend $16.19 CPM for a 30-second ad when I could spend $5.32 for a 6-second bumper ad?" That's not a terrible question, and if you only had a little money to spend on one thing, you would probably be totally justified in only buying the 6-second ads.

But also remember to compare these results to other TV advertising. Now we are almost 4 times more expensive than Fox TV… but did you catch what the major difference is? The 59,000 people who watched our ad on YouTube actually watched the entire 30 second ad—even when they had every opportunity in the world to skip it! Then remember that these are precisely targeted people, both geographically and demographically. That's definitely worth a premium.

I won't go into as much detail on Facebook advertising; suffice it to say that the mechanics—as well as the advantages—are very similar to YouTube, even though they offer some different kinds of ad formats.

They point of this chapter is not to exhaustively cover all the details of YouTube and Facebook Advertising, but rather, to open your eyes and your mind to additional options to reach your target market.

Once you increase your radio and TV budget to at least 30% of your total advertising budget, I recommend spending at least 10% of that 30%+ on YouTube or Facebook advertising. Again, think of them like alternative TV stations, and make them a part of your advertising mix.

CHAPTER 43
No-Risk Radio & TV

Now that we've covered media advertising in detail, I want to reveal what might be a secret weapon for some companies. I want to emphasize *some* companies because there are a range of factors used to determine whether or not a given company is qualified to participate. I'll cover those factors momentarily.

If you read the chapter on No-Risk PPC with interest, you'll like this chapter, too. I'm going to show you a way to participate in radio and TV lead generation with little risk... or in many cases, *no risk at all.*

We call it No-Risk Radio & TV.

That means we can generate leads for you on radio and TV as follows:

- No money required by you up front; we use *our* money to place ads on your behalf.

- We guarantee a fixed cost per lead of between $100 and $300 each (depends on market conditions).

- We handle all the ad writing, production, and placement.

- The leads come to you directly, in real time, by phone or email notification.

- The leads are 100% exclusive—they only go to you, and no competitors.

- You pay for the leads you receive twice a month.

- There are no contracts; if you don't like it, you can quit.

If that sounds like a "Vegas jackpot" kind of deal, it is.

Let me explain how we do it:

We commit to purchasing large blocks of highly discounted airtime on many of the biggest radio and TV networks in the country. That includes radio networks like Cumulus, Entercom, iHeartMedia, CBS Radio, and others… plus all the major TV networks. By highly discounted I mean 50% to 80% off regular prices. And I don't mean discounts off the inflated "rate card" prices; I mean 50% to 80% less than the best prices we can negotiate using the tactics used in the previous chapters.

The networks are willing to sell us large blocks at a huge discount for two major reasons:

First, it gives them a large guaranteed sale—in advance—on an annual basis. Then it becomes *our* problem to go out and find advertisers to fill the space. We do this by selling space to companies in all kinds of industries, not just home improvement and home services. We work with advertisers in diverse industries such as home alarm systems, business opportunities, mortgage companies, legal, insurance, medical devices and more.

Second, we give the networks' stations the flexibility to run our spots at times that are best for them—and they have the right to refuse our spots if they have better offers from other higher-paying advertisers at any given time.

Let me give you an example:

Let's say a news talk station in your market is averaging $9 CPM across all advertisers during its morning drive daypart. That means that some advertisers might be paying as little as $5 CPM (the ones who negotiate like a pro using the principles in the previous chapters) and as much as $20 CPM from advertisers who don't know jack squat about negotiating media.

We will offer to pay that local station $2 CPM based on our nationals contract with their network. If they have open inventory, they'll accept our offer and run the ad. That's a 60% discount off the BEST prices on the station. If their inventory is a little tighter, they might counteroffer $3 or $4 CPM—still a good price.

This type of negotiation is not available to you, because you don't have the large commitment annual contact with the national networks like we do. If you called a station and said "We'll pay you $2 CPM if you have open space," they will simply say "NO."

Now here's the downside:

If the inventory on that station in our example is tight, they don't have to sell us the discounted spot. They can refuse it, and the spot won't run. In many cases, they will accept the order, but if better offers come in at the last minute, they'll *bump our ad* in favor of the higher-priced advertiser. And even if they do run our spots, they may only run a very limited number of them.

The result is that **we sacrifice consistency and frequency for a lower price.**

For this reason, we only use No-Risk Radio & TV for direct response campaigns—not identity or brand-building.

Instead of running ads that are full of identity points that educate the market and brand our clients over time, we run ads that have a very specific offer—usually an exceptionally good offer—and we usually don't even mention the advertiser's name.

The leads that come in are delivered in real-time on a fixed-cost, per-lead basis, with lead costs ranging from $100 to $300, depending on the type of product and the market. The lead costs are always determined up front so there is no guesswork.

The reason we don't use the clients name is a tracking issue: If I run an ad that mentions your company name 6 times, a good percentage of people who respond will do so by going to your website (either directly or via Google search), and we lose the ability to track that lead. If we can't track the lead, we can't sell the leads to you on a per-lead basis, and the program won't work.

So instead, we only mention you company name zero or one times and provide either a special tracking phone number (not your normal phone number) or a web address that takes people to a special landing page that we create. Either way, we can then track the leads and accurately charge you for the leads that come in.

We ask our No-Risk Radio & TV clients to commit to a minimum of 50 leads per month—but because of the uncertainty of availability discussed above, in some cases we may deliver fewer than that.

The inability to run identity-based, branding advertisements is why none (read: ZERO) of our largest clients use our No-Risk Radio & TV for lead generation. The two key factors in long-term business-building advertising—consistency and frequency—are not available. If you are trying to build a relationship with an audience over a long period of time, it is imperative that you reliably talk to them over and over and over again. You can't do that with No-Risk.

Also, for branding, it's important to attach your name to your identity points. Over time, the dollars you spend tattooing your name and identity into peoples' brains is worth something. Think about it: if you spend $1MM to $5MM a year for 10 straight years advertising your name and identity in the marketplace, what percentage of people are going to know who you are? How many phone calls and Google searches will you get just because people already know to call you when they need what you sell? The answer is a lot—a whole lot.

So, then... who can/should use No-Risk Radio & TV for lead generation?

- **Smaller Companies:** Our No-Risk program is a good way to generate a lot of high quality, low-cost leads for companies who are just starting out, or for ones that are stuck in the mud and could use a boost. In these cases, we still recommend that you begin to allocate a portion of your advertising budget to REGULAR identity-based radio and/or TV. At the very least, allocate a portion of the profits generated from No-Risk advertising into regular identity-advertising.

- **Augment Regular Leads:** Larger and more established companies can also use our No-Risk program as a way to augment their regular lead flow. In these cases, you can think of these leads like Home Advisor or Angie's List leads… in the sense that the person responding to the ad was responding to <u>an offer</u> and <u>not your company</u> specifically. But unlike Home Advisor and Angie's List, your No-Risk leads come directly to you and to none of your competitors, which is why they are a little more expensive and a lot more valuable.

- **Special Offers:** One of the requirements of the No-Risk program is that you must have a really good offer—usually one that has to do with a price promotion. The idea is to get the phone to ring, then have your sales people sell and upsell. That's not a good fit for all companies… if not, then No-Risk probably isn't a good fit.

Bottom line, No-Risk Radio & TV can be a great way to generate a lot of high quality, low-cost leads. If you want more information, or if you'd like to discuss if it's appropriate for your situation or not—and to read some FAQs about the program, just go to our website at UnlimitedLeadFlow.com/book.

SECTION 6
Other Marketing Fundamentals

F OR PRACTICAL PURPOSES, this book is done. You have the formula, and you have enough details to get you going. Execute on this formula and you will thrive.

That being said, there are still many, many other marketing topics that are important to building a solid foundation for your business. Remember, the first thing we talked about in this book is the $10MM Mindset, and specifically, chapter 5 "Demanding Excellence." If you truly demand excellence, then you'll want to make sure that you master multiple other things that I am going to cover in this section.

This section is not comprehensive—there are plenty of other topics that could be covered as well. But there is only so much space in a book, and you've got a business to tend to. So in this last section, I'll cover a few important topics that I sincerely hope will benefit you.

CHAPTER 44
Handle Your Leads Properly

M Y MOTHER KILLED every single houseplant she ever owned. She was a notorious murderer of all things foliage. If killing plants was a crime, she'd be wanted in seven states for mass herbicide.

When she'd go to the local garden center to choose a new "victim," all the plants would run and hide. They knew what awaited should she pick them.

My mom swears it wasn't her fault her plants always died. She'd blame it on the dry air. Or a bad batch of fertilizer. Or the store from which she bought the plant.

In her mind, she was a dyed-in-the-wool green thumb—a plant connoisseur fit for the cover of *Better Homes and Gardens*. There was just NO WAY it was her fault.

Sometimes it's hard to see our shortcomings. Right, mom?

Odds are, the way you handle leads is similar to how my mom treats plants.

You think you're awesome at answering your phone. You think you follow up with your leads like gangbusters. You think you do enough to nurture them from a seedling (a prospect) to a fully blossomed Tiger lily (a sale).

But here's the harsh reality: You're probably nowhere near as great as you perceive.

I know what you're thinking: *"Rich, you don't know my company from Adam. How do you have the nerve to say I'm not handling leads properly?"*

There are a few reasons I can say this with bet-my-kids'-college-funds confidence.

First, you're reading this book. This tells me you want to make more sales. And one of the best ways to get more sales is having a well-oiled system for handling leads.

Second, I've been in the contractor-marketing game a *LOOONNNGGG* time. I've worked with hundreds and hundreds of remodelers, builders, and contractors. And if there's one common theme among them, it's how disastrously they manage their leads. (I'll show you some real-word examples in a minute that'll make you shake your head).

Third, my company, Unlimited Lead Flow, began our No-Risk Pay Per Click program in 2016. (See Chapter 28: PPC – Problems, Difficulties… And *Solutions*). Since we charge clients by the lead, we monitor and transcribe their incoming phone calls and online chats. This direct line into how contractors handle their leads has been an eye-opening experience. It's blown me away seeing how badly even highly successful companies botch their leads.

If you remain unconvinced that you need to clean up your lead-handling protocols, that's okay. You COULD be one of the few companies that does do EVERYTHING right. But I strongly suggest you read this chapter anyway. It never hurts to make 100% sure you're maximizing your lead-to-sales ratios.

Why Speedy Lead Follow Up Matters, And How To Actually Pull It Off

Question: At what moment are your prospects MOST in the mood to buy?

Believe it or not, it's <u>not</u> during the sales meeting.

It's when they first pick up the phone to call you, or fill out a form online to request information.

Think about it for a second: At that precise moment, something in their brain said, "I have enough pain with my current situation that I'll risk calling a stranger and give them a chance to SELL me something to fix my problem." That's a big deal.

At that moment, the prospect WANTS you to convince them to buy from you. Some of them will even be on their proverbial hands and knees, begging you to tell them why you're the right person to solve their issue.

Even though this sounds like the ideal situation for landing a sale, most contractors make a COLOSSAL mistake during this moment of truth: Failure to follow up with leads fast enough.

Now, if you're one of the few companies that manages to answer every single phone call you get, you don't need to worry about this.

But the vast majority of contractors do not answer all of their phone calls. And for the calls they miss, they are way too slow in following up.

What's "too slow" to follow up with a lead? Anything more than five minutes.

Yes, really. This goes for following up with online-form submissions, too.

You might think someone's a jerk for not waiting more than five minutes for you to get back to them. I mean, you're up to your eyeballs in work! How the heck can you be expected to field every single call you get?

But here's the thing. While YOU are busy, the PROSPECT who called you has a problem. One that—in their eyes—can't wait.

While you may be the best of the best in your area, guess what? Literally dozens of other contractors are in the vicinity. A prospect WILL move on to the next company—and you'll have lost that lead FOREVER—if you don't follow up with them IMMEDIATELY.

This isn't just me shamelessly trying to strike fear in you. TONS of studies and statistics prove that it pays to **STRIKE WHILE THE IRON IS HOT.**

Speed Counts: The Geniuses At Harvard Back Me Up

In 2007, *Harvard Business Review* and MITperformed different studies on lead response. They studied tens of thousands of leads across different industries.

Here are the shocking results:

- For inquires submitted on the web, <u>78% of sales go to the first company to respond</u>.

- The likelihood of contacting a prospect <u>decreases by a factor of 100 TIMES</u> from five minutes to 30 minutes after they become a lead. ONE HUNDRED TIMES!

- The qualification rate of a lead <u>decreases 21 times</u> from the five-minute mark to the 30-minute mark. In other words, you're 21 times less likely to get that lead if you wait 30 minutes or more to follow up.

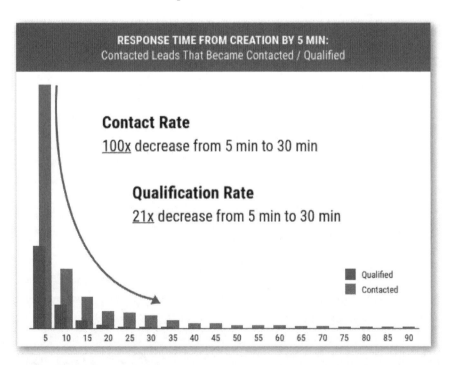

Bottom line: Your spellbinding advertising, awesome website, and killer Google rankings mean jack squat if you wait too long to follow up with your leads.

And these studies were done in 2007! Remember that prehistoric time? Mobile devices weren't quite yet ubiquitous. People didn't have a million and one apps and avenues contact companies instantly. And humanity's collective attention span was still longer than eight seconds.

You can bet that if these studies were done today, the results would be even more dire for contractors who don't follow up within five minutes.

If you think following up with leads within five minutes is Mission: Impossible, you're really going to flip at what I'm about to say…

Five Minutes Is TOO Long; Shoot For 10 Seconds

Not 15 seconds. Not 22 seconds. Not 10.5 seconds. TEN.

Why is 10 the magic number? Because that's the time it takes for someone to hang up after leaving you a voicemail, scroll down the search engine page to the next company, and start dialing *their* phone number. My advice: Don't even give leads a CHANCE to call someone else.

With the proper follow-up system—which I'll reveal in the next section of this chapter—10 seconds is more than doable.

And if you <u>can</u> do it, why <u>wouldn't</u> you?

3 Reasons Leads Shrivel Up And Die If You Don't Reach Out Instantly

1. **Quick-Draw Competitors:** If you wait 11 minutes to call a web lead, you've given your competitors an 11-minute head start. Like I mentioned a second ago, the internet gives instant access to thousands of options—you can bet your prospect has reached out to others besides you.

2. **Avalanche!:** This is first cousin to "quick-draw competitors" above; not only have others reached your prospect first,

there's a pretty good chance the prospect has actually been overwhelmed by TOO MANY competitors reaching out to them. This is particularly true for prospects who have unwittingly filled out an online form that they didn't realize was going to be converted into a "lead" and distributed to the 77 highest bidders (See Chapter 32: Third-Party Lead Sources for the dirty details about lead aggregators). If your return phone call comes 22 minutes and 13 competitor calls after the fact—you're invisible.

3. **The Law of 9,344:** Even if the prospect doesn't call 5 of your competitors, they're still going to be overwhelmed by life. I figure that most people have approximately 9,344 things going on in their lives… from the extremely mundane (e.g., "Where are my car keys?"; "Look at all this junk mail!") to the extraordinarily important (e.g., "Mom fell and broke her hip"; "My daughter just got an art scholarship"). If you don't capture them IN THE MOMENT, mentally, they'll shift gears (attention) rapidly to something else. They'll forget about you when they finally do remember that they need remodeling work (More on this in a minute).

Here Are The Steps To A Fast & Effective Lead Follow-Up Program:

1. **Make Instant Follow Up Your Culture:** Let everyone in your company know that the most important person in your company is the prospect who just filled out the form or called in. Let them know that fresh prospects are more important than current customers, current prospects, sales meetings, installing stuff, accounting stuff, or any other stuff. Weave this philosophy into the fabric of your culture and make sure it sticks. If that sounds tough, try waiting 11 minutes to follow up your leads and see how tough life gets.

2. **Use Technology:** Get off your dinosaur and utilize computer automation to detect and route leads instantly to the right person on your team (more on who that should be below).

Software like MarketSharp is inexpensive and BONEHEAD-PROOF—there's no excuse for not using it. You can instantly route leads via email, phone, text message, or courier pigeon (not really), and you can also instantly reply to the prospect by those same means. Not doing this is just proof that you hate yourself, your customers, and your business.

3. **Designate A Follow-Up Person:** I'm not a fan of distributed duties—like having "whoever is available" handle critical tasks like talking to fresh prospects. The fact is that whoever does talk to your prospects is going to have a profound impact on whether or not they ultimately buy or not. You simply cannot afford to have the wrong person taking that call. We'll cover who it should be and what they should say in detail in the section below. *Spoiler alert:* It should be a capable, high-caliber sales person.

4. **Get A Reliable 24/7 Live Answering Service:** A live receptionist is best (see #3). But make sure your phone system has a rollover call center that IMMEDIATELY picks up if the main receptionist does not pick up within three rings. This is nonnegotiable. Otherwise, you're missing calls and losing sales. PERIOD. I wholeheartedly recommend AnswerConnect. They provide turnkey phone-answering solutions, so you NEVER have to worry about missing a call from a lead again. Their services are completely customizable for your specific needs. Whether you want them to take calls and answer messages—or even set appointments themselves (don't worry, they are 100% reliable, professional, and qualified)—they can help you.

If You Think You're Already Doing Well…*Trust Me, You're Not.*

Most contractors philosophically agree with me on the points above, even if they're unwilling to put the time and effort into actually fixing the problem. The most common objections are "It's hard to manage a large number of leads that way" and "We simply don't have the time and/or manpower to do this."

Hey, it's your leads, your life, and your business. The fact you don't like that this is the best way to handle leads is irrelevant. The solution still remains the same: If you don't make <u>instant follow-up</u> part of the fabric of your company's culture (#1 above), you lose.

I'll show you an example from my client files.

This client was spending $60,000 a month to generate leads via radio and TV for four offices. The ads directed prospects to an online landing page, where they could either fill out a form or call a phone number.

About 90% of the prospects filled out the online form to become a lead, leaving about 10% who called the phone number instead.

For the leads who called, we discovered a major problem. The client had their receptionist answer the phone. She would take the calls on her office phone, and have calls rolled over to her cell phone when she was out of the office.

On the surface, that's a good thing—like I said, you want a person dedicated to answering calls from leads. But this client did not have an answering service. As a result, all 10 calls the client received in the first month of the campaign went unanswered.

Oops!

Here's a look at their call report for that period (identifying info is blurred out):

I feel especially bad for poor Louie—the dude called four times with no answer! He was practically begging our client to take his money.

Do you think Louie moved on after that fourth unanswered call? Gee, I wonder…

Let's face it: Receptionists sometimes get overwhelmingly busy. They may not be able to take every single phone call (Or in this case, any phone call). You see how having a reliable answering service could have solved this client's problem, right? They could have had seven additional leads and the possibility of adding tens of thousands of dollars in sales for the month. All by simply having an answering service that costs a dollar or two per call.

You might be thinking, *"I'm not THAT terrible at answering the phone, Rich."*

Maybe not. But go back to the beginning of this chapter where I talk about my mom, the mass plant murderer. And then consider this: Just ONE extra sale from an answering service provides a ridiculously high return on investment for contractors. **When your average sale per project is $8K, $15K, or $20K+, paying $150- $500 per month for an answering service is peanuts.** It's downright dumb NOT to do this.

But wait, this story gets worse.

Remember the 90% of leads that came in from an online form? Everything about their lead follow up from those leads was reprehensible. There was no instant call back. There was no automatic email sent out. We even discovered at one point that they FORGOT to input three weeks' of leads into their system.

Now imagine an image of me huddled in a corner crying.

No, That Lead Is Not A Crack Head…

Unanswered calls and un-followed-up-on web submissions are just one problem we see regularly. Another major issue is companies squander perfectly good leads because they think/assume that certain leads suck.

During one of the first billing periods for a window company's No-Risk radio campaign, we generated 17 phone calls for them. Out of those 17 calls, the client claimed only *seven* of those were qualified leads.

Here's a list of the phone calls the client sent me, and their reason why some of them weren't leads:

Here are the results from the calls we received. I have a total of 17. With 7 qualified leads

Name	Status	Note		Rep	Reason
Darell	Pending		17-Sep	Jeff	qualified
Scott	Pending		7-Sep	John	qualified
Grayline	Pending		17-Sep	Jeff	qualified
Frank	Dispute			John	Less than 3 window lead
Bob	Dispute			John	Less than 3 windows and not homeowner
Caroln	SOLD	Financing		Jeff	qualified
David	Dispute	Only a phone call		Jnet	We don't sell the brand of window they want
Roscoe	SOLD			Jeff	qualified
Billy	SOLD		$2,000.00	John	qualified
Scott	Dispute			Jnet	wrong state
Gavin	Dispute	Appointment 9/19		Jeff	phone disconnected
Ron	Dispute	not homeowner		Jeff	one window
Robert	Dispute			John	Single Picture Window
Todd	Dispute			Jeff	2 windows
Kathy	Dispute			Jnet	storm windows
Hollace	Pending	Stood up		Jeff	Crack house
Yvonne	Dispute			Jnet	wrong state

Knowing what I know about how badly contractors sometimes botch perfectly good leads, I decided to play detective. Since we track all of a No-Risk Radio client's leads in our system, I donned my Sherlock Holmes hat, stuck my Calabash pipe in my mouth, and called some of these "non-leads" myself.

The results were as I expected.

See that guy Gavin on the list? I called him up to see if the phone was actually disconnected or not. I couldn't fathom that somebody would hear a radio ad, call to set an appointment, then give a bad number. Guess what? It was not a bad number. Gavin answered my call on the first ring. (Maybe he should switch careers and be a receptionist at a remodeling company!).

I told him I was doing a follow-up customer service call, and that there was a note in my system that we couldn't get in touch with him because his phone was disconnected. He told me that he had set an appointment when he first called in (via the call center). Our client called him back when he was at work, so he asked them if they could call back later that night.

Gavin said nobody ever called back and nobody ever came. I have no idea how or why my client marked the call "disconnected." It should have been marked "head up our butts."

I asked Gavin if he would still give "us" (i.e., my client) a shot. My phone call came about 10 days after the original lead (not 10 seconds lol!), so Gavin told me how he had already purchased windows from somebody else. Twelve windows, to be exact. At $1,100 each.

For real.

But let's talk about the one you really want to hear about on this list: **the "crack house."**

I called Hollace, who purportedly runs/live at/smokes crack at the crack house. I once again posed as a customer representative doing follow-up at my client's company.

When Hollace answered, he asked me if I was calling because I needed a fix.

Just kidding. He was actually quite upset because nobody showed up for the appointment he had set with my client. He explained that he was in the process of FLIPPING THE HOUSE and so he had set the appointment for a time he knew he could be there. He showed up at the appointed hour, waited for 15 minutes, then left when nobody came. He had places to be and people to see. He was *pissed*.

When I confronted my client with this information, they checked their notes and admitted they had been "about a half hour late" for the appointment. But when they arrived and saw the house was torn up and uninhabited—and not in a great part of town—they noted "crack house" in their notes and promptly forgot all about this prospect.

Fortunately, when I had Hollace on the phone I had apologized profusely and practically begged him for a second chance. He reluctantly agreed, so my client was able to get back out there and sell the job.

Bad leads, my a$$.

Maybe you think I cherry picked this story. You think that you'd never treat your leads like that. Unfortunately, this story isn't even close to cherry picked. Almost every client we deal with is throwing away money by poor lead handling.

We were struggling to get a good cost per lead for a major gutter protection company with our No Risk PPC program. We double checked everything—ads, landing pages, keywords, bids, budgets—everything. Everything appeared to be perfect, yet lead costs were running 20% to 30% higher than they should have.

Then we discovered that they were routing all phone calls through a phone system that had an auto-attendant. You know—"push 1 for sales, 2 for customer service, 3 for accounting" and so forth. Fully 35% of the callers were hanging up when they got a computer instead of a human on the phone. Think about that: THIRTY-FIVE PERCENT were hanging up!

But the story gets worse!

This company was operating 13 offices across the country, and spending MILLIONS on advertising—the majority of which we had nothing to do with. Every single call they generated via phone was being routed through that auto-attendant torture chamber. They were losing at least 30% of all leads accords all advertising methods.

But the story gets worse!

When we brought this to the CEO's attention, he argued with us about it! He said that's how they'd always done it, and it worked just fine, thank you. He reasoned that if somebody wasn't patient enough to push the right button on the auto-attendant, then they weren't a serious prospect in the first place. I have no words for how insane this reasoning is.

We told him that if we couldn't route OUR calls (for our No-Risk PPC and Radio) through a live human answering service, we were done. Feel free to spend YOUR money generating calls that hang up, but I'm not doing that with my money.

Respect your leads! All of them! They cost a ton of money!

This is why we now explicitly check how our No-Risk leads are going to be handled, and we insist that a 24-hour call center be in place to handle leads anytime, day or night. We will never assume that because a company is big that they "must know what they are doing." These didn't. Most don't.

This is also why we have extremely strict rules about what "counts" as a lead in our No-Risk Lead Generation programs. If the person gives their name and contact information, that's a lead—period. It's *your* job to follow-up in a timely manner and have a sales staff that can squeeze water out of a rock if necessary. Our strict rules force our customers to treat each and every lead with respect.

Some of our prospective clients take issue with our rules for counting leads. Honestly, these are the kind of people I want nothing to do with—and are generally the kinds of companies who are stuck for a reason. If you can't even respect your own leads that you are paying your own good money to generate, how could you possibly be expected to tread leads that somebody else is paying for with respect?

One last plea—treat all your leads with respect!

Okay, Now What To Say When You DO Answer The Phone

Assuming you actually answer your phone in a timely manner (or follow up web leads quickly), we need to talk about how to treat them when you get them on the phone.

Most contractors look at a prospect's first phone call as a strictly transactional situation. The person calling in wants to set an appointment... and you've got a person on your end of the phone to handle the logistics of setting that appointment. They typically gather normal contact information, confirm a time for the meeting, and hang up.

That's a good start.

You need to remember that the vast majority of your prospects are <u>scared to death</u> when they call you. They've just taken a huge risk to call an unknown company in an industry with a bad reputation to come to their house for an obvious selling situation.

You need to read that sentence again.

They've just taken a <u>huge risk</u> to call an <u>unknown company</u> in an <u>industry with a bad reputation</u> to come to their house for an <u>obvious selling situation</u>.

Really, truly think about that. The public at large views remodeling companies in the same light as lawyers and used-car salesmen. When someone calls you inquiring about your services, they are oftentimes already bracing themselves for a bad experience.

That's why your receptionist needs to be more than an appointment setter. They have to put the potential client at ease, reinforce the idea that they called the right company, and set expectations about what is going to happen during the appointment.

Let's look at the three steps to accomplish this:

Step #1: Setting The Prospect At Ease

Right off the bat, you want to make prospects feel comfortable. To chip away at that barrier they've built around themselves because they just know FOR SURE they're in for a bad time because they called a remodeler.

So you appointment setter's first job is to be FRIENDLY. This sounds obvious. Yet most receptionists have a tone in their voice that says, *"Why are you bothering me?"* when they pick up the phone. Don't think prospects who call you don't notice—they absolutely do.

You want your appointment setter to answer the phone with (natural-sounding) enthusiasm. Spunk. Verve. Like the prospect calling just made their day.

Next, your appointment setter needs to be conversational. As if they're talking to a friend about replacing their windows... not like a monotone robot with the emotional range of The Terminator.

Lastly, use SOFT language. Soft language isn't threatening because it doesn't sound like it's trying to sell anything.

Soft language says *"When were you thinking you might want to replace your windows?"* instead of *"When are going to replace your windows?"*

Soft language says *"Did you have a budget range in mind?"* instead of *"What's your budget?"*

Less abruptness; more smoothness. The difference is subtle, but tangible.

My suggestion: Hire naturally friendly people with warm, inviting voices. You don't want to have to train this into people.

Step #2: Reassuring The Prospect

The next thing you want to do is make the prospect feel confident that calling you was the right choice. The easiest way to do this is by having and communicating a powerful, precise IDENTITY.

Write a little script that your receptionist will READ (i.e., not ad lib) that lets people know who you are, why you're different and better than others, and what they can expect when doing business with you.

Here's an example:

Appointment Setter: How much do you know about Revive Remodeling?

Prospect: Uh, not a lot, really. I just found you on the internet.

Appointment Setter: Okay, great—then you must have seen where it says, "If you're persnickety, fussy, demanding, and hard to please... then we're the right remodeler for you." Do you remember that?

Prospect: (laughs a little) Yeah, actually I did see that. That's why I called!

Appointment Setter: Well, it's true. When it comes to remodeling, it's all about the details—and we're obsessed with them. We go above and beyond the call of duty to make sure that everything is always done exactly right every time... with no exceptions. We're basically OCD. We're not the fastest remodeler around... and we're not the cheapest. But according to our clients... they say we're the best.

We've already talked at length earlier in this book about identity. You've got to develop yours, and then put it into all your marketing. From your ads to your website to your brochures to your phone script. And make sure your appointment setter puts some PASSION behind those words!

When a prospect hears that phone script, they breathe a sigh of relief. They feel like they're talking to somebody special. Somebody who cares and *will take care* of them. They don't feel like you're "just another remodeler." This is the beginning of increasing your closing ratios.

Step #3: Setting Expectations

Finally, you've got to let the prospect know what to expect at the appointment.

More specifically, I recommend setting a clear expectation that you WILL NOT be putting any sales pressure on them during the appointment. I also recommend setting time expectations.

Here's a little script:

Appointment Setter: Mrs. Johnson, I appreciate you calling Revive Remodeling today. We're really looking forward to seeing you on Thursday at seven. I want to be clear up front: When we come to your home, we're coming to help you make the best remodeling decision possible for your situation. If you end up going with us, we'd be honored to have your business. But even if we discover that it's not a great fit—that's okay, too. We're not into high pressure-sales. We don't twist arms. Our meetings typically run about an hour to an hour and a half, depending on how many questions you have. At the end of that time together, it will be completely up to you what you want to do next. Our only goal is to help you make the right choice for YOU.

Some people read all these scripts and think that they'll take too long. Or your receptionist won't read them. Or that they won't have time because there are too many calls coming in.

Nonsense.

Don't let the 5% of the time you're too busy to handle calls this way be an excuse to NOT do it the other 95% of the time. Call overflow is why you invest in a reliable answering service, like I mentioned above.

With regards to this script, training and role-playing will get your people up to speed in a matter of just a day or two. I've found that small rewards such as restaurant gift cards can be very effective in gaining employee compliance.

Don't discount this small adjustment out of hand. Once you recognize that the moment of truth—the most important point of contact—is the initial phone call, you'll be able to capitalize by following these simple suggestions.

What To Do With Prospects Who Drag Their Heels (The Law Of 9,344)

I'm not sure you noticed... I've kind of made a big deal about instant follow-up with leads in this chapter.

Here's the part where I add a big old "BUT."

It's true that many leads <u>do</u> shrivel up and die if you don't call them back immediately... **BUT** not all of them.

These leads are in hibernation. If you proactively—and consistently—poke them during their slumber, they'll eventually wake up and give you their business.

A second ago, I mentioned the Law Of 9,344. A prospect has so many things on their plate (9,344, to be not so exact) that you're wiped from their memories the instant after they leave you a voicemail. When they eventually <u>do</u> get around to their remodeling project, they'll have forgotten all about you and go with someone else.

But not if you incessantly follow up with them the moment they contact you.

Need proof?

Picture this...

Several years ago, I was driving home from work trying to figure out what to do with my kids.

It was the end of October—that wretched time of year when it starts getting cold outside and dark at 5:30pm. For my and my wife's sanity, I wanted to find something to keep our then-still-young kids occupied in the evenings.

Then the proverbial lightbulb popped on: Lifetime Fitness.

It's a gargantuan family friendly fitness center that has an AWESOME kids play place—tons of toys, computers, video games, arts & crafts, and sports equipment. We had been a member a few years before and my kids loved it. We had only quit because the drive was a bit too far, and we had gotten a little burned out on it. But now, three years later, I was ready to give it another try.

I pulled a U-turn at the next stoplight and drove straight there.

When I entered the facility, I found a 20-something membership-salesman named Jason. He seemed genuinely enthusiastic and answered all of my questions. He told me that he would honor our previous membership rate of $140 a month. That's way cheaper than hiring a babysitter, so I was definitely interested.

I told Jason I needed to go home and talk it over with my wife. He gave me his card and thanked me for coming in.

The next day, my wife told me some guy named Jason called from Lifetime Fitness while I was at work. I had forgotten to discuss the membership with my wife the previous night (The Law Of 9,344 strikes!); but she agreed that joining again sounded like a good way to keep the kids occupied a couple times a week.

The following day, Saturday, I was taking my family to lunch when my cell phone rang. It was Jason. He wanted to know if I had discussed a membership with my wife. I said, "Jason, thanks for calling. But it's really not a good time to talk right now. I am literally backing my car out of my garage right now with my entire family in it on our way to lunch. Is there any way you could call back later?" The Law Of 9,344 strikes again!

Jason agreed, and I zoomed away to lunch with my family.

Fast-forward three months: I suddenly realized I'd never gotten around to joining Lifetime Fitness. It had completely slipped my mind. By that time, my kids were up to their ears in basketball games, cub scouts, and a hundred other things. I mentioned the Lifetime Fitness membership to my wife, who shrugged it off. Oh well, maybe next fall.

Here's the important part to you...

Jason never called back after that day I took my family to lunch. He likely figured I was brushing him off. So he gave up after that second time he called.

That's too bad for old Jason. It's not that I was brushing him off—I was genuinely interested in a membership and was THIS close to joining. I simply had—you guessed it—9,344 things going on in my life. Had Jason called a few more times, I'm positive I would have signed my family up. All Jason had to do was keep in front of my face through regular follow up and catch me at that moment when I had the time to talk.

Moral of this story: Don't assume that because leads won't talk to you that they're not interested in buying what you're selling.

As counter-intuitive as that sounds, it's true.

For proof, here are some stats from an Inside Sales.com study (this isn't specific to home improvement and remodeling sales, but it paints a clear enough picture):

- 38% of sales reps will attempt to call a prospect just ONE TIME
- 28% will try twice
- 11% stick it out for three calls
- 8% will try four times
- 6% will dial five times
- 4% will call the prospect six times

Now consider these mind-blowing stats from the same report:

- If you call one time, you have a 38% chance of getting though
- Two calls raise your chance to 61%
- Three calls – 71%
- Four calls – 82%
- Five calls – 90%
- Six calls – 92% chance of getting through

In other words: The more you call, the better your chances of closing the sale.

I know what you're probably thinking: These stats fly in the face of the studies I mentioned earlier about how your chances of closing a lead decrease exponentially if you don't call back in five minutes.

But remember: **These aren't the leads that shriveled up and died five minutes after contacting you; these are the leads that pulled a Yogi Bear and went into hibernation.** They are NOT in the same category.

The truth is you should focus heavily on BOTH. Make sure you call in the first 10 seconds. And make sure you continue to have somebody call the ones who aren't responsive. I'll talk about what I call "hopper systems" in an upcoming chapter… which is using email and direct mail to nurture stubborn prospects. For now, keep calling.

Now let's break down how much money you can make with consistent follow up.

Assume you get 20 leads per week, and can set 15% more appointments with diligent follow up. That's three extra set appointments, which is ONE extra sale, assuming a 33% closing rate. **If your average gross profit is $5,000 per sale, that's an extra QUARTER-MILLION DOLLARS IN GROSS PROFIT PER YEAR JUST BY <u>NOT GIVING UP</u>.**

This isn't rocket science, and I'm not Elon Musk. This is simple sales and marketing for contractors. And like I mentioned a minute ago, the right software (e.g., MarketSharp) and systems in place allow you the best chance of success.

So call prospects. Then call again. And again and again. Who knows what's going on in somebody's mind at the moment when you call. It could any one of 9,344 things. My recommendation is to KEEP CALLING until the prospects flat-out tells you "no." Until then, your unwillingness to be persistent is very likely costing you hundreds of thousands of dollars a year.

Just ask Jason. He learned the hard way.

Recap (The "Too Long; Didn't Read" Version Of This Chapter)

This is a jumbo-sized chapter for a reason: a crappy lead-handling protocol kills sales… while an awesome, systemized, well-oiled lead-handling protocol will boost sales by hundreds of thousands of dollars every year—and put you on the path to $10MM.

Trust me, as you grow and spend more money on marketing, seemingly small flaws in your system will just cost you more and more money.

If you take anything away from this chapter, let it be this: Be open to the possibility you may be losing out on business because…

A) You don't follow up with leads fast enough.

B) You make snap judgments about what are "good" and "bad" leads.

C) You're not properly setting prospect expectations—and making them feel comfortable—the first time they call you.

D) You don't follow up enough with the prospects who drag their heels.

And here's a quick recap of what you need to do to solve these problems FOR GOOD:

1. Have a reliable 24/7 call center backing you up.

2. Don't have "whoever is available" set appointments—have specific, trained appointment setters do it.

3. Call people back within 10 seconds of them becoming leads. NO exceptions.

4. If you don't get somebody on the phone, have a system for calling them back FOREVER until they tell you to quit bothering them. **Buy or die.**

5. Put prospects at ease the first time they call you. Remember, they're scared to death because they've heard all sorts of bad things about the remodeling industry. Prove them wrong by killing them with kindness, compassion, and understanding.

6. Don't write off a lead that you just assume is "bad" (or a crack house). You are—with 100% certainty—losing out on business because of your preconceived notions of what a lead should be. People who were trying to call a different company... people who want one window when your minimum is three... people who want brand ABC when you sell brand XYZ... these are **all** viable leads. But only if you make them.

Now if you'll excuse me, I've got to go to my mother's and save a new royal fern she just took prisoner bought.

CHAPTER 45
What To Do With Prospects Who Don't Close

Pop Quiz: What is the <u>number one reason</u> deals don't close during the initial sales meeting?

I've asked this question to thousands of people at seminars, and believe it or not, it's not all the usual answers everyone thinks, and your sales people would like for you to believe. Answers like "no money" and "needs more information" and "bad timing" and "didn't like the salesman" are all good answers, but they are not even close to the number one answer.

Really.

The main reason people don't buy during the first meeting (which drastically drops their likelihood of ever buying at all) is: **You are asking them for a lot more money than they were expecting you to ask for.** This is not the same thing as "can't afford it"—it's actually VERY different. It's simply a matter of out-of-whack expectations.

Sticker shock.

You're around windows or roofing or HVAC or kitchen remodeling all day, every day. You know exactly how much that stuff costs. But homeowners who have never bought it before have no idea. They're feeling their way in the dark. They have no idea how much it should cost.

Sticker shock.

But contractors are a lot more likely to cling to their beliefs that the non-closeable prospect was simply "stupid, broke, or both."

Let me prove that mindset wrong by role-playing for a minute.

Let's Go On A Disney Cruise!

Imagine you are watching TV with your spouse and you see a commercial for a Disney cruise. You've got 3 kids, and you and the misses (or "mister" as the case may be!) get to talking about how you've been wanting to take the kids on a REAL vacation, and how they are right at that perfect age for Disney. You've even been saving up some money, so on the spur of the moment, you decide to take the plunge.

The next day, as you're driving to the cruise specialty travel agent, you discuss the plan with your spouse, and try to figure out your budget. Here's what you discuss:

- You're not sure how much a 7-day Disney cruise will cost, but you're assuming it's going to be expensive because let's face it, everything Disney is expensive.

- You have friends that have been on a Disney cruise before, and they swore on a stack of Bibles it was the greatest experience ever. But the cost of their Disney cruise never came up in discussion.

- You have another friend who took her family on a Carnival cruise and loved it. Your friend is the kind who "finds deals" and told you their cruise was only $370 per person for a week, all-inclusive. That's $1,850 for 5 people. This is now your benchmark.

- Since you know Disney will be more, and you know your friend is a bargain hound, you're assuming that the Disney Cruise will probably be about DOUBLE the cost of your friend's cruise—maybe even as much as $4,000.

- You also know there will be airfare to get to Florida where the ship launches… at $300 to $400 per person, that will add another $1,500 to $2,000.

- You also budget $500 for miscellaneous things, bringing your total maximum budget to $6,500.

- That number scares you a little, but since you've already saved up $3,000, and you think you can save another $1,500 prior to the trip, and you'll just put the other $2,000 on a credit card that you'll pay off as soon as you can.

- Great—you're all set to talk to the travel agent.

The travel agent, of course, is thrilled to see you. She asks about your travel dates and plugs all the information into her computer. The following conversation ensues:

Travel Agent: Okay. It looks like that will be… $10,343.60, including taxes. That's a stateroom with a verandah.

You: Gulp. What's a stateroom with a verandah?

Travel Agent: Stateroom just means room; verandah means it has a little balcony you can sit on to view the ocean. Here, take a look at this picture (turns computer monitor around).

You: Uh, okay. That might be a little out of our budget.

Travel Agent: Well that's actually the cheapest sailing in June. There are 3 others sail dates that range from $11,500 to $12,400. It all depends on demand, you know.

You: (Realizing that the travel agent hasn't even considered airfare) Uh, okay. Are there any, you know, less expensive staterooms? Maybe without a verandah?

Travel Agent: They do have interior rooms without a view or balcony for cheaper; usually about $7,000 to $8,000. But they're sold out for the entire month.

You: Uh, okay. Um, uh.

Travel Agent: Well, if you could go later in the year, like in October, then the cheaper rooms would be available. Or you could go on a different cruise line—we have a Carnival Cruise in June for only

$4,400. Or you could take a shorter Disney Cruise that's only 4 days that would be less money. But it's sold out too.

You: Uh… uh… (exchanging hurried glances with your spouse)… yea, okay. We need to think about it.

Travel Agent: Well, I'll tell you what. I have been authorized to give you a 10% discount on any of these cruises if you decide and buy right now. Because, you know, if you do that, then I don't have to waste time calling you back later. So which cruise do you want?

You: I… don't know. I'd really like some time to think about it.

Travel Agent: Well you know we can finance it. Just give us $1,000 down, and we can do 0% financing for up to 18 months. Then you can afford the Disney Cruise you want. Which date would you like to book?

You: Heh, yea. Okay. I think we want to think about this. We'll get back to you.

So let me ask you this—whose fault is it that you didn't buy? Maybe the travel agent didn't "sell" the benefits of the Disney Cruise enough. Maybe she didn't ask for the sale in a firm enough fashion. I'm sure if the travel agent's sales manager asked, the blame would be placed on YOUR shoulders: you were broke and indecisive. You couldn't and wouldn't make a decision, even when you were given multiple options in your price range and financing was offered.

This role-play scenario is a microcosm of the ordeal many (probably MOST) contractors force their customers to go through in every sales meeting:

- You ask them to pay way more money that they were anticipating.

- You use words and vocabulary that are foreign to them.

- You give them a bunch of choices that are hard to sort through.

- You try to make them decide something right away when they realistically need some time to process the information.

- Your last-ditch effort to sway them with low-payment financing can't overcome the sticker shock.

Here's the point—there are *real* reasons why people don't buy right away that have absolutely nothing to do with your salesmanship or closing skills.

But here's another critical point: Just because they didn't say yes RIGHT NOW doesn't mean that they won't say yes later on.

Most contractors assume that customers who don't buy from them turn right around and immediately buy from somebody else—ostensibly, from somebody with a cheaper price.

In some cases, that's true. Some people do decide to take the Carnival cruise instead of holding out for the objectively better (for children) Disney cruise.

But guess what? Lots of people want Disney, and are willing to wait and save up so they can buy Disney.

And guess what else? Lots of people want to buy from you, too!

Especially since you've got such a great identity that they've latched onto and want. They realize that your competitors are unworthy, and they're only hesitating because they mentally budgeted $9,000 for a new HVAC system, not $18,500. Or $40,000 for their new kitchen, not $62,000. Or $6,000 for their new windows, not $10000.

In other words, they're WILLING to pay your asking price, they're just not ready—mentally, financially, or both—to pull the trigger quite yet.

A lot of companies have, in theory, what they call a "re-hash" department, where they have somebody call back leads that didn't close (AKA "sit no sales" or "pitch 'n miss") and try to convince them to reconsider, sometimes with another price drop to sweeten the pot.

The reason I say "in theory" is because most rehash programs, in my experience, don't actually operate. Somebody is supposed to be making those calls, but nobody actually ever gets around to it.

And why do you think that is? Because very few people who had sticker shock are going to change their mind within a day or two. That means when you DO make your rehash calls, they seldom result in sales. So people quit making them. Which further reinforces the idea that people who didn't buy simply don't want to buy from you. (Or that they are stupid and broke—or both).

There is a better way—a way that works. But it takes patience.

What if you set up a system that send emails and postcards to those who didn't buy?

I can build a rock solid case for you that this is a good financial decision, and I'll use the real-life example of a window and door company in Washington DC to illustrate it:

This was a $10MM+ company that was generating and running about 700 leads a month. Their closing ratio was about 30%, for an average of about 200 sales a month. Their average sale was about $6,000, with a gross profit of about $3,000 per sales.

Pretty good, right?

Well, here's what nobody ever wants to talk about. When they close 200 sales out of 700 leads, that means that there are 500 prospects who DO NOT close.

That is a staggering number when you think about it that way. Roughly 6,000 people a year essentially told the salesman, "Thanks, but no thanks."

Why? Because they broke and stupid, obviously! Or maybe it was sticker shock.

Now consider this: If this company spends an average of $200 for leads, that means they are spending $140,000 a month in lead generating costs. And at a close rate of 30%, that means that the average SALE costs them $667 in advertising cost.

Let me state that differently: This company is perfectly willing to spend $667 in advertising costs to get a new customer.

Hold that thought.

Next question: What percentage of the 500 prospects a month that DO NOT close do you think MIGHT be recoverable on the back end? How many of them had a severe case of sticker shock? How many of them froze like a deer in headlights? How many of them didn't immediately jump to a different, lower-priced competitor?

If it were 10%, that would be 50 new customers. If it were just 5%, that would still be 25 new customers. Even if it was just 3%, that's still 15 new customers.

Would it be worth your time, effort, and money to attempt to recover 15 to 50 customers who didn't buy during the first appointment?

Let's be conservative and shoot for 15. That's 15 out of 500. Does that sound reasonable?

We already determined that this company is perfectly happy to spend $667 in advertising costs for each new customer they recruit.

So if we allocate $667 each to recover 15 customers, that would give us a budget of $10,005. Since there are 500 prospects, simple math would tell us that we now have a budget of $20 per prospect.

So what do we do with that money?

First, email is (practically) free. What if you had a series of 25 emails that went out once a week? What if you wrote 2 or 3 different subject lines for each of those 25 emails? You could hit them with an email a week for a year! Then repeat it the next year.

Of course, some people would opt out of your list. Others would never see them for a myriad of reasons that hinder email deliverability. But besides the time and effort to create the emails and set up the system—what's the downside?

Next, send postcard mailers.

You might be thinking, "Postcards? Why would you send postcards? Wouldn't a letter be more effective?" And the answer is usually NO—letters won't work for a Wall Drug-type of campaign, because people will start to recognize ANOTHER letter from you and they won't even read it.

I like postcards though, because of a principle I call "Left hand, right hand, trash can," which means from the time they pick it up, see what it is to decide what to do with it, and then throw it in the trash, you can deliver a message. Assuming you've got a good identity that's articulated with power, precision, and passion—and IF you send them out consistently over time, you'll move the needle. A single postcard, or a few postcards aren't' really going to do much.

If postcards cost you 50 cents each, you'd have enough budget so send 40 postcards. Space them out every 10 days (consistency and frequency) and you have enough budget to keep your postcards flowing for 14 months. Or if you only sent two per month, you could keep going for almost two years.

To see some samples of email and postcard series for remodelers, go to UnlimitedLeadFlow.com/book and take a look.

Here's another way to think about it.

What do you think will happen if you follow up with 500 prospects with weekly emails and 40 postcards?

For the contractor in our example, an extra 15 sales a month would be worth an extra MILLION dollars a year in sales.

What do you think would happen if you only sent 10 postcards and no emails?

What about zero postcards and zero emails?

This Wall Drug idea is financially sound, but in my experience, I know that **the overwhelming majority of contractors won't do it.**

They send out 2 or 3 postcards and nobody calls, so they conclude that it doesn't work, and they quit.

Don't be that guy. You should seriously explore this idea of following up missed sales with marketing.

CHAPTER 46
Lead Generation With Direct Mail

Y OU CAN USE the same math and logic to do other kinds of mailing campaigns as well. It's a simple as:

- Determining a targeted group of people to mail to.

- Determining an allowable marketing cost per sale.

- Setting a budget based on conservative estimates of how many sales you can get.

- Putting a system in place to mail the target market consistently.

The last three steps from above are the same for all types of mailing campaigns. Let's discuss some of the different target markets briefly.

New Movers

"Because that's where the money is."

That's the famous answer prolific bank robber Willie Sutton gave when asked why he robbed banks.

Then, he added, "It couldn't be more obvious. Go where the money is, and go there often."

When it comes to direct mail for remodelers, it's pretty where the money is: NEW MOVE-INS.

Just look at the data. According to a Scarborough report, new homeowners are more likely than established homeowners (those who have lived in their home for over 3 years) to spend on the following items for their new home:

- 53% more likely to repair or replace flooring
- 47% more likely to add or replace heating and cooling systems
- 47% more likely to have the interior of their home painted
- 45% more likely to remodel the home's kitchen
- 34% more likely to replace siding
- 33% more likely to add on to the home
- 32% more likely to remodel the bathroom
- 29% more likely to replace windows
- 24% more likely to upgrade the home's exterior
- 14% more likely to repair or replace the roof

It only makes sense, right? When people buy an existing home, they're not always going to be crazy about the condition, the colors, the design, or the look. That's when the checkbook comes out and the spending starts.

And that's where you come in.

One way to capture these eager spenders it is to make sure that you're killing in with your online marketing. You should already be investing in SEO, and you need to make sure you're king of the pay-per-click mountain in your local area.

So yes, internet marketing. That goes without saying.

But now let's go out and GRAB THOSE NEW MOVERS, shake them a little, and make sure they come your way before they can even think about Google.

The obvious thing to do is to send mail. The less obvious thing to do is to focus on consistency and frequency. In other words, if you send one or two mailers to new movers, you're probably going to be pretty disappointed in your results. But if you have the patience to stick with it a bit, you can see some good results.

So how many mailers should you send, and how often?

Answer: More than you think, and more often than you think.

But instead of giving you some arbitrary numbers, let's (surprise, surprise) work our calculators a little:

First, figure out your allowable marketing cost per sale. This is the exact same process we went through earlier when we talked about following up with prospects who didn't close. The operable question is how much money do you normally spend on marketing to generate a sale? Not a lead—a sale.

In our previous example, the company was normally spending $200 per lead, and you closing at a rate of 30%, for a cost per SALE of $667. This is the critical number that allows you to set a budget.

Next, estimate what percentage of new movers you think you can convert to sales if you consistently send them a high volume of mailers on a frequent basis? I know you don't KNOW... but come to think of it, you never really KNOW what results any marketing activity will bring. So we have to use common sense and logic to estimate.

Just for grins, let's say that number is 1%. In other words, you think you can sell one job for every 100 people you consistently send a high volume of mail to. I'm not talking about a single stab in the dark with a single mailer. I'm talking about piling it on with frequency and consistency.

That would give you an insanely high budget of $667 for every 100 new movers to cover mailing costs.

Think about that for a second: If mailers cost 50 cents each, that means you can afford to send all 100 of those new movers THIRTEEN mailers ($667 x $0.50 / 100 people).

Sound familiar? It should. It's basic Wall Drug—consistency and frequency.

So here's my recommendation. If you think it seems reasonable to net one new sale from NEW MOVERS for every 100 homes you target with a veritable mountain of mail, I recommend you send one postcard every 10 days for 4 months.

This gives you enough time to:

- Establish a rapport with the homeowner; make yourself a familiar name.

- Educate them about who you are, what you do, and why you're better than everyone else—IDENTITY.

- Let them get settled into their new home and start a project when they're good and ready.

- Nudge them into taking action on the project they know they want/need to do.

- Outlast all the other remodelers who send paltry one or two mailers (or none!).

Now here's the kicker:

Hire a guy and give him a clipboard with the names and addresses of all the new movers on the list that you've been mailing to every 10 days for at least 2 or 3 months.

Have him drive around and knock on the doors of these folks and see if they're interested in a home improvement project. When you do this, you'll find that people are surprisingly open and willing to talk. Why? Because a sizeable percentage of them ACTUALLY NEED AND WANT WHAT YOU SELL... RIGHT NOW!

I've placed some sample postcard series on our website at LINK so you can get a feel. Notice that the language and images on these pieces are more tailored to the new move in.

That's it! Now let's rinse and repeat with a couple of other targeted markets...

Proximity or "Radius" Mailers

Radius mailers or proximity marketing.I'm talking about sending mailers to the neighbors of your current customers. The idea is simple: If your customer needed (whatever you sell), maybe their neighbors will to because of the relative age and condition of their homes.

Whatever you call them, they actually usually don't work very well for most contractor companies.

In fact, in live seminars, when I ask for a show of hands how many people successfully use this tactic, I almost NEVER get affirmative hand raises. More usually, I hear "we used to do that," or "it doesn't work anymore."

The problem is the tired old "send three postcards" routine simply doesn't work anymore (if it ever did). As you are probably already well aware by now, hitting somebody once or twice (or three times) with a mailer doesn't give enough consistency and frequency (Wall Drug) to get the job done.

Understand The Real Situation: First realize this: just because your customer bought windows (or siding or a furnace) from you doesn't mean that his neighbors are automatically thinking about the same thing. Stated differently, if your neighbor buys a new TV or hot tub (or whatever), do you automatically want one too?

To get these neighbors on board, you're first going to have to get their attention, your best bet is to use a multi-touch approach that's geared to hit them repeatedly until they can't help but deal with you. That sounds a bit roughshod—and maybe it is—but hey, you gotta do what works.

Get Your Customers Involved: Next, give your customers a little incentive to help you out. Maybe a little price discount, or a gift card to a local restaurant. But you're going to need their help.

Ask them if you can put your sign in their front yard—that's obvious. But don't stop there; also put a "take one" box next to the sign that is filled with flyers that tout your Identity. Your customer's job is to keep the box full. Also have your customers agree to let you send a testimonial letter out with their name signed to it (discussed below) as well as post photos of their job on your website, as well as on your mailers (also below). Finally, you need them to agree to take phone calls from prospective customers in their neighborhood as a reference. See, you need to give them a little SOMETHING since you'll be putting them to work!

Let The Fray Begin! After the jobsite sign and take-one flyers, you will next send out a series of three postcards. But not just any postcards! Don't send those stupid "We're in the neighborhood" ones that nobody reads or cares about. Send three different cards, in succession, that talk about your identity, give references (with phone numbers), and any offers you have. You shouldn't expect a big flurry of calls from this—you are just softening up the ground at this point. Breaking through the clutter. Getting a foothold.

Unleash The Heavy Artillery: Once you've hit them with the 3 postcards, now it's time to break out the bigger guns. First up is a check mailer—it's a mail piece that's designed to LOOK like it's a check. It tends to get opened, and when it does, you make them an offer (in the form of the check) and communicate your Identity points (in the letter attached to the check).

This can be effective, but still isn't going to make the phone ring off the hook. Next up is a testimonial letter—remember above, you were recruiting your customers' help? This is a letter that YOU write on behalf of your customer and have them sign. It talks about—surprise!—your company's identity and the great experience they had with you. It invites the neighbor to call your customer to ask questions. This works exceptionally well because the letter is delivered in a plain white envelope with a real stamp and your customer's return name and address on it—which is ostensibly and noticeably nearby.

Send In The Ground Troops: This is where the rubber hits the road. It's the same concept we just discussed with New Movers: Print off a list of all the neighbors that you've been mailing stuff to over the last couple of weeks (usually about 40 to 200 names) and hand the list to an attractive, well-groomed, well-mannered young man between the ages of 18 and 25 years old. We call this guy the "micro-canvasser."

Tell him to knock on the doors of the addresses on the list and identify himself as a representative of your company. Have him hold a fanned-out-and-stapled-together stack of the 5 mailers you've sent out, and have him show the people at the door. They should have at least a glimmer of recognition.

Create an oversized "big bill" (17" x 7.3") printed on one side with any denomination that you are willing to offer as an incentive (say, $500) and on the other side, your...... IDENTITY! We've found that when you actually get in front of peoples' faces AFTER having softened them up with the mailers, THEN you're in a good position to set appointments and get sales.

Final Word: This takes time, effort, money, and discipline to pull off. Don't run wild at first. Instead, pull all the pieces together and try it on 50 to 100 neighbors for 1 or 2 of your customers. You will find that the effort is well worth it as your "micro-canvasser" is welcomed into homes and appointments are set.

You can see samples of all of these pieces on our website at UnlimitedLeadFlow.com/book.

Neighborhood Mailers

In this version of mailing, you are trying to identify neighborhoods of homes that share a common need for whatever it you are selling.

I once worked with a sunroom company near Hilton Head, South Carolina. There was a huge community there of 6,000 homes affectionately called "Senior City," so named because they only allowed senior citizens 55 or older to live there. By HOA rules, children were not allowed to visit for more than 7 consecutive days. And these people LOVED sunrooms.

Based on everything we have talked about in the last chapter and a half, can you figure out how we managed that? If not, I have failed you.

Similarly, I've worked with roofers who target neighborhoods that have older roofs that need to be replaced. And window companies that target older homes with inefficient windows. You get the idea.

Let me share a story with you about an HVAC company who I challenged to use an aggressive mailing campaign based on the information they gave me about a neighborhood they serviced:

It's Just Math, People

This HVAC company in the northeast wanted to target homeowners whose heat pumps were likely to fail within the next few years with a postcard campaign. When they called me, they were already planning to send a series of six postcards every six weeks to a targeted list of 1,000 homeowners whose units were between 10 and 12 years old. They wanted me to help write the postcards.

The idea was to have them replace their units now, *before* they failed—which would most likely happen in the dead of the winter—and cause the homeowner to endure 2 or 3 days in a **freezing house** while the (seasonally) busy HVAC companies would hopefully squeeze them into the overcrowded service rotation.

Makes sense, right?

As we discussed his strategy and some of the identity for the headlines, I became concerned that this campaign was just going to be a miserable failure. I explained in no uncertain terms that a campaign geared toward getting people to spend a lot of money—$8,000 on average—for a problem they <u>might</u> have in the future was a major uphill battle. The business owner's rationale of "the longer they wait the bigger the risk of failure is" was refuted by my rationale of "the longer their heat pump works the more convinced they become that it will never break."

Then he said something that drastically changed the playing field. Big-time drastically. He told me that it wasn't accurate to say that these heat pumps <u>might</u> fail; it was accurate to say that they <u>would</u> fail with nearly 100% certainty. He went on to say that these particular heat pumps—installed by the home builders in that area when the homes were new—NEVER last more than 13 years, and that homeowners with a 10-year-old pump would FOR SURE need one within 1 to 36 months... end of story.

Hmmm. I wanted to know: "How sure are you that the pumps will fail? Would you be willing to bet your life that 100% of the pumps will fail by the time they reach 13 years old?" He assured me that he'd be willing to bet his life that at least 90% would fail by that time.

Time to break out the calculator.

I found out the average sale was $8,000 with a gross profit of $3,500. That means for 1,000 homes on the target list there is $3,500,000 in gross profit at stake over the next three years—$3,150,000 if you factor out the 10% of heat pumps that might <u>not</u> fail for some reason. Think about that for a second—a guaranteed $3.1 million in gross profits over the next 3 years just sitting there for the taking.

How much would you be willing to spend to accrue $3.1 million in gross profits? If it were me, I'd be willing to spend at least 10% of that amount—a cool $310,000.

Let's take a Wall Drug approach.

For starters, I'd send one 6" x 11" inch postcard per week to each of the 1,000 prospects. That's a whopping 52,000 postcards a year, times 3 years... which is a total of (roughly) 150,000. If each card cost 50 cents to send, the total cost for the 36-month campaign would be just $75,000.

That's **chickenfeed** compared to the anticipated gross profit, so I'm going to go ahead and bump it to two postcards per week—a little more than 100 per year per prospect. That's going to cost me $150,000— not including all the customers who we'd take <u>out</u> of the prospecting database once they actually become customers and we quit sending them stuff. And we've still got $160,000 and change to spend.

Ignore me if you're getting bored by the repetitive nature of these discussions.

Next I'd hire a college-aged kid, stick him in a brightly colored company shirt, and have him go **knock** on each of the 1,000 doors *every* month. If the door knocker knocked 5 days a week, he'd have to knock just 50 doors a day—an easy feat given that all the homes are in a reasonably close proximity. After a few months, my door knocker would instantly be recognized as the guy from the company that sends all the postcards that keeps coming by and knocking on the door. Anytime there was no answer, I'd have him leave a giant "Big Bill" door hanger (more on that later). If I paid that door knocker $3,000 a month, that would take $108,000 of my three-year budget—leaving me with a paltry $52,000 to play with.

So let's think of something fun to do with the remaining fifty grand. How about creating something for my door knocker to hand to people when he knocks their doors? Like fridge magnets. Or calendars. Or an **ice cream scooper**. Something, for crying out loud!

Notice that we haven't even discussed what messages to put on all those marketing touches. With this kind of frequency, it *almost* doesn't even matter what I put on there as long as it's something sort of like "Hey we can replace your flipping heat pump when it goes out?" Seriously—this is a lot more about what the <u>calculator says</u> than the <u>marketing messaging</u> says.

So now let's look at all this from the perspective of the prospective customer. I really want you to put yourself in his/her shoes for a minute and think about this. Image getting two postcards a week from an HVAC company warning you that your heat pump was almost certain to fail in 3 years or less. How many weeks would it take you before you started to notice the postcards? I mean really notice that "hey, these guys are sending me a ton of mail!"? Probably about 4 or 5 weeks.

Think forward 18 months. Now you've received two pieces of mail from the HVAC company every week for a year and a half, and the college kid has knocked on your door almost 20 times, and handed you three fridge magnets, two ice cream scoopers, and a six-pack of Dr. Pepper.

Is there any chance at all that you're not aware of who this company is? Is there any chance that you don't know why they are pestering you, and what you need to do next? Of course not!

That's called Wall Drugging 'em!

Don't brush this aside and say "But my company is different. We don't sell heat pumps, and we don't know exactly who our customers will be." Instead, take a look at your numbers—how much can you spend for each new sale that you get? How could you best spend that money? Use your calculator to find answers to these questions. You just might find a formula for success that you hadn't expected.

CHAPTER 47
Maximizing Home Shows

OST REMODELING CONTRACTORS I know (and some service companies) rely heavily on home shows for an annual or semi-annual spike in leads and sales.

The purpose of this chapter is not to give you an exhaustive set of guidelines on how to run a show... but to give you a few tips that might help you add 20% to 50% more leads than you would otherwise get.

Is It Even Worth Your Time?

Remember the good old days when there was one main show that came to down every year that attracted more attendees than you knew what to do with? Now most cities have multiple shows at different times of the year—and fragmented attendance. The last thing you want to do is pay a ton of money, staff up, then sit around twiddling your thumbs for 3 days.

So if you're not sure if you should go to a given show or not, do a little bit of detective work. It's pretty simple: contact the show organizer and ask them for references from last year's show that you can call, then actually do you due diligence.

Call at least 5 companies and ask them how many years they've attended, what the attendance patters have been in recent years (up?

Down? Steady?), how last year's show was, how responsive the attendees were, and whether or not they're going back. Those questions should loosen the lips, so to speak, and you should be able to gather a wealth of information.

If the organizer won't give you information on previous attendees, you can often find them by searching on the show organizer's website—frequently the information from last year isn't updated until just before this year's show. Of course, if they won't give you the info, that's just weird—and a really bad sign.

Location, Location, Location

If you do decide to participate, booth location can make or break your show. Try to get a booth as close to the front as possible, and as close to the center as possible.

This can get a bit tricky, because home show attendees will frequently come in and automatically turn to the left or the right and start on one of the sides, grocery store style. This makes booths on the side a gamble—if you end up on the side where somebody STARTS walking, you'll grab them while they're still fresh. But if you're on the other side, they may never make it to you. Middle is better—some people plow right down the middle anyway, and even if they start on one side, most people won't give up before making it back to the middle.

If possible, position your booth close to one of those huge booths from a national company that attracts a lot of attention. Other locations to consider include near food, near beer, and near bathrooms. You want to avoid that row of booths that always seems to be tucked somewhere near the back that is occupied by small-time players who can't afford real backdrops who collectively scream "Rinky Dink Alley!"

Should you pay extra for premium booth location? In most cases the answer is YES. And generally speaking, you can accurately judge a booth's value by simply looking at the pricing matrix; trust me, these organizers know which booths are worth the most money, and they're going to charge accordingly. Just like any other advertising media, position does matter—put some thought (and wallet) into this decision.

Think about it this way: If you have to pay an extra $1,500 for a premium spot, how many extra leads and sales do you need to get to cover that? Yea, probably ONE. Don't skimp on this.

Rent Two Booths

If you really want to make a splash, get two booths. This is a no brainer if you have multiple products—you can have a window booth and a siding booth. Or a kitchen booth and a bathroom booth.

My clients who have taken this advice swear up and down that it's no-brainer ROI. Just make sure that your two booths are on essentially opposite ends of the convention floor to maximize foot traffic from all directions.

Identity Integration

Your booth should give even casual passersby a good indication of your company's identity—a powerful, precise, and passionate articulation of who you are, why you're different and better, and what people can expect when doing business with you. Then I strongly recommend professionally designed, high quality tension fabric backdrops and pop-up banners with strong headlines that grab prospects and draw them in. On the following pages are a few examples. To see them in color, go to UnlimitedLeadFlow.com/book.

Use A Big Bill

One of the biggest problems you'll have at a show is just getting people to pay attention to you. Lots of companies use lame handouts like candy, pens, rulers, and the like to "entice" people into the booth.

The best tool I know is what I call the "Big Bill." I've already mentioned it a couple of times in conjunction with door knocking and micro-canvassing.

Simply put, it's an oversized dollar bill that's Photoshopped into a denomination that's consistent with a promotion you are running or a discount you want to give. So if you have a $10,000 giveaway, create a $10,000 bill. If you're offering a $2,000 "show discount," print up a $2,000 bill. The opposite side should have your company's identity information and an offer consistent with the Giveaway.

Here's why it works: Most people at home shows are pretty cautious about who they make eye contact with and talk too—there are hundreds of booths and they have limited time, so they don't want to get sucked into a conversation with everyone.

The Big Bill is a way to snap them to attention—it's an ice breaker. As somebody walks by, just say "I'd like to give you two thousand dollars"... then lean forward and extend the bill out to them. The bill is so big that you can do this without infringing on their personal space. And the bill is unusual and interesting enough that 80% of the people will reflexively reach out their hand and grab it. When they do this, let them take the bill, then tell them to turn it over... and say something like "yea, we're giving a $2,000 home show discount on our windows because they are 2,000% more air tight than other windows. Do you feel drafts in your house in the winter from your windows?"

Ask Qualification Questions

I'm talking about a simple progression of 6 to 10 questions you ask the prospect to check for interest and urgency. Or in other words, if you ask them 2 or 3 of the questions and give short, rushed answers as they start edging away from you like they want to leave... that's a pretty good indicator that they're not interested. On the other hand, if they become engaged in the conversation, that tells you something as well. The questions should always start general, and work toward more specific; they should also be asked in non-committal language so you don't put the prospect on the defensive (example: "How long have you been *thinking* about replacing your windows?"... instead of "When are you going to replace your windows?").

Here's an example of some qualification questions you could ask if you sold windows:

- How old is you home?

- Are the windows original to the home?

- Is there anything, specifically, that bothers you about your windows?

- Do you think your energy bills are too high?

- Do you get drafts?

- Have you here at the show actively looking for windows, or are you just browsing?

- Do you have any idea how to tell good windows from bad ones?

- How long have you been thinking about a project like this?

- Have you ever gotten a bid?

Set Appointments On The Spot

If you find interested people, you should attempt to set appointments on the spot. This might sound like "no duh" advice, but you might be surprised how many contractors settle for "leads" and don't ask for appointments. You may want to offer "show specials" or incentives to people who set on the spot… after all, if they do commit to an appointment, you've effectively taken that prospect off the market, so to speak, to a certain extent. With easy access to online scheduling software, there's no excuse for not doing this.

We've also found the Big Bill to be a good appointment setter. Just let the prospect know that in order to get the $2,000 discount shown on the bill, they have to set an appointment here at the show. It works like a charm.

Follow Up!

Finally, don't forget to actually follow up with the leads you get from the show. Most companies are pretty good at following up with hot leads, but fail miserably when it comes to the "shoebox full" of other leads.

Case Study

You know the old story about the "cobbler's children have holes in their shoes" and "the barber's kids desperately need haircuts"? That's kind of how I felt when I met Kathi, owner of LoneStar Property Solutions, and looked at her marketing—and her home show materials, in particular.

I quickly recognized that Kathi was no ordinary remodeler. Her background and passion was design… and she had an uncanny ability to reach into peoples' brains, grab a clear picture of what they were hoping to achieve, then deliver exactly what they wanted. Clients were always thrilled with the final results, and would often say things like "It's exactly like I imagined it would be—except it's BETTER!"

So as I worked through the identity creation process, the challenge was—as usual—to find an interesting, engaging, and compelling way to communicate her unique abilities. Here's what we came up with for headlines:

Most Remodelers Are Order Takers.

They Say, "Tell Me What You Want And I'll Make It Happen."

I'll Guide You Through An Exhilarating Brainstorming Session Where I'll <u>Pick Your Brain</u>, Throw Out <u>Tons Of Ideas</u>, Show You <u>Dozens Of Materials</u>, And Help You Discover What You <u>Really</u> Want.

Beautiful. We integrated that message into her website, brochures, and business cards.

Then it was time for the first of her two annual home shows in Fort Worth, so I asked her to send me a picture of her booth so I could get a feel for what she'd been doing. Remember the cobbler's children's' shoes? Yikes! Take a look for yourself—a dark, drab, dreary, non-inviting, dungeon-esque home show booth if I've ever seen one!

Talk about a disconnect! Here is the woman with perhaps the best eye for design in the entire Dallas-Fort Worth area, and she's designed her home show booth to look like a 3rd grade science fair project.

Let's fix this (final result below):

Step 1 – Colors: For heaven's sake, let's take her company colors and create something that's bright, airy, colorful, and that is consistent with her brand and image she's trying to build. It's amazing what you can do with orange and purple. Go to UnlimitedLeadFlow.com/book to see this in full color!

Step 2 - Identity: Integrate the identity! The headline from the website sums up why she's different and better, and the reaction that clients have to her work. So let's use that as a starting point!

Step 3 – Backdrops & Banners: Create a main backdrop and pop-up banners: The main backdrop should communicate the identity, and the pop-ups should be a derivative of it. Notice how we used opposite colors for each banner, and how the messages compliment that main backdrop nicely.

Step 4 – Supporting Materials: Kathi also used a Big Bill to stop people in their tracks and start conversations about their potential projects.

The Results: Kathi reported that she would normally expect to get about 15 to 20 good leads at a typical home show, then have to battle through the usual process of trying to convince people that she was different and better and worth her price.

In her first show after the overhaul, her lead count shot up to 60, then in August (generally lower attendance), she netted 50 good leads. **All told, her results TRIPLED.**

But what's even more impressive is her prospects' attitude about her company. Many of them never even bothered to investigate her competitors because they already knew—based on her identity—that they wanted to use LoneStar. Almost every prospect commented that they "kind of knew what they wanted, but needed some help getting it out of their brain."

By simply pointing out that her company, in fact, specializes in just that, she won. Big time.

A few comments from Kathi:

- "Before, most people walked right by and didn't want to stop and talk...we felt like we had to either be pushy, or let them walk right on by..."

- "Now our Identity sets the pace for everything we do now—EVERYTHING; it's the reason clients choose us over our competitors."

Are you involved in home shows and/or events? Then don't wait another second—get moving on creating a strong identity and integrate it into your show materials. Then integrate scripting, pre-show mailings, follow-up materials, and more. All of these things working together will increase your results and MAKE YOU MORE MONEY!

CHAPTER 48
Billboards

Y ou already know from my story about Wall Drug that I'm a fan of the billboard.

But you don't have to have 115 billboards in a 50-mile stretch of road for them to be a meaningful contributor to your marketing plan. With a little research and a good, creative message, billboards can work for medium to larger-sized remodeling companies. Here is my best billboard advice:

To Billboard Or Not To Billboard

Don't start thinking about the specifics of your billboard campaign until you've first carefully evaluated whether or not billboards even make sense for your marketing situation.

Billboards, almost by definition, are more of a branding/farming activity than a direct response one. With the exception of directional billboards (exit here for a restaurant, hotel, etc.), billboards should be part of a larger marketing campaign that will serve to extend your brand's reach and nudge people to remember what they already know about you from exposure to your other advertising.

Radio and billboard go well together since both are experienced (primarily) while driving. The key here is to educate people about your company and identity (brand promise) in other media so they already know who you are, what you stand for, and why you're a good choice to buy from. Then the billboard does its job by triggering that pre-existing information in their brain.

What this really means is you probably shouldn't use billboards as the first or second item on your advertising checklist. Consider setting a strong foundation with radio, TV, direct mail, newspaper, etc… then "boost" their effectiveness with a billboard campaign when your budget allows.

Put Some Eyes On It

Never buy a billboard that somebody you trust hasn't seen with their own two eyes. Yes, I know the billboard companies will provide pictures, but you can't always tell the full story from those.

Your best bet is to get a "right hand reader," which means the billboard is on the right side of the road, and therefore closest to the cars that are passing it… and in the natural line of sight for a car's passengers.

Second best is a "cross-reader," which is a billboard on the left side of the road, which might make them harder to see. But neither one is a sure bet to be good or bad—you have to see the entire context of the position of the board to know for sure. I've seen plenty of right hand readers that were placed just after a bridge, which only allows people a split-second view. Some cross readers are plainly visible and will work fine. Just make sure you see it before you buy it so you know for sure.

Get Out Of The Crowd

Generally speaking, the more billboards on a given stretch of road, the worse.It's common sense: if there are 10 billboards in a mile stretch, they're more likely to blur together and go unnoticed by drivers. Ideally, your billboard will be the only one that is clearly visible from a range of 100 yards.

Brand Consistency

Make sure you billboards have a consistent look and feel both with each other and with your other marketing materials. You should already have a definitive brand color and color scheme that appears on your website, print materials, advertising, trucks, etc.... Remember, your billboard should be triggering their brain to remember what they already know about your company, so your color, look, feel, style, and themes will enhance that recognition.

Keep It Simple

It goes without saying, but billboards present some significant challenges for the readability of your message. Billboards should generally be limited to 3 to 7 main words (i.e. not including phone numbers, web addresses, etc.) so that people can read it at 60 MPH and absorb the message. Don't fall for thinking that people will pass the billboard several times a week and therefore have a chance to "read the rest of the sign." Also make sure: the words are big enough to read; there is enough color contrast so the words pop off the billboard; the font is clean, clear, and simple; don't put words on top of images (EVER! Not just on billboards!).

Funny Business

Like any other advertising, getting noticed is half the battle. Since space is limited anyway—I'm a fan of using cute, clever, and creative words and images to capture attention. Don't go crazy with this; and don't delve into obnoxious... but see what you can come up with. Here are a few ideas I came up with for a home services company:

- PhD in PDQ (fast service)
- Greased Lightning (fast service)
- Quick. Fix. (fast service)
- Orange YaGonna Call Us? (picture of their signature orange trucks)
- Faster Than A Speeding.... (picture of signature orange truck)

Phone &Web Address

Anytime you utilize a non-print advertising method, you need to make sure you've got a good, memorable phone number and web address. You can research good phone numbers at TollFreeNumbers. com; I highly recommend going toll-free due to the large number of area codes in most areas. Don't worry, for most parts of the country (small towns excepted), people won't be scared off by 800 numbers. Also make sure your web address is easy to remember!

Keep It Going

Billboards are not for those who want to put a toe in the water! As stated above, they are more of a branding tool to be used in combination with other advertising. Don't run billboards for a month or two (or six!) then quit. Find a good spot, put up a good message, and let your silent salesman sit there and remind everyone about you for years to come. Change up the messaging every 4 to 6 months (negotiate this into your contract) and you will find success.

Rolling Billboards

Last thing.... if you've got trucks rolling around town, I highly recommend spending the money to get them wrapped so you can turn them into mobile billboards. I was with the client mentioned above (with the signature orange trucks) one morning driving with him in his car to his office. During the short 10-minute drive, I counted 11 plain white service trucks from his competitors. PLAIN WHITE! The few thousand dollars it costs to wrap vehicles will pay off many times over in found sales!

CHAPTER 49
Why You Never Get Referrals

MY BROTHER-IN-LAW JARED is a big dude. Like Grizzly bear big. Like lumberjack big. Pretty much like Sasquatch big. Big enough that he calls me "Tiny" even though I'm a fairly average 6 foot tall, 180 pounds.

So I was a bit surprised when Jared improbably announced he was going to begin training to run a half marathon… and asked if I wanted to join him. That's how I found myself with him on an early July morning sweating out what was supposed to be an easy 40-minute jog. Afterwards, when I asked Jared how it went, he said he felt great—except he felt a shin splint coming on, which he blamed on not having the right shoes.

In business, this is the perfect setup for what you'd call "The Referral." Sure enough, he asked, "What kind of shoes do you have? I need to get some new ones."

He shouldn't have asked. Can I just tell you, I love my running shoes. Nike Zoom Vomero. I found them at Academy Sports & Outdoors priced at $109 and instantly fell in love with them the moment I tried them on. They were so soft, so comfortable, so incredibly awesome; I seriously considered wearing them out of the store like a 5-year old with a new pair of Buster Browns. Okay, I did wear them out of the store.

Unfortunately, Jared couldn't try mine on since I wear an 8 ½ regular and he sports the Dolly Parton of shoe sizes with something like a 27 quadruple H. But I told him what they were called and where to get them and encouraged him to at least give them a try.

He must've gotten busy, because almost a month after our run together, I got this text from Jared: "What kind of shoes were those you said I needed to check out?" Another golden opportunity for a referral.

And believe it or not, *hidden in this story lies the key to unlocking the mystery of getting referrals*: the vast majority of your real referral opportunities are going to come from your customers' routine conversations with their friends, family, and associates well <u>AFTER</u> the moment of sale.

But conventional referral-getting wisdom says just the opposite, doesn't it? It says the best time to get referrals is to simply ask for them right there when the customer is buying from you. I'm not saying you shouldn't ask for referrals at the point of sale, but I am saying that **the vast majority of referral opportunities occur much later, after the sale.**

To understand why, Imagine for a moment, hypothetically, what would have happened if the shoe salesman would have asked me for a referral when I bought the shoes. I would have shrugged my shoulders and said "Nope, can't think of anyone." <u>And I would have been telling the truth, too.</u> I don't walk around with a mental inventory of everyone I know who might need running shoes at a given point in time. Or telephone service. Or a laptop computer. Or a new swimming pool. Or any of the 716 things I might happen purchase during the course of a year.

Most salespeople are all-too-familiar with the "I can't think of a single soul who would want one of these" problem. That's why almost every sales person quit asking for referrals at all, and why referrals for your company probably don't exist. And even if you do get one once in a while, it's more like finding a $20 bill in a jacket you haven't worn since last year. Not exactly a product of careful planning.

The secret to getting lots of referrals, then, is to make sure that your customers are ready and willing to recommend you when the topic of conversation naturally makes it way around to whatever it is you sell.

Making this happen takes a little effort, but is very doable. Here are the five main steps:

First, Get Real

The first thing you've got to do is align your expectations with reality. Your customers have better things to do with their time than sell crap for you. Think about things you've bought and how anxious you were to go out and get your friends to try. Not very anxious, right? And even if they are anxious, they still don't honestly know anyone right now who needs what you sell. This is called reality. Deal with it.

Create & Promote A Powerful Identity

If your customers know up front WHY they should do business with you… if they buy from you on purpose because they WANT to buy from you…. if they know the EXACT reasons you are different and better than your competitors… then the chance of them recommending you to their friends goes up exponentially. On the other hand, if you fail to communicate these things with them (even though you perform on them), they won't notice and your impact will be greatly diminished. Identity isn't optional.

The real key is this: Did you customer have a good enough experience that 2 years later they remember you well enough to recommend you when the situation comes up? Or do they say "Yea, the guy who put my roof on was pretty good… what was his name again? I can't remember."

Focus On Communication

The number of referrals you get will depend heavily on how good you make the customer experience. Smile a lot. Answer the phone promptly. Over-communicate… tell people what to expect and when to expect it. Send emails with updates. Have somebody call just to check in and ask if everything is okay. This will go a long, long way toward getting referrals.

Pro-Actively Reward Your Customers

Send your customer a thank you gift. It serves two purposes: 1) it's a good way to say thank you (duh!), and 2) you can thank them in advance for getting the word out about you to their friends and associates. The gift should be something of real, tangible value that's commensurate with the size of the sale or the likely size of the lifetime value of the customer. You can't go wrong with a restaurant gift card, and if you're feeling extra saucy, send them something that's a literal gift in a box.

The idea here is to invoke the law of reciprocity—you've done something nice for them, now they'll feel obligated to do something nice for you. They'll be sitting there eating at Chili's on your nickel and start to feel guilty if they don't help you out somehow. If you think that sounds sneaky and manipulative, you're probably not married. Or at least not happily married. This is called human nature—it's how we operate.

I recommend that you have one specific person in your office that's responsible for the gifts, and I strongly recommend that you keep this program simple. Make sure the gift goes out within a day or two of the transaction so it lands while the customer is still thinking about the purchase. If you've done a good job delivering a great customer experience, this gift should have the effect of being a giant exclamation point at the conclusion of a good experience.

Ask For Referrals In A Systematic, Consistent Way

You can hope that your sales people remember to ask for referrals at the point of sale, or you can take it on your shoulders to pro-actively ask for referrals on an ongoing from the corporate level. As has been stated above, people are going to get busy with their lives, and 12 months after they bought from you, they might not even remember your company's name. So fix that by sending them a steady barrage of mailers to remind them. Not just emails—regular mailers too.

Send them <u>at least one postcard per quarter</u> thanking them again for their business, and asking them to mention your name if the situation comes up. You might even want to send more gifts later on.

For example, a pool company I know about sends their customers an annual anniversary present—a pool toy or towel or goggles or something—as a way of keeping in front of their customers' face. Top of mind, so to speak.

The idea is simple—by using this five-step methodology, you'll anchor the customer to a good experience with the innovative company and thank you gift, then remind them on an ongoing basis that they had a good experience. Then the next time the topic of (what you sell) comes up naturally in conversation—BAM! Referral.

Or you can just leave it to chance and see how that works out. It didn't work out to well for Academy Sports & Outdoors—by the time I bothered to return Jared's text a few days later, it was too late. He had already bought another pair of shoes from another store. A store, it turns out, that sells shoes in size 27 quadruple H.

Run on, Sasquatch!

CHAPTER 50
Social Media

L AST YEAR ONE of the biggest kitchen fixture companies in the world asked me to do a webinar for their customers on the topic of social media. I put together the first draft of the webinar and sent it over to them for review. Their reaction was immediately negative—they hated my webinar.

Why? Because they wanted a webinar that tapped into the mainstream hysteria about how social media was the marketing savior of the world. They wanted a webinar that would show remodelers 5 quick steps to social media riches. *They wanted to tell people what they wanted to hear—that Facebook and Twitter and Pinterest were the missing link in the evolution of their marketing plan.*

Instead, I gave the REAL facts about social media—far less sexy that all the hype you've heard. I talked about what remodelers can realistically expect from social media, and how hard it is to keep up with it. I talked about nuts and bolts of creating interesting posts and avoiding mistakes.

They wanted charts and graphs that proved that everyone was using social media as their new source of information. They wanted to show how easy it is and how effortless it would be to find money online.

And the end of the day, they wanted what they wanted, and they were paying the bill. They completely rewrote the webinar to fit their agenda, and in my opinion, the webinar was watered-down at best. It wasn't that the information was WRONG or BAD or MISLEADING, it's just that it didn't focus on what remodelers really need to know in real life about social media.

So guess what you get here in this chapter? That's right—the real scoop. Let's go!

Begin With The End In Mind

When you hear the "experts" talking about social media, the discussion always centers around all the new customers you can create with social media if you just do it right. While it's true that social media CAN bring you new customers, as the saying goes, "don't hold your breath."

First of all, very few people just randomly find and follow remodeling companies out of the blue. Instead, most people who decide to "like" or "follow" your company on social media will do so at a point when they are actively in the market to buy what you sell. Social media is about nurturing people along; most of the people who follow you are ready to buy now. True, you can nurture them for the NEXT sale, but this timing issue is troubling for those who want a bunch of sales from social media RIGHT NOW. I'll address how to nurture people along to generate maximum sales below—if you do it wrong you'll never get ANY new customers—but just realize it's a slow process that's unlikely to become one of your main lead sources. It's farming. Slow farming.

So then why even bother? Two reasons: SEO and leads.

Hey! I though you just said not to expect a ton of leads from social media! That's true… but if you are consistent in your efforts, over time you will steer people in your direction. It takes time; be patient. You'll also be the go-to answer for your followers' friends who post things like "I'm looking for a window company" or "Anyone know a good kitchen remodeler?" Just be patient; I've used the word nurture 3 times already above for a reason.

But SEO is a whole other ball game—and probably the best reason to get involved with social media. Google eats GREAT CONTENT for breakfast, lunch, and dinner. Every time you create a social media post, you're creating a little bit of content that Google can gobble up. If you consistently post good content (see below for tips on content), then you're going to help your website rank higher in search. Make sure your posts include a fair amount of links to your site (30% minimum) because Google eats good links for snacks.

So if you're ever discouraged because you don't have that many followers (yet!)… or because you don't seem to be getting a lot of leads from your social media efforts, know that it is working—but maybe just in ways that aren't as readily apparent. Keep the faith—it's working.

Facebook First

There are plenty of social media sites to choose from—Facebook, Twitter, Pinterest, Houzz, Instagram, SnapChat, and LinkedIn, just to name seven—so you might feel a bit overwhelmed. Here's my advice, start with Facebook, and don't even worry about the other ones for a while. The number one problem I see that remodeling companies run into when getting into social media is that they simply CANNOT KEEP UP WITH IT, so they quit. It's a heck of a lot easier to keep up with it if you are only focusing on one thing instead of two or three or seven.

So why Facebook? Simply put, it's where the largest number of your customers are actively participating in social media. For most remodeling companies, "your customers" means adults in the age range of 40 to 60. Naturally, that varies, but I can safely say that there are more 48-year olds replacing their windows than there are 8 or 18 or 28-year olds. Twitter is a young person's game for the most part. Look at the number of fans/followers for a popular (but not remodeling related) blog I read that's geared toward this same age group (of which I am a member!):

Clearly, 15,710 people is a lot of people, but it's not even 10% of the number of Facebook followers. Google Plus isn't even on the radar yet. Pinterest is a good idea for companies that deal in more visually important areas of remodeling—kitchens, baths, design-built, etc.—but should still be tackled AFTER a strong and consistent Facebook presence is established. Note: if you have a 3rd party company handling social media for you, they may indeed put you onto multiple platforms at once, and that's great. They very likely have the resources (read: skill and manpower) to handle this.

Tip 3: Entertain, Engage, & Educate

Answer this question: why do people even use Facebook in the first place? For your target market (remember from above, adults in the 40 to 60 age range), the number one reason is… to legitimately keep in touch with people and things that are important to them. Poll teenagers about their social media habits, and you'll see that social media is frequently a game of "who can get the most followers." Most teenagers follow hundreds or even thousands of people—most of whom they only peripherally know, but who they are happy to follow because those same people are following them, thus boosting both parties' all-important follower list.

Adults, on the other hand, usually only have a couple hundred Facebook friends at the most. Those friends usually include siblings, parents, cousins, and uncles. They frequently include old college friends and roommates, and a few friends from high school or even elementary school. You'll also see current friends from church, work, the neighborhood, or volunteer organizations. But not just ANY friend or family member… only ones that they legitimately care about keeping up with.

You'll also see a smattering of things that they are FANS of… from sports teams, to retail stores, to rock bands, to charities. The common denominator of these various entities is that people genuinely CARE about them. Adults don't have time or patience to filter through a bunch of junk to see the stuff they really want to see. They self-filter it out.

All of which brings us to YOU. If you happen to be LIKED by one of your customers or prospects, you should consider that a great honor. That's really saying something; they care enough about you to actually be willing to follow what you have to say—right there in the same feed where they're looking at their nephew's graduation pictures. Treat that relationship with the respect it deserves. You have to be super careful WHAT YOU POST or they will "unlike" you in the proverbial NEW YORK MINUTE.

First rule: don't post too often. I'll cover this in detail in a minute, but for now, just know that nobody wants to hear from a remodeling company 5 times a day. They barely want to hear from their aunt who constantly rants about politics or pugs 5 times a day, let alone some remodeling company.

Next, remember that good content is all-important. You should aim to entertain and educate people so that they become engaged with your company. I've posted several sample posts below to give you a better idea; for now, think in terms of funny, interesting, newsworthy, posts that make people say to themselves "I'll spend 30 seconds to click that and find out more." You are creating your own little content channel—no different than Yahoo or MSN or USA today. You'd better be interesting or people will ignore, or worse, unfollow you.

Create A Plan... Ahead Of Time!

Social media is a terrible place for "winging it." Inevitably, you will commit one of the two major social media sins when you resort to making up your content as you go along: 1) You'll post crappy content that nobody's interested in, or 2) You'll have huge gaps between your posts... or quit altogether. It's really hard to nurture something (remember: consistency & frequency!) when you're not paying any attention to it!

The solution is to create a social media plan and stick to it. Every two weeks sit down and decide how many posts you want for the next month, and then specifically research and write those posts. If you do it every two weeks, you should perpetually be writing content for TWO WEEKS FROM NOW, which will keep you well ahead of the game.

I recommend 3 to 10 posts a week... more if you are researching good stuff to post about, fewer if you're not. Just map it out on a piece of paper or a spreadsheet:

- Monday, 2 pm: Post about Beyoncé's recent home remodel; link to blog posting on our site, with link to TMZ site's article.

- Tuesday, 10 am: Post about the Stephens' kitchen remodel with link to our website with photos.

- Tuesday, 6 pm: Post funny quote about CHANGE from comedian Tim Hawkins

- Wednesday, 3 pm: Post free ticket giveaway to Thursday's Texas Rangers game.

- Thursday, 10 am: Post winner of Rangers ticket giveaway.

- Thursday, 7 pm: Post link to 5 new customer reviews on our website.

- Friday, 1 pm: Post "5 funky restaurants you've probably never tried" article

- Saturday, 10 am: Post "Parade of Homes" info/link

- Sunday, 8 am: Post inspirational quote from Oliver Wendell Homes

There you have it; 9 posts in 7 days on a variety of topics, with a variety of themes. Do this every two weeks and make sure you've got a plan for a solid month. Boom.

Solicit Followers Everywhere

Of course none of this matters if you don't have followers seeing what you're posting. Start immediately to solicit followers anywhere you can—on your website (on every page), on your advertisements, in person at home shows or during canvassing or while in the home selling. Ask people to follow you when you're on the phone with them. Always be thinking about gaining followers. Then when people do look you up on Facebook and see you've got interesting, relevant, engaging content, they'll hit LIKE and you'll be in business.

Don't Post Too Frequently

Besides me and my kids, my wife's #1 love in life is Anthropologie. Not "the study of humans past present, and future." I'm talking about the woman's clothing, doo-dad, frou-frou and knick-knack store that is the frequent beneficiary of half my paycheck. 90% of her closet and half the stuff in my house originated from that store.

Her next love in life after me, my kids, and Anthropologie is Pinterest. You know, the social media network that caters (mostly) to women by letting them "pin" photos of stuff they like to "boards" that they can then share with their friends. My wife pins stuff constantly, and checks to see what other people have pinned approximately 713 times a day.

So when I asked my wife recently if she follows Anthropologie on Pinterest and she said NO, I almost fell over and died on the spot.

When I asked why she told me that Anthropologie posted stuff on Pinterest 4 or 5 times a week, but when they do post, they don't just post one thing. Nope. They post 20 to 30 items at a time, effectively clogging her Pinterest feed. That's sort of like your favorite restaurant bringing you 25 hamburgers every time you order—a bit too much. Sorting through that many posts all at once was somewhere between mildly annoying and intensely frustrating. So she unfollowed Anthropologie. Unbelievable.

Now here's the bad news: I guarantee you that people like your company <u>way less</u> than my wife likes Anthropologie. People simply do not want to hear from a remodeling company THAT MUCH. Your target market uses Facebook to keep in touch with people and things that they genuinely like; overplaying your hand by posting too much starts to make you feel burdensome and salesey, not interesting, fun, and entertaining. They will hide your posts or unlike you.

I recommend remodeling companies post 3 to 10 times a week depending strictly on how much interesting stuff you have available to post. Read that carefully: if you can't think of anything particularly interesting to say/post, you're better off keeping quiet. Speaking of which...

Avoid Self-Serving Or Boring Content

Self-serving or boring posts are the kiss of death for social media. REMEMBER! People have invited you to their social media feed because they think there is something interesting and worthwhile about your company. You should literally feel honored that they "like" you. Respect that and you'll do fine.

The worst thing you can do is repeatedly post sales-oriented, price-oriented, offer-oriented stuff. Rule of thumb: 1 post out of 10 can make an overt offer... but your other 9 posts better be good enough for your followers to cut you some slack. Another common sin is reposting the same thing over and over. This shows a lack of imagination AND common sense. What if one of your actual friends posted the same thing over and over again on Facebook? That's just not how this works.

The third worst thing you can do (reposting was #2!) is post boring stuff. The internet is great at using provocative headlines and images that make you want to click and read stuff. Take a look...

These are ads that appear on the bottom of an article about the San Antonio Spurs; their sole purpose is to temp me to their website by giving me interesting bait like "Celebrities you didn't know were Asian" and "16 celebs who don't drink."

The point of this example is not to say copy these ads verbatim. It's to help you realize that your Facebook feed is like your own personal billboard that's competing with thousands of other billboards for eyeballs and clicks. You have to treat it like your own personal Yahoo or USA Today. I'll give some detailed sample posts in the next chapter… for now, think INTERESTING!

Don't Focus Too Much On Followers

Having tons of followers (or Fans) is a good thing. Unless most of those followers don't actually pay any attention to you. There are plenty of experts out there who will teach you how to get more social media followers, and often, their advice works. Except that most of the followers that come from "trying to get a ton of followers" aren't worth having.

Several years ago when Twitter was really starting to take off, I decided to experiment with it, just to get a first-hand feel for how it worked. I read up on how to get a lot of followers and discovered that if you find other Tweeters who are in a similar industry/interest sphere as you, you can go into their list of followers… stay with me here… and follow their followers. Then those people you follow, in theory, will "reciprocal follow" you—meaning, they will follow you for no other reason than you are following them. Follow that?

The funny thing is it actually worked. I followed the formula and followed about 1,000 people, of which about 800 followed me back. 800!!! Wow! I must be really popular! I referred back to the "experts" and they recommended a 1:1 follow ratio… so I was a bit out of whack… so I went back and tried to figure out who the losers were that failed to follow me back so I could unfollow them.

At the end of the story I had a bunch of followers who essentially paid no attention to me whatsoever. Fake followers. Followers for the sake of numbers. Hollow followers.

Here's what you want: Real followers and fans. These have to be earned. Know up front that it's going to take time to build up a following, and that you have to reward them with interesting, entertaining content. Post your social media icons on your website, on your newsletters, on you advertising, and on your trucks. Put them on your business card and your invoices and your jobsite signs. Encourage people to take a look… and then make sure you have interesting stuff, or you're dead before you even start.

That's a good primer on social media. Now let's explore how to create good posts.

CHAPTER 51
Sample Social Media Posts

S OCIAL MEDIA IS kind of like exercise. It's easy to get all gung-ho for a while... then regular life seeps in, saps your will, smothers your desire, and kills your plan. Lack of planning is the kiss of death for social media.

I previously stated that you should post 3 to 10 times a week, and the variation depends on how much interesting stuff you have to say. If you decide on 8 posts a week, that's 32 a month... no small task.

Here are some ideas to help you out:

- Decide on a tone and a voice. This will vary depending on the personality of your company... some companies are more serious, others more fun... others aspire to be inspirational. Find your voice and then you can start to look for content that matches.

- Keep a notebook (or notes on your phone) about interesting things you see/hear that might make good posts. Think about it while you're surfing the web... and just in conversation with people. There are good ideas all around you if you just keep your ears and eyes open.

- Decide on post categories, then schedule them out. By categories, I mean things like:

- o Quotes
- o Jobsite photos
- o Customer reviews
- o News-oriented articles
- o Celebrity stuff (related to your industry)
- o How to
- o Lists (8 ways to…)
- o Blog postings
- o Giveaways/contests
- o Offers
- o Etc.

- Once you have the categories, it becomes easier to put together a skeleton outline of your posts for the month… you choose the frequency of each category… I'm just trying to help you see an easy, systematic way to approach this.

- Hold a planning meeting (with yourself or your team) every two weeks and make sure you have SPECIFIC posts planned out for at least 30 days. You should spend most of this meeting planning out the posts for the 3rd and 4th week out (since ostensibly you already did this 2 weeks ago for the upcoming 2 weeks).

- Designate a specific person to make all the posts. All hands on deck is not a good approach to social media… more people means less likely to actually get done. Put somebody in charge, then hold them accountable.

Let's take this all to the next logical level by creating sample posts in multiple categories; these posts could then be calendared out in whatever frequency and interval you want.

But before we get started, just a couple of notes: 1) these are SAMPLE posts; use them for inspiration, not verbatim; 2) these posts will be written for multiple kinds of remodeling companies… don't be confused that a post that talks about window replacement is followed by one touting kitchens.

The idea is to write multiple posts in multiple categories, then create a schedule that mixes them up and keeps the type of post fresh.

Okay, here we go! These categories are not in any particular order.

Category 1: Quotes – You know, quotes! The quotes you post should be consistent with the image you want to portray. Find quotes that suit your identity, your personality, your products, and your mood.

- Service, quality, or low price: pick any two.

- I've missed more than 9,000 shots in my career. I've lost almost 300 games. 26 times I've been trusted to take the game winning shot and missed. I've failed over and over and over again in my life. And that is why I succeed. –Michael Jordan

- Twenty years from now you will be more disappointed by the things that you didn't do than by the ones you did do, so throw off the bowlines, sail away from safe harbor, catch the trade winds in your sails. Explore, Dream, Discover. –Mark Twain

- People often say that motivation doesn't last. Well, neither does bathing. That's why we recommend it daily. –Zig Ziglar

- When I was 5-years-old, my mother always told me that happiness was the key to life. When I went to school, they asked me what I wanted to be when I grew up. I wrote down 'happy'. They told me I didn't understand the assignment, and I told them they didn't understand life. –John Lennon

- Fall seven times and stand up eight. –Japanese Proverb

- What's money? A man is a success if he gets up in the morning and goes to bed at night and in between does what he wants to do. –Bob Dylan

- What's money? A man is a success if he gets up in the morning and goes to bed at night and in between does what he wants to do. –Bob Dylan

Category 2: Customer Success– You've got customers, right? And you do good work for them and make them happy, right? Well… show and tell about your great customer experiences!

- We just finished the Johnson's kitchen remodel; this was one of the most technically challenging projects we've ever attempted—we had to use all four of our master craftsmen. Check out the photos and let us know if you like it!

- It's not for everyone! This is one of the most colorful kitchens we've ever created… nothing dull and boring and typical going on here. Do you have the nerve to go BOLD!?!

- 14 windows installed in one day! It took two crews and 54 man hours, but the Simms's home is now energy efficient, safe, and beautiful!

- The Davis' new roof LOOKS like a regular roof; but it's guaranteed to last 50 years, no exceptions. The secret is superior material and strictly "by the book" installation.

- The Guymons wanted a bathroom that LOOKS like stone and tile, but lasts longer and cost a lot less. This entire project came in under $9,000. What do you think—does it look like real stone and tile?

- We just installed our 1,000th window, and Mark & Debbie Hunsaker got their entire job for FREE! Check out the details and pictures!

- What are the best home improvement shows on TV? Click here to see the top 19…

Category 3: News-Oriented – Keep an eye out (or a Google alert!) for anything in the news that's related to home improvement or remodeling… then report it to your fans. You are basically acting as a curator for relevant information.

- Another home improvement scam BUSTED! Be careful… unfortunately this kind of thing is more common than you think: Read the article here.

- Can your marriage survive a remodeling project? The stress and emotion tied to remodeling can be a minefield. Read the full article here.

- Want to get discounts on home improvement projects? Channel 13 ran a story last night about how to find DIY remodeling materials at a discount. Watch it here.

- Wondering what a home improvement project will look like BEFORE you spend the money? Lowe's has new "Holoroom" technology to let you do just that. See it here.

Category 4: How To – Everyone wants to know how to do stuff… so your job is to figure out what kind of stuff would be interesting to teach them… then give <u>write an article on your blog </u>that you post about on Facebook.

- How to choose the perfect cabinets for your new kitchen.

- How to set a realistic budget for a kitchen remodeling project.

- How to tell how if new windows will REALLY save you money on your energy bills…

- How to save money on your energy bills without turning off the lights and without becoming an "energy miser."

- How to build a sunroom that won't cook you in the 100 degree Texas summer heat.

- How to destroy the value of your home with the wrong siding.

- How to drive your marriage to divorce by choosing the wrong remodeling company…

Category 5: Numbered Lists – You know how you see those numbered lists all over the internet? "10 Child Stars From The 80's Who Are In Drug Rehab" or "12 Places You Must Visit In Europe Before You Die" The reason they're so darn popular is they are easy to write and fun to read. So make some lists, write some articles for your blog, and post away!

- 7 home improvement scams that you won't recognize until it's too late.

- 9 different kinds of siding—which one is best for your home?

- 14 things to look for when hiring a remodeler... read our "Contractor Code of Ethics"

- 5 "before and after" kitchen remodeling photos—vote for your favorite.

- 8 inexpensive kitchen upgrades you can do to avoid the cost and hassle of a full remodel

- 4 ways to save money on bathroom remodeling including 3 things you can do yourself.

Category 6: Time of Day/Week-Related – Besides being interested in home improvement, your fans and customers are also interested in.... life in general! Help them out by giving them tips and inside info about places to go, things to do, and activities to participate in.

- We'll be participating in the Leukemia Foundation 5K run tomorrow at Bicentennial Park in Eastridge. The entry fee is $35 and includes a t-shirt, snacks, and a chance to win a Ford F150 pickup truck. Read more about here (link).

- Just had the most amazing Pepper Steak and Mushrooms at Ling & Louie's... RUN, don't walk, to try this outstanding dish. The secret is they use Filet Mignon instead of strip steak like most Asian restaurants (link)

- How To Train A Dragon 2 was a fun movie with stunning special effects. Highly recommended. Read a full review here. (link)

- It's Friday night! If you don't have plans, we've got 5 fun things to try in Fort Worth that you may not have heard of before... including a dueling piano bar, a 5-man improve comedy show, and a music show you won't forget. (link)

- Did you know that Yogurtland offers 3 ounces for free on Mondays? Head over there tonight and treat yourself—you deserve it!

Category 7: Giveaways & Contests – You know, quotes! The quotes you post should be consistent with the image you want to portray. Find quotes that suit your identity, your personality, your products, and your mood.

- Guess how much this bathroom remodeling job cost within $100 and we'll give you a $100 gift card to Chili's. Hint: It's probably a lot less than you think! First 3 who get it right only… hurry!

- It's almost time! Every year, whoever buys the 1,000th window of the year from us gets their entire order for FREE! We don't announce the winner until it's time to pay the bill, so no cheating! Right now we've sold more than 700 but less than 900 windows… anyone you know need windows?

- We've got 5 pairs of Rangers Tickets to tonight's game vs. the Angels. Just comment on this post with your name and email and we'll get you the tickets.

- March Remodeling Madness! Vote on which one of our 64 all-time best remodeling jobs is your favorite… Today's bracket: Kitchens (link)

- We're giving away $250 worth of fireworks for the 4th of July! Write a comment on the topic of "my dream remodeling project" to enter the contest. The winner will be chosen on July 1st.

Category 8: Offers – Use offers sparingly—you don't want your social media feed to be perceived as just another chance to sell people something. But every 10 to 20 posts, give your fans an offer.

- July Facebook special: Buy any 5 windows, get the 6th one free. Click here for details (link)

- Thinking about remodeling but not sure if the timing is right? Here's a "toe in the water" offer… For the first 10 who request it, we'll do our $995 consultation and PRELIMINARY PLANNING MEETING for free. We'll evaluate your needs and wants, sketch out rough plans, estimate a ballpark budget, and bind the results in a 15-page "dream remodel" project book. Feel free to share with your friends.

- Appliance Upgrade Event! During the month of February, we'll automatically upgrade all appliances in your full kitchen remodel to premium Sub-Zero and Bosch for the price of regular appliances. See our site for details (link).

- Today only! Set an appointment to talk about your window, siding, roofing, or deck needs and we'll give you a $100 gift card to Ruth's Chris steak house. Feel free to share this offer with your friends (link to site).

Category 9: Jokes – You know, quotes! The quotes you post should be consistent with the image you want to portray. Find quotes that suit your identity, your personality, your products, and your mood.

- Joke of the week: At a motivational seminar 3 men are asked to come up to the stage. They are all asked, "When you are in your casket and friends and family are mourning upon you, what would you like to hear them say about you? The first guy says, "I would like to hear them say that I was the great doctor of my time, and a great family man." The second guy says, "I would like to hear that I was a wonderful husband and school teacher who made a huge difference in our children of tomorrow." The last guy replies, "I would like to hear them say…… LOOK!!! HE'S MOVING!!!!!" (source)

- A doctor says to his patient, "I have bad news and worse news".

- "Oh dear, what's the bad news?" asks the patient.

- The doctor replies, "You only have 24 hours to live."

- That's terrible," said the patient. "How can the news possibly be worse?"

- The doctor replies, "I've been trying to contact you since yesterday." (source)
- Just google "good clean jokes" and you'll find a ton….

Category 10: Ponderables –You know, quotes! The quotes you post should be consistent with the image you want to portray. Find quotes that suit your identity, your personality, your products, and your mood.

- Can vegetarians eat animal crackers?
- Why is it that rain drops but snow falls?
- Why is "abbreviated" such a long word?
- Is it OK to use the AM radio after noon?
- Why isn't there a mouse-flavored cat food?
- Why isn't phonetic spelled the way it sounds?
- What was the best thing before sliced bread?
- How do you tell when you're out of invisible ink?
- Why do people like to pop bubble wrap so much?
- If the #2 pencil is the most popular, why is it still #2?

There you have it! Just do a little research, a little pondering, a little thinking… and you'll have plenty of content before you know it. Remember, the key it to think it all out in advance, so you have a plan. The worst thing you can do is try to "wing it" with social media. Do you have other ideas? Other categories? Just make sure they're interesting and relevant… and go for it!

CHAPTER 52

Wrapping It All Up – Make The Jump To $10MM

W<small>E HAVE COVERED</small> a tremendous amount of ground in this book, and in doing so, I have presented a blueprint for growing your remodeling or home services business to $10MM or more.

Let's revisit the 4-Step formula I introduced at the beginning of the book:

1. **Sell awesome stuff that people genuinely love.**

2. **Charge high prices.**

3. **Master the internet.**

4. **Use radio & TV advertising.**

I am here to tell you from many first-hand experiences with clients all across the country in every kind of remodeling and home services companies that *this formula works*. But you have to diligently apply all of the principles. You can't shortcut any of the steps. If your prices are high but your stuff isn't awesome, you're doomed. If you try to advertise on radio & TV, but your prices aren't high enough, you'll run out of money and patience before you actually unlock unlimited lead flow and make the jump. And if you don't master the internet, well, you're just letting your competitors walk all over you.

Don't hesitate to reach out to us if you have any questions or if you need help implementing anything covered in this book. You can always find us at UnlimitedLeadFlow.com.

Thank you for reading. I really appreciate it.

Made in the USA
Columbia, SC
27 September 2019